JOHN RAWLS

JOHN RAWLS

The Path to a Theory of Justice

ANDRIUS GALIŠANKA

Harvard University Press

Cambridge, Massachusetts
London, England
2019

First printing

Library of Congress Cataloging-in-Publication Data
Names: Gališanka, Andrius, author.
Title: John Rawls : the path to a theory of justice / Andrius Gališanka.
Description: Cambridge, Massachusetts : Harvard University Press, 2019. |
Includes bibliographical references and index.
Identifiers: LCCN 2018041449 | ISBN 9780674976474 (alk. paper)
Subjects: LCSH: Rawls, John, 1921–2002. | Justice (Philosophy) | Liberalism—
United States—History—20th century. | Political science—Philosophy. |
Ethics, Modern—20th century. | Rawls, John, 1921-2002. Theory of justice.
Classification: LCC B945.R284 G35 2018 | DDC 320.092—dc23
LC record available at https://lccn.loc.gov/2018041449

CONTENTS

JOHN RAWLS

Introduction

T HE AMERICAN POLITICAL PHILOSOPHER John Rawls (1921–2002) has shaped contemporary responses to democratic disagreement. In particular, Rawls's understanding of political philosophy as a search for shared beliefs and values is still a guiding light for Anglophone liberalism. According to this view, heated and persistent disagreement obscures a shared conception of justice. Political conflict is a result of a misunderstanding, which philosophy should correct. It is a failure to notice that which we all share or, at least, that which we all can share. This vision of political philosophy has had a vast influence on liberalism, and even important political figures have arguably drawn on Rawls's ideas.[1]

Despite the wave of creative work Rawls inspired, liberal political theory is currently in crisis. Most of all, liberal political theorists find it difficult to show the possibility of agreement on principles of justice. Moreover, in trying to show this agreement they idealize actual citizens, turning them into "reasonable persons." Thus, even if agreement among reasonable persons can be shown, it is not obvious whether it is of much value to actual citizens who may not recognize themselves in the image of "reasonable persons."

The first problem of liberalism stems from its conception of freedom. Believing that citizens are free when they are governed by laws to which they all can agree, liberals have struggled to show that this agreement obtains. How can one look at seemingly persistent and deep disagreement and yet find some shared grounds? On the one hand, we can try setting aside as many of the underlying disagreements as possible, hoping to eventually retreat to a ground we all share.[2] This requires that political questions be independent from these disagreements, and, as we know from contentious political issues, such as immigration and abortion, this seems at least sometimes hardly possible. In part because of this difficulty, some liberal theorists do not even attempt to justify laws to those with radically different views, addressing their arguments to those who already accept the liberal norms.[3] Alternatively, we can try to use concepts that all can accept—such as liberty and equality—ignoring the different interpretations of those concepts and the reasons they generate.[4] This path is problematic as well, since different interpretations of concepts also lead to practical disagreements.

For its attempt to uncover shared grounds and use these grounds to justify constitutional restrictions, critics call Rawlsian liberalism "high liberalism."[5] They point to the reasons for which such shared grounds cannot be attained. Those who describe themselves as political realists and agonistic democrats argue that "high liberalism" misunderstands politics and political philosophy.[6] It leaves the "political" out of "political philosophy." For these critics, disagreement is always part of politics. It can be overcome—sometimes, on particular issues—but the attainment of agreement should not be an expectation or even a hope. On their view, Rawls's focus on shared grounds is misguided and potentially dangerous precisely because it overlooks the permanent fact of disagreement. Instead of repeating to ourselves that we will discover shared grounds and end disagreement if only we dig deep enough, we should compromise with our political opponents and search for legitimate ways to compete politically.

The second problem of liberalism is related to the first. In trying to avoid the problems of disagreement, Rawlsian liberals have moved further and further away from justifying the principles of justice to actual citizens. Instead, the principles are typically justified to "reasonable persons"—those willing to consider all sides of the argument, having knowledge of the question at hand, and able to exclude considerations irrelevant to the question at hand. As a result, it may be said that liberalism respects the persons' better beliefs—those beliefs people may arrive at after fuller consideration—rather than their actual beliefs. One might even say that liberalism respects beliefs rather than persons who try to articulate them.[7]

Indeed, this is what critics of liberalism allege. According to these critics, respect for citizens' autonomy or self-rule is respect for their actual decisions, including decisions that are mistaken. Rawls's lifelong interlocutor and critic Michael Walzer expressed this contrast poignantly. As he put it, philosophical conversations about what reasonable persons would decide aim to produce "conversational endings" that shut out actual citizens.[8] A democratic conversation, Walzer argued, is one in which we accept people's actual decisions, even if we view those decisions as mistaken: "As a citizen of a democratic community, I must wait for the people's decision, who have a right to decide."[9]

This book focuses on John Rawls and his intellectual development that led to *A Theory of Justice* (1971), the classic work that reinvigorated "high liberalism." It does so in order to understand the nature of the questions and problems Rawls considered, hoping that these historical explorations will also illuminate the problems of contemporary liberalism and perhaps suggest solutions to these problems. Rawls was aware of the fact of disagreement throughout his career. In fact, he wrote the book during the civil rights movement and the antiwar protests. He offered his political vision as an attempt to find shared grounds precisely to escape this disagreement. Believing that our natural feelings lead us all to largely the same principles of justice, he thought that we only need a proper point of view—the "original position"—from which we can see this. Moreover, he thought that the agreement one can attain will be narrow and fragile. Nonetheless, he thought, that was the most we can get given the differences in the way reasonable persons view the world and their place in it. Analyzing Rawls's account of natural feelings and the proper point of view, and understanding the fragility of the expected agreement among reasonable persons, we can decide how feasible his solution is and what we can take from it for the future. For both his followers and his critics, it might be worth returning to Rawls.

This kind of intellectual history of Rawls has become more possible only recently. With Rawls's private papers open to the public at Harvard, Princeton, and Cornell University Archives, we can now situate Rawls in the political and philosophical movements of the time and understand him better. This book draws on archival documents extensively. They contain thousands of pages of Rawls's work, including lectures, drafts of essays and books, correspondence, and books from his personal library. These are marvelous resources for understanding Rawls as a person and also for uncovering the intellectual contexts in which he wrote, therefore illuminating the development of his political and philosophical thought.

The book has two central tasks: to explore Rawls's political and philosophical visions. Focusing on the political vision, I ask: How did Rawls conceive of political philosophy as a search for agreement? Following Rawls's intellectual development from his early years to the publication of *A Theory of Justice,* this book narrates the origins and history of Rawls's political vision. Despite Rawls's influence, this history is poorly understood. Too often, Rawls is seen as a lone figure, ignoring the contemporary philosophical landscape and looking back to the social contract tradition, Kantianism, and, at his most modern, the emerging field of game theory.[10] These narratives fail to explain the novelty of Rawls's philosophical approach and consequently misunderstand the character of the political vision he made prevalent.

Outlining the development of Rawls's conception of philosophy is the second central task of this book. It aims both to explain the origins of Rawls's political vision and to show the originality of his philosophical framework. "Conception of philosophy" is an intentionally broad formulation. I will understand it as encompassing two suitably broad questions: What is political philosophy about? and What, if anything, makes one political judgment or argument better than another? Answers to these questions rely on views about human beings, their place in the world, their ability to make ethical and political judgments, and the nature of valuable things.

The book focuses on two aspects of Rawls's conception of philosophy: its nonfoundational modes of justification and its aim to organize our ethical judgments in terms of a theory, or a list of ordered principles. The history of political philosophy contains numerous examples of foundational arguments that derive a political vision from a certain foundation that needs no further defense. Plato's independently existing forms, Kant's noumenal realm, intuitionism's objectively existing values—these are standard examples of foundational arguments in philosophy.[11] Rawls's vision of philosophy contained no such certain foundation. Instead, he conceived of political philosophy as having a task—to offer a conception of justice that can solve disagreements—and considered that task complete if citizens could agree on one such conception. If there were no objections, the philosophical conversation could stop, for the time being. As we will see, this is another remarkable fact about Rawls's philosophy. Not only did he aim to show the possibility of agreement among reasonable persons, but he also thought that this agreement can be generated from the combination of many considerations that are uncontestable and yet weak by themselves.

A *Theory of Justice* was Rawls's offering of such vision and an explanation of how we might come to accept it. Rawls thought political philosophy could achieve this task by producing a conceptual framework that organizes our considered judgments correctly. This process of organizing takes place on both the individual level and the social level. As individuals, we all make judgments about the justice of our political system. Some are more confident, such as that slavery is wrong, while others, such as those about the justice of the living conditions and earning potential of the poorest, are not as firm. Often, however, we are not sure what reasons lie behind even the firmest of judgments. According to Rawls, political philosophy should offer principles of justice that explain why each of us makes these judgments. On the social level, these principles should explain the considered judgments of all citizens. Rawls called the state of affairs in which the considered judgments of all reasonable persons converged the state of "reflective equilibrium," while the balancing between judgments and principles was seen as the "process" of achieving reflective equilibrium.[12] As Rawls indicated, any such equilibrium is tentative, as any particular judgment that supports it can be changed. When reason giving stops, it stops not because we attain certain knowledge but because for the time being we agree on relevant propositions.

Rawls's philosophical vision relied on the assumption that all reasonable persons share at least some considered judgments and that these considered judgments are made for the same reasons. Why did he think so? By drawing on Rawls's historical development, this book attempts to explain why Rawls believed that all reasonable persons might agree in their judgments. It shows that, throughout Rawls's early writings, there is an undoubted assumption that reasonable persons do not have radically different conceptual frameworks. Later, Rawls started emphasizing natural feelings, such as sympathy, which all human beings were expected to have. He set aside the doubt that different cultural contexts might change the expressions of these feelings. Certain reasons, Rawls thought, can be more or less detached from the nonpolitical parts of our conceptual frameworks.

The book also focuses on the second aspect of Rawls's vision of philosophy: his conception of ethical and political theory. Rawls believed that a theorist should explicate ethical judgments of reasonable persons in terms of a list of ordered principles. He proposed two such principles: that each person have an equal right to the most extensive system of liberties (the first principle of justice), and that social and economic inequalities be arranged so as to bring the highest benefit to the least advantaged, with the condition that offices be open to all under conditions of fair equality of opportunity (the second principle of justice).[13] The principles were lexically ordered: the first trumped the second in all situations where the two conflicted.[14] Initially it might appear that this is a conception of justice of impressive scope and order: all reasonable persons can agree on the two principles and the order in which they apply. In fact, however, the possible agreement Rawls expected to show was much narrower and looser than his critics assume. As Rawls liked to say, philosophy guides politics only in a general direction. Philosophical analysis can determine what justice requires in some clear cases, but the more particular and contested questions of justice are left for citizens to decide. In these complex cases, principles of justice serve as guides to discussion, not as premises for deduction. If so, Rawls's philosophical vision leads to a more democratic picture of justice than his critics assume. In many cases, it leaves it to actual citizens to decide how our society should look. I trace the development of Rawls's view on this question.

While important in its own right, the philosophical narrative also illuminates Rawls's political vision. Rawls is known primarily as a political philosopher, but for much of his life he was a philosopher first. Inquiries into the nature of ethics and political philosophy—what questions these disciplines raise, how they answer these questions, and how they back up the answers—were his central concerns. They posed his main questions and tasks and often were responsible for changes in his political worldview. Until the late 1950s, Rawls's primary opponent was not a political but a philosophical tradition—emotivism. Only later did questions of political philosophy—about liberty, equality, desert—become the center of Rawls's work. Thus, to tell the intellectual history of Rawls's political vision most faithfully, we should also examine his changing understandings of philosophy.

Tracing the development of the political and philosophical visions of *A Theory of Justice,* the book analyzes many aspects of Rawls's thought and some aspects of his personal life. Much is to be learned in the archives about Rawls's dedication, creativity, and love for precision. However, I do not intend this book to be a complete intellectual biography. I focus on the political and philosophical visions of *A Theory of Justice* and narrate Rawls's intellectual development and life as these help us understand these visions. Other stories can be told about Rawls's philosophy and life. My main goal is to clarify what kind of agreement among reasonable persons Rawls hoped to attain and why he thought they might agree on anything at all.

The Argument

I argue that Rawls's conception of political philosophy as analysis of the considered judgments of reasonable persons was influenced by a variety of currents in analytic philosophy. Logical positivism, Wittgensteinian linguistic philosophy, and Quine informed Rawls's thinking that philosophy is analysis. Although, as we will see, Rawls thought the function of the principles of justice was to generate agreement, it was not a pragmatic agreement that Rawls sought. There is a sense that, throughout the years, Rawls was searching for a political vision that is implicit in our considered judgments. The uncovered political vision is not a coincidence of contingent historical and cultural factors, and it involves no compromise used with the purpose of arriving at consensus.

Moreover, Rawls's view that philosophical analysis is not only the discovery of the political vision but also its justification was also informed by these same traditions. As Rawls argued, once we show that we all agree on a political vision and there are no standing objections against it, we have done all we can do. Further doubts about the solution to the philosophical puzzle are no longer real doubts.

The central belief of Rawls's philosophical and political visions—that all reasonable persons can be shown to agree in their core political judgments—is the result of a twofold influence. The first is an analysis of natural feelings, prompted by Ludwig Wittgenstein's argument that there exists a human "form of life."[15] Inspired by Wittgenstein's argument, Rawls argued that human beings have the capacity for natural feelings, such as love, sympathy, and affection. He believed that if these feelings can be expressed freely, they would lead every person to agree. They needed only to think about the question from a suitable point of view. Because of Rawls's infrequent references to Wittgenstein in *A Theory of Justice*, this influence has not been noticed. Indeed, Rawls's nearly 200-page investigation of moral psychology in *A Theory of Justice* has received the least attention and sometimes has gone entirely overlooked.[16] It was Rawls's favorite part of the book, and it stemmed from one of the most creative periods of his career.[17] Clearly, Rawls also thought that analysis of natural and moral feelings was the core of his argument, describing *A Theory of Justice* as "a theory of the moral sentiments (to recall an eighteenth century title)."[18]

The second influence, shaped first by biblical essentialism and then various strands of analytic philosophy, was the assumption that parts of reasonable persons' conceptual frameworks are sufficiently independent from others. Their understandings of liberty and equality, Rawls thought, are at least somewhat detachable from their other beliefs. So, Rawls thought that there are some judgments that are basic and made by all reasonable persons. These assumptions are evident already in Rawls's early religious years and are then reinforced by various sources in analytic philosophy, including logical positivism's concept of "basic statements" in the 1940s. Rawls's interpretations of other thinkers reveal this way of thinking. Drawing on Wittgenstein, Rawls emphasized the commonality of our experiences—the human form of life—rather than differences stressed by thinkers such as Stanley Cavell. Similarly, creating the final version of reflective equilibrium, Rawls drew on Quine, who emphasized the shared and fixed points of our experience, rather than on the more historicist Thomas Kuhn.

Rawls's political vision in *A Theory of Justice,* as I show, was formulated mainly by drawing on Kant. However, it is important to emphasize that Kant's influence was preceded by others and, especially, that it changed over the years. To show that reasonable persons can actually agree, Rawls thought, we needed to take a certain point of view. Throughout his career, Rawls worked on versions of what later became the "original position," or a thought experiment meant to bring out the shared conception of justice—the content of our shared considered judgments. In 1958, as Rawls once again started drawing on Kant, the "original position" became a point of view from which one could analyze what it means to respect moral persons. Justice was a way of respecting persons, and this respect was informed by Kant's formula of humanity: respect persons as ends, never as means only. Only in the mid-1960s did Rawls interpret this respect in terms of autonomy. Respect now required treating persons solely as moral beings, independent of the particular contingent facts about themselves and the societies in which they lived. The decisions they actually made, if these were not consistent with their moral nature, were to be rejected.

Uncovering these influences and their timeline, intellectual histories can be useful for contemporary concerns. To address the dilemmas of liberal political theory, we can ask how plausible Rawls's argument about overlapping moral principles is, and how possible it is to show that the political parts of our conceptual frameworks are at least in some cases independent of our broader beliefs about the world and our place in it.

Should such defenses fail, we can point out that, at least initially, Rawls did not see respect for persons as necessarily connected with autonomy. This suggests that, on Rawlsian grounds, it was possible to respect decisions that stemmed from the contingent facts about ourselves. Moreover, as I show, the agreement Rawls thought possible was actually narrow and fragile. Rawls discussed a shared conception of justice, and this discussion has overshadowed the limited agreement he expected to achieve. The shared principles of justice could determine the clearest cases of justice, such as the injustice of slavery, but they were not determinate even on the justice of the core economic institutions, including the debate between capitalist and socialist means of production. Realizing this narrow reach of the principles of justice is helpful in contemporary liberal debates. Rawls's conception of autonomy allowed disagreement on many issues. Respecting a person did not require showing that every law can be agreed to by reasonable persons—in part because sometimes we could not say whether the law was just or unjust.

If respect for persons did not require respecting their Kantian autonomy and if that autonomy did not require showing agreement on all questions, this intellectual history allows us to ask if respect for persons is detachable from Kantian autonomy altogether. This is the claim the realist critics put forth: respect for persons is respect for their actual decisions—decisions that stem from contingent and perhaps not wholly reasonable parts of our persons. The goal of this intellectual history is not to argue one way or another. However, showing the roads not taken by Rawls, it can suggest paths to be explored.

I narrate Rawls's intellectual development in the chapters that follow. Beginning with Rawls's undergraduate years before the Second World War, I show that, like many liberals of the time, Rawls started out as a religious thinker.[19] Despite the ubiquity of such stories, it came as a surprise to many that the author of *A Theory of Justice*—a book that relies on no religious claims—started his intellectual career with an undergraduate thesis "A Brief Inquiry into the Meaning of Sin and Faith," filed in 1942 and published as a book in 2009.[20] Analyzing the thesis, I argue that Rawls's intellectual lineage started in two theological traditions. A core aspect of Rawls's political vision—respect for persons—was developed drawing on the neo-orthodox framework that dominated American theology in the 1940s. Agreeing with the neo-orthodox emphasis on the sinfulness of human beings, Rawls nonetheless argued that human beings are all made in the image of God and should therefore all be treated as persons capable of communion with God and fellow human beings. Rawls's philosophical vision, however, found its origins in a different theological tradition: liberal Protestantism. Preceding neo-orthodoxy, liberal Protestantism insisted on the primacy of lived Christian experiences, such as personal revelation, conversion, and guilt. Inspired by his liberal Protestant professors George F. Thomas and Theodore M. Greene, Rawls also conceived of theology and philosophy as analysis of Christian experiences. He took Christian experiences as the ultimate grounds in ethical arguments and expected that all persons—Christians and non-Christians—could share these experiences.

Part of the interest in Rawls's Christian story lies in its influence on his later secular thought. Having served in the army on the Pacific Front during the Second World War, Rawls lost his faith. From then on, he no longer framed his arguments in terms of religious concepts. Instead, as I describe in Chapter 2, he turned to analytic philosophy. Ironically, this story begins with logical positivism. In traditional accounts of the revival of political philosophy, Rawls is portrayed as freeing the discipline from logical positivism, a tradition that typically considered ethical statements as unjustifiable expressions of emotions. While Rawls indeed spent much of the 1940s and 1950s criticizing logical positivism, his own formulation of secular ethical theory drew on that tradition. Rawls's goal was to fashion ethical theory on logical positivism's conception of scientific theory. In another ironic twist of history—since logical positivists also considered theological statements as meaningless and therefore unjustifiable—logical positivism was a fitting framework for crucial aspects of Rawls's liberal Protestant conception of theological inquiry. Having understood theology as an empirical inquiry, Rawls followed the philosopher Curt John Ducasse in modeling ethical inquiry after scientific inquiry.

Viewing ethical inquiry as scientific inquiry, Rawls aimed to explicate the considered ethical judgments of reasonable persons, or those judgments in which reasonable human beings are most confident. He borrowed Karl Popper's concept of "basic statements," or statements the truth of which every observer could verify, to describe our basic ethical judgments. Like Popper, Rawls believed that all reasonable persons would agree in making identical basic judgments if only they were placed in the right contexts. Moreover, as in his liberal Protestant conception of philosophy, Rawls believed that the result of such philosophical analysis—this time a secular liberal framework—is justified insofar as it explains the actual judgments of actual reasonable persons.

Over the years, as Rawls reacted to post-analytic themes in Ludwig Wittgenstein's writings, Rawls's picture of ethical theory evolved, and much of the early positivist influence fell away. The first such change took place during the academic year of 1947–1948, which Rawls spent as a graduate student at Cornell, studying under Wittgensteinians Max Black and Norman Malcolm. I describe this development in Chapter 3. While constructing his conception of ethics as empirical inquiry, Rawls also introduced the concept of "absurdity." Drawing on debates about the justification of induction, he argued that certain doubts—about ethics as about induction—are absurd. If we cannot elaborate a concrete criticism of a theory, Rawls thought, then we have no reason for doubt. This development helped Rawls respond to the skeptic who challenged Rawls's conception of justification.

Chapter 4 outlines Rawls's first secular political vision. In a general way, this vision drew on Rawls's liberal Protestant belief that our society should respect persons. This time, however, the account of personhood was secular. Drawing on Kant, Rawls argued that the highest aspect of human beings is their ability to follow the moral law. As he argued then, a political system should protect and foster this capacity. Drawing on game theory, which was developing at Princeton with John von Neumann and Oskar Morgenstern's *Theory of Games and Economic Behavior,* Rawls argued that respect for persons was respect for one's capacity and right to decide what kind of life one should pursue.[21] Rawls would combine these two aspects of personhood in the later years, but they appeared separately in his writings already in the late 1940s and early 1950s. Moreover, in this same period Rawls formulated the first version of what would become known as the "original position" thought experiment in *A Theory of Justice.*

Chapter 5 turns to Oxford, where Rawls spent the 1952–1953 academic year, and to the preceding academic year at Princeton. This period saw Rawls fully immerse himself in the thought of Ludwig Wittgenstein, his students, followers, and interlocutors. Among these was Stephen Toulmin, whose *The Place of Reason in Ethics* impacted Rawls the year before.[22] These encounters led to significant changes in Rawls's philosophical vision. In particular, the new influences changed Rawls's explanation of reasonable persons' agreement. Rawls's unpublished notes indicate that he struggled to explain why reasonable persons might reach this agreement, despite the various explanations he gave. Explaining this possibility was easier in his religious framework: there Rawls argued that if we are all made in the image of God, then our experiences—whether those of grace or sin—will be the same. Wittgensteinians' conceptual framework helped Rawls deal with this problem. Rawls now focused on the concept of "practice" and the related argument that if practices are to continue, there must be some agreement about them. Thus, if making ethical judgments is a practice, there must be some agreement about what ethical judgments are appropriate in what situations.

Chapter 6 continues the story of Rawls's changing philosophical framework. It focuses on Rawls's Wittgensteinian investigations in moral psychology—some of the most innovative thinking in Rawls's career. Rawls's seminars at Cornell in 1958 and Harvard in 1960 and 1964 give us a picture of naturalistic ethics and political philosophy. At the center of these naturalistic arguments is an attempt to demonstrate the link between our natural feelings and our moral feelings and conceptions. Who we are as human beings affects the moral views we hold. As Rawls phrased it, moral reasons are extensions of natural feelings that all human beings are expected to develop in normal circumstances of human life. These naturalist explorations helped Rawls explain why all reasonable persons would agree on their considered judgments of justice. Rawls now argued that, given the roughly shared background of natural feelings—what he, following Wittgenstein, called a "form of life"—"all moralities . . . have this sort of family likeness. They resemble one another in their <u>principles</u>."[23] This statement shows well the mixture of Rawls's Wittgensteinian naturalism and the legacy of his positivist belief in the basic experiences. The historical and cultural traditions in which these beliefs form do not significantly affect the content of the moral conceptions. Natural feelings, if unobstructed, were expected to express themselves in principles that show family likeness. Later in his career, Rawls would qualify the statement and claim that principles of justice apply only to a "democratic society under modern conditions."[24] In the late 1950s and in *A Theory of Justice,* however, Rawls's analysis of justice applied to all human beings. A theory of justice was a theory of moral sentiments, not moral sentiments of a particular culture or a time period.

This Wittgensteinian influence is unnoticed partly because, unlike other Wittgensteinians, such as his Harvard colleague Stanley Cavell, Rawls emphasized not variations but commonalities in the human form of life. This perhaps unusual interpretation of Wittgenstein is due to

Rawls's early philosophical visions, which took for granted that ethical judgments of reasonable persons are stable despite their possibly varying cultural backgrounds. Rawls's belief that moral psychology can uncover something akin to human form of life is an intelligible elaboration of the idea.

Chapter 7 turns to the final evolution of Rawls's philosophical framework before *A Theory of Justice*. It begins with Rawls's engagement with the work of his Harvard colleague W. V. O. Quine, a naturalist and the "greatest logical positivist."[25] Drawing on Quine, Rawls argued that justification proceeds by gathering the "fixed points" in the judgments and beliefs of all reasonable persons and selecting a theory of justice that explicates most of these fixed points. This argument was the final touch to his account of reflective equilibrium. Rawls now believed that the defense of a political vision consisted in showing that it faces fewer problems than its main alternatives. However limited and unsatisfying that vision may be, it is ours until we have a better alternative.

Chapter 8 analyzes the 1960s with the focus on Rawls's political vision. This period reveals Rawls's turn to the social contract theory and the newly acquired emphasis and importance of Kant's political thought. I argue that Rawls placed different emphases on Kant's moral philosophy in different periods. In 1958, we see him drawing on Kant's formula of humanity, or the requirement to treat "humanity, whether in your own persons or in the person of any other, never simply as means, but always at the same time as an end."[26] In the mid-1960s, however, Rawls started emphasizing Kant's formula of autonomy, which required us to govern ourselves by a will that "makes universal law."[27] Only then did respecting persons become for Rawls respecting their autonomy, understood as acting on principles that are not dependent on contingent facts about ourselves, such as our gender, race, or vision of the good life, or contingent facts about our societies, such as their level of economic and cultural achievement.

In Chapter 9, I show how all the previous developments help us better understand *A Theory of Justice*. The picture of Rawls as an analytic philosopher reformulating his views to respond to more contextualist and naturalist themes can help us reject some common misinterpretations of Rawls. Contrary to Richard Rorty's suggestion, Rawls's liberalism does not rest on pragmatism.[28] Rawlsian liberalism is in fact committed to a "philosophical anthropology"—a "philosophical account of the human self."[29] Resting on an account of moral feelings, this philosophical anthropology was not noticed because of its limited conclusions: according to Rawls, natural feelings are compatible with a variety of moral views.

Moreover, Rawls's intellectual development bears out Walzer's criticism that respect for citizens' self-rule is respect for their better beliefs and self-understandings—those beliefs that could be arrived at after reflection and thought experiments. It is not respect for the perhaps mistaken beliefs and understandings that citizens actually hold.[30] At the same time, however, this history qualifies Walzer's criticism by showing the limited scope of agreement that Rawls hoped to achieve. As he acknowledged, political philosophy can guide political practice only in a general direction: it restricts our alternatives but cannot by itself lead to particular judgments about justice in a mechanical way. At such boundaries of philosophy, it is actual citizens who interpret the conception of justice.

Relying on the philosophical story given thus far, the epilogue gives a brief account of Rawls's transition to *Political Liberalism*. In the decade after the publication of *A Theory of Justice,* Rawls was forced to admit that the expectation that all reasonable persons might agree was mistaken. Reformulating his theory, he drew on his earlier themes, familiar from his early engagement with positivism. Rawls now hypothesized that reasonable persons can agree on the parts of their framework that are relevant for political questions, but not on other statements that required reference to citizens' comprehensive doctrines—their beliefs about the world and their own place in it. This was the genesis of "public reason"—a reason that relies only on a publicly accepted political conception of justice.[31] This concept continues the idea that was implicit in his early writings as well—that parts of our conceptual frameworks are independent of other parts of those frameworks.

I conclude by observing what lines of thinking Rawls rejected and thus what lines of thinking are potentially open for liberal thinkers. In particular, I suggest that, for Rawls, respect for persons was possible without respect for their autonomy understood in the Kantian way, and that respect relied on only narrow and fragile agreement. Perhaps, then, liberals can develop an account on which it is possible for citizens to respect each other even if they hold incompatible conceptions of justice. This might bring liberalism closer to critics, who interpret respect for persons as respect for their actual decisions, but it would retain the core of Rawls's ideas.

Rawls inspired liberal political thought with his theory of justice, and many creative minds elaborated on his arguments and took them in their own directions. Showing how Rawls dealt with the most important questions of political philosophy, I hope that this intellectual history can give both liberal political theorists and their critics new grounds and inspiration in inquiring what it means to treat persons as free, self-governing, and equal.

1

Protestant Beginnings

J OHN BORDLEY RAWLS was born on February 21, 1921, in Baltimore, Maryland, to what he called a conventionally religious family.[1] His father, William Lee Rawls, was a Southern Methodist but frequented the Episcopalian Church, the congregational home of his wife and John's mother, Anna Abell Stump. Rawls's family was also engaged in politics. His father, a self-educated lawyer, was an unofficial adviser of Albert Ritchie, the Democratic governor of Maryland (1924–1936).[2] His mother was the Baltimore chapter president of the League of Women Voters and worked for the campaign of Wendell Wilkie, a former Democrat who challenged Franklin D. Roosevelt as a Republican in 1940.[3]

Religion did not seem to play a crucial part in Rawls's early life, however. He attended the Episcopalian Kent School from 1935 to 1939, but in his decision to enter it, he seems to have followed his brother William rather than a religious calling. Rawls described his experiences at the Kent School as unremarkable.[4] This relative lack of deeper interest in religion continued in his first two undergraduate years at Princeton, which he entered in 1939, again following family tradition. Initially, Rawls planned to major in art and architecture, taking classes in free-hand drawing, ancient art, painting in Italy, and ancient and medieval architecture.[5] He also wrote and served as news editor for the school newspaper, the *Daily Princetonian,* covering wrestling and football in his first year and then music in the later years.[6]

Rawls did, however, develop an interest in politics while at Princeton. This interest started emerging in his sophomore year and was motivated in large part by the Second World War and the puzzling popularity of the Nazi movement. Rawls's concern with the war is evident in his first political writing, "Spengler's Prophecy Realized," published in June 1941 in Princeton's *Nassau Literary Magazine,* now the *Nassau Literary Review.* In this uncharacteristically despairing and sarcastic essay, Rawls argued that the Western world is living out Oswald Spengler's prophecy that it would fall. On the one hand, he argued, we are witnessing "the rise of great individuals to power" and thus the diminution of democracy.[7] In Germany, "Herr Hitler has made true the fears of Spengler," and in the United States, attributing greater power to President Roosevelt, "a so-called free people are giving their freedom to become exploited pawns in a new war."[8] On the other hand, Rawls thought, machinery is making redundant the virtues of human beings. Given Germany's leadership in the latter area, Rawls concluded that "there is no hope for a successful revolt against the Nazis in Europe; at least not at present."[9]

Rawls's interests changed in his junior year. His interest in politics assumed a more ethical perspective, focusing not so much on actions but on the ideals that motivate them. His interest in religion and theology sparked. In the fall of his junior year, he took a religious history course titled Christian Thought to the Reformation.[10] The course was part of the Committee on Religious Instruction, created in 1940. It was taught by George F. Thomas, hired to be the formative person of the committee, which would soon become the Department of Religion. The course discussed "the origins of Christian beliefs about God, Creation, Man, Evil, and Salvation as expressed in the Bible" as well as the influence of Greek philosophy on the development of these beliefs.[11]

The influence of this course is evident in Rawls's second publication, "Christianity and the Modern World," also in the *Nassau Literary Magazine.*[12] The content and character of this essay differed noticeably from the first. Rawls now focused not on the concentration of power and the effects of technology but on the beliefs of Western societies. He argued that the Western world has departed from Christian principles. He attributed to Christianity beliefs that would reemerge in his senior thesis:

God is a person; each person has equal value because of their "ability to enter into the relation of union between Nature and Grace"; and human beings inevitably fall into sin and cannot be kept from it without God's grace.[13] According to Rawls, no religion based on reason alone could understand the "radical evil" that was present in human beings.[14] Hence Rawls's solution to the problems of the Western world was a return to Christianity. "There are but two alternatives," he wrote. "Either we become Christian or we become pagan." To return to Christianity, Rawls argued, we must start with education that introduces Christianity to students, which should be followed with individual conversions.[15]

In the spring of his junior year (1942), Rawls took Social Philosophy with Norman Malcolm, an analytic philosopher and Ludwig Wittgenstein's interlocutor, who served as instructor at Princeton from 1940 to 1942 and then again in the spring of 1946.[16] The course had religious-ethical undertones: Malcolm framed it around the topic of evil, assigning Plato, Augustine, Bishop Butler, Reinhold Niebuhr, and Philip Leon. According to Robert Scoon, the chair of the Princeton philosophy department, Malcolm "has prepared himself for the course in Social Philosophy . . . to such an extent that we know of no other young man to whom we would prefer to give this work."[17] Much later, Rawls singled out this course as the most influential course in his undergraduate career.[18]

Rawls's interest in the ethical aspects of religion, and to a lesser extent politics, peaked in his last undergraduate semester, the fall of 1942, at the end of which he submitted his senior thesis, "A Brief Inquiry into the Meaning of Sin and Faith." It contained political and philosophical visions that would lay the basis for his later thinking, even when he rejected these visions in their original theological form. Politically, Rawls affirmed a nonnegotiable stance of equality: everyone was to be treated equally because everyone was created in the image of God. Philosophically, Rawls took it for granted that a philosopher's task was analysis of experience, and that the results of this analysis—a conceptual framework—were justified insofar as they explain the Christian experience correctly. In their broadest forms, these political and philosophical visions would shape the development of Rawls's later secular commitments and his arguments in *A Theory of Justice*. Respect for persons would eventually transform into the "inviolability founded on justice that even the welfare of society as a whole cannot override," while reliance on Christian experience would make Rawls receptive to analytic accounts of nonfoundationalist justification.[19] These developments would take time, but they were influenced by the place in which Rawls's story began.

Here, I want to explain Rawls's seemingly sudden interest in theology, the nature of his early philosophical and political commitments, and his eventual loss of faith. These developments are best understood against the background of American theology enmeshed in the debate between liberal Protestantism and neo-orthodoxy. Liberal Protestants understood Christianity as a movement that focused on Christian experiences and defended its theological frameworks by appeal to Christian experiences, such as those of grace, sin, and conversion. Neo-orthodoxy rejected this reliance on personal experience and brought back the emphasis on revelation that happened only once, through Christ. Debates between these traditions shaped Rawls's teachers and, in turn, the questions Rawls raised in his thesis.

Most of the existing literature on Rawls portrays him as neo-orthodox. Eric Gregory and Robert Adams emphasize neo-orthodoxy's influence on Rawls's view of God as a person and on his claim that full knowledge of God is possible only through his self-revelation.[20] David Reidy calls attention to Rawls's statement that the Bible is "the last word in matters of religion," a statement he interprets as a typical neo-orthodox theme.[21] One cannot deny the neo-orthodox influence on Rawls, especially on his political framework. However, it is worthwhile to trace the liberal Protestant influence on Rawls's philosophical vision. It helps us explain the core aspect of this vision—his reliance on Christian experience to justify political views—and therefore illuminates his eventual commitment to reflective equilibrium.

Philosophy and Religious Instruction at Princeton

While the Second World War must have prompted Rawls's interest in religion, his focus on theology emerged during interactions with his philosophy professors. Princeton's philosophy department in 1939 was unusual given the dominance of analytic philosophy at the time. It was a group of philosophers of different intellectual interests and approaches.

Robert Scoon, the department's chair, was a classicist who started his Princeton career as a professor of Latin in 1919 and transferred to the philosophy department in 1923.[22] Along with the introductory courses, he taught Plato, the history of philosophy influenced by Plato, and the philosophy of religion. Walter Stace was a former administrator of Ceylon (now Sri Lanka), who turned philosophy from a hobby to a vocation when he joined Princeton in 1935. An empiricist, he taught mainly twentieth-century philosophy. Theodore M. Greene, writing mostly on aesthetics, taught Plato, ethics, and aesthetics. David Bowers covered Kant and American philosophy, while Andrew Ushenko taught logic and the philosophy of science. Norman Malcolm would join in 1940 to teach social philosophy.

If there was one theme that united most of these philosophers, it was their interest in religion and their belief that religion was compatible with philosophy, even if only in complicated ways. Many but not all philosophers at Princeton were liberal Protestants. Stace, for example, assigned religion to the category of mysticism. Of the Protestants, Scoon and Greene worked closely together. As an Episcopalian minister, Scoon spoke at Princeton's chapel as early as 1917, frequently leading its services. His Philosophy of Religion course reflected his way of life. As part of this course, he offered lectures on the bases of morality, the conception of value, mysticism, individuality, sin, salvation, and soul.[23] Greene, a Presbyterian, led the first religious discussion with juniors at Princeton, focusing on the foundations of religious thought. He participated in various university-organized talks on the relationships between religions and the place of religion in the liberal arts education.[24] One of these conversations was published as an edited volume.[25] Greene's interest in religion and its compatibility with philosophy is also evident in his translation of Kant's *Religion within the Limits of Reason Alone*.[26]

Scoon and Greene played an important part in the founding of the Committee on Religious Instruction, which later developed into the Department of Religion. Scoon served as an assistant clerk in writing the 1934 Report on Religious Education. He and Greene were part of the six-person committee that recommended instituting two new courses at Princeton: the Development of the Religious Thought of the Hebrews and Religious Thought in the Gospels. The Committee on Religious Instruction was formed to oversee these courses, and George F. Thomas was hired as the lead lecturer in this new program, giving his inaugural lecture, "Religion in an Age of Secularism," in the fall of 1940.[27]

Given Scoon's and Greene's involvement in religion and religious education at Princeton, it is not surprising that Rawls took a course in theology in his junior year. By that time, he had already completed two introductory courses in philosophy—Ethics and Plato—the latter of which was taught by Greene. Rawls received a first (the highest grade) in Greene's course, so it is likely that Greene took an interest in Rawls's development and suggested Thomas's course to him. In the later years, at least, Rawls was known and highly regarded by his professors at Princeton. In his 1947 letter of recommendation, for instance, George Thomas wrote that Rawls was "one of the best students" he has taught at Princeton.[28] In a letter of recommendation from the same year, Scoon remarked that he had met Rawls "on a good many informal occasions. [Rawls] has also consulted me frequently with regard to his courses."[29] Rawls was the only student in 1942 to graduate with the highest honors in philosophy, and his graduate school assessments five years later described him as exceptional.[30] It is fair to conclude, then, that Rawls's interest in religion arose as he sought advice and discussion from philosophers who labored to bring religious instruction to Princeton.

Explaining Rawls's early religion, most commentators emphasize Malcolm's influence. There is something to be said on behalf of this argument. Rawls took Malcolm's Social Philosophy in the spring of 1942, a course that discussed "the nature of social values and standards, their relation to the structure of society and social institutions, to political authority and law, and to political and economic rights."[31] In his 1947 application to Cornell, Rawls described this course more personally than others, giving the reader Malcolm's own view. As he wrote, the course was "in what Prof. Malcolm liked to call 'philosophical anthropology,' i.e. study of some of man's views of himself, accent on Plato, Augustine, Schopenhauer, Adler, Niebuhr and others."[32] While this description may have been affected by the fact that Malcolm was at Cornell at the time of Rawls's application, we will see that the authors assigned in Malcolm's course strongly featured in his senior thesis, showing Rawls's genuine interest.

However, Rawls had already acquired an interest in religion by the time he took Malcolm's course. According to his transcript, Rawls took

Thomas's Christian Thought to the Reformation in the fall of 1941. In his application to Cornell, Rawls described it as a course "in Medieval Religious thought reading Augustine, Anselm, Thomas, Eckhart." He also listed two additional courses, also taken with Thomas, that are not noted on his transcript: one "in Church Fathers with concentration on Justin Martyr, Origin, Clement, Tertullian, Marcion" and another "in Reformation and Rationalism as Theology with study of Luther, Calvin, Zwingli, Locke, Hume, Kant as religious thinkers."[33]

Moreover, Malcolm was no longer at Princeton when Rawls actually wrote the thesis: he resigned from his appointment on April 16, 1942, before finishing the course Rawls was taking, to join the U.S. Navy.[34] Writing his thesis, Rawls worked with professors whose intellectual background drew at least in part on liberal Protestantism. Theodore Greene was one of his advisers (Stace another), and, given how much Rawls's philosophical commitments matched those of Greene and Thomas, the classes with Thomas must have been influential as well.

The philosophical commitments of Greene and Thomas are also reflected in Rawls's thesis. As we will see, they show a mixture of liberal Protestant and neo-orthodox themes. Both Greene and Thomas agreed with the neo-orthodox that knowledge of God depends on God's self-revelation, but thought that God reveals himself in a variety of ways, including through personal experiences. To understand Greene and Thomas—and so the intellectual milieu in which Rawls wrote his thesis—it is helpful to look at the development of liberal Protestantism and neo-orthodoxy in Europe and the United States. This story shows how, by the time Greene and Thomas worked with these frameworks, they were highly intermixed, and the notion of experience had become broad and almost all-encompassing.

Liberal Protestantism and Neo-Orthodoxy

Greene's and Thomas's philosophical visions are marked by the claim that the truth of the Christian message rests on its ability to explain the experiences of the Christian community rather than on an external authority such as the Bible. Their arguments also have elements of neo-orthodoxy, which emphasizes the personal nature of God and the importance of revelation in acquiring knowledge of God. But to explain the reliance on experience—a commitment that would become central to Rawls's vision of philosophy—one needs to turn to liberal Protestantism.[35]

Different currents of liberal Protestantism interpreted the Christian experience in different ways and attributed to it different philosophical significance. The core currents—the Ritchlian (what I call biblical historicist) and Harnackian (biblical essentialist)—arose in the nineteenth and early twentieth centuries in part as a response to the dilemmas raised by the studies of biblical contexts. Revealing that the Bible was written in different times by different people, these studies questioned the Bible's status as a record of a revelation that happened once and was written at once.[36] Biblical scholars were forced to conclude that the Bible was often historically inaccurate, going as far as to say that "not one of the historical books of the Old Testament has any historical value."[37] Having lost the Bible as a source of authority, liberal Protestants justified Christian truths by their ability to accord with Christian experience. Those drawing on the writings of Albrecht Ritschl (1822–1889) emphasized the historical development of the Christian community, while those drawing on the work of Adolf von Harnack (1851–1930) sought to find the essence of the Christian experience.

Ritschl's and Harnack's reliance on Christian experience differed, and these differences are important for understanding American Protestant theology and Rawls's early thought. Harnack insisted that the Christian community—past and present—has shared experience. This Christian experience, according to him, had a "kernel" or an "essence"; as he wrote, "certain fundamental ideas of the Gospel have never been lost and have defied all attacks."[38] As this essence was not apparent in the different historical expressions of Christianity, Harnack argued that it was the task of a theologian to study these different expressions and reveal the commonality that hides in them. Ritschl, on the other hand, appealed to neo-Hegelian historicism to claim that Christianity is the end of all religions. For him, it was not important if Christianity significantly differed from other religions or its own earlier expressions. Instead, he argued, "in Christianity the tendency of all the [historical religions] finds its perfect consummation."[39] Ritschl was historicist whereas Harnack was not: Ritschl thought that the very development of history made a difference, since Christianity in its most defensible form would be found only at the later stages of historical development. Harnack, on the other hand, saw historical differences as dross that should be shed to reveal an essence common to all Christian doctrines.

It was Harnack's biblical essentialist current that had the most influence in the United States, on Rawls's teachers, and, eventually, on Rawls himself. Due to this influence, American liberal theology was not primarily historicist. Historical research was used to discover the essence of Christianity, but historical development was not deemed important for the truth of the Christian doctrine.

American Protestant theologians borrowed from their European counterparts, and by the early twentieth century Harnackian biblical essentialism had taken root in the United States.[40] Theologians such as Charles Briggs, William Adams Brown, Henry Churchill King, and Shailer Matthews sought to uncover the essence of Christianity by purifying it "from all dross, brushing away the dust of tradition."[41] They thought that this essence would consist in shared Christian experiences. Brown, King, and Matthews all stressed that Christ's person should be understood as a living spirit revealed in the history of Christian religious experiences.[42] As Brown wrote, "If we are to understand the nature of the Christ of whom we speak, [we must] study the effects which he has produced in human life. Here our own experience gives us invaluable help."[43] Biblical essentialists understood Christian experience—and thus revelations of God—broadly. Thus, Brown thought that God's presence is experienced in daily life, but also in the more dramatic experiences of conversion in which "the Christian life begins."[44]

Liberal Protestant emphasis on experience and Harnack's essentialism are also evident in the writings of Rawls's teachers Greene and Thomas. Greene understood God as a person who revealed himself through the historical figure of Jesus, but also "in the distinctive religious experiences of mystics, saints and prophets, and, more particularly, in the individual and corporate experiences recorded in the Bible."[45] Greene placed the weight of his argument on the more direct religious experiences of the Christian community: trust in the truthfulness of these experiences was warranted, he thought, because they were shared by all Christians.[46] Answering the question "Is the Christian picture of God true?" Greene wrote: "The only reasonable response to this claim would seem to be to study the alleged religious experiences and the Christian interpretations of these experiences."[47] Given this justificatory primacy on experience, the Bible was not the standard of truth to be accepted unquestionably, but "the chief record of God's Self-revelation" through this variety of experiences.[48]

For experience to show the existence of God, it had to meet certain conditions. First, the object of the experience (God) "intrudes itself upon our consciousness with a character of its own which we ourselves cannot change but must accept for what it is." Second, this experience of God has to be made "coherent with some order of reality"—our other experiences. And last, this experience has to be public, or shared by others: "only that is judged undeniably real which others, at least those who are qualified to do so, can also experience and interpret in the same way."[49]

So, it was important for Greene to show that Christians did have common experiences. He did not do this in the article but gave reasons for his belief that the existence of this common experience can be shown. "The large measure of agreement among the prophets and saints of the Hebraic-Christian tradition is impressive," he wrote. "They confirm one another's testimony again and again. They agree that the God whom they claim to have encountered presented Himself coercively to them with a character of His own; they agree in broad outline in their interpretation of these coercive experiences."[50]

Thus, for Greene, theology was an interpretation of the Christian experience: an attempt to discover a conceptual framework that would explain this experience. As he wrote, "The relevant experiences are correctly described as 'encounters' with the Deity in direct communion with Him and through His revelation of Himself and through His revelation of Himself to man in Jesus Christ. The relevant interpretation of these encounters is theological interpretation."[51]

Thomas, much like Greene, was also influenced by liberal Protestantism and especially its biblical essentialist current. He argued that to understand the Christian faith we need to pay attention to Christian experience.[52] As he wrote, "Especially if God is *living* and *personal,* as Christian experience indicates, He can be expected to disclose Himself to the finite persons who are His sons and who are in need of light for their darkness, as a human person in friendship willingly discloses himself to another person."[53] Moreover, Thomas believed that experiences of God come in personal moments and are not limited to special persons or special circumstances. Because God reacted to human beings and their condition, persons who seek God could expect communication with God: "Revelation comes to men who are actively seeking light in their darkness to guide their people and who bring to bear all of their faculties of feeling, imagination, and reason."[54] Such experiences of God are thus expected to continue as long as there are persons in need: "God is of such a nature that He does not wait for man to find Him but *takes the initiative and discloses Himself* to man."[55]

This reliance on experience gave Thomas the same understanding of theology as that of Greene. Theology was analysis of the Christian experience, and this immediate experience was taken to be prior to any interpretation. As he wrote, "The *intellectual interpretation* of the Christian faith, though important, is *secondary to the Christian experience* and must be understood in the light of that experience."[56]

Greene and Thomas were drawing on liberal Protestantism that had sustained heavy criticism from neo-orthodoxy both in Europe and in the United States. As a result, liberal Protestants modified their positions, often incorporating themes from neo-orthodoxy. This was true in one crucial respect: liberal Protestants' conception of God and the Bible. These accommodations to criticism are also evident in the writings of Rawls's teachers and Rawls.

Liberal Protestants in general, and Greene and Thomas in particular, allowed that God could reveal himself in a variety of contexts and ways. Although this may seem like a repetition of the original liberal Protestant criticism, it in fact shows how this doctrine adapted to neo-orthodox emphasis on God's revelation through Jesus alone. The neo-orthodox such as Karl Barth (1886–1968) portrayed Jesus as "the *risen one*" who carried a supernatural revelation of God.[57] This contrasted with the original liberal Protestant understanding of Christ as an exceptional human being. In response to such criticism, liberal Protestants now allowed that both personal revelations and Jesus's revelation are part of the broader Christian experience.

The same was true of neo-orthodoxy's understanding of God as a person who reveals himself at will. Neo-orthodox theologians argued that since God is a person, no natural theology or experience of the world as God's creation can give full knowledge of God. Liberal Protestants accommodated this criticism by allowing that God is a person and arguing that, given that God is a person, he also responds to human persons' calls in the more personal and everyday revelations. These, of course, were precisely the positions of Thomas and Greene. They followed the typical neo-orthodox understanding of God as a person, but did not restrict our communication with God to one particular instance, the person of Jesus Christ.

The same was true of the liberal Protestant understanding of the Bible. Neo-orthodox theologians put forth a conception of the Bible as the Word of God.[58] This was meant to redirect the theological conversation from the Christian personal experiences to God.[59] In response to such criticisms, liberal Protestants now portrayed the Bible as the fullest record of Christian experiences. The Bible still conceptually depended on Christian experiences, but was recognized as the most accurate representation of God.

In sum, Rawls's intellectual milieu at Princeton included philosophers who in their visions of the world combined the various positions of liberal Protestantism and neo-orthodoxy. They borrowed from both traditions to form their own views.

Rawls's Early Political Vision

Rawls's religious political framework is best explained by appealing to the themes of neo-orthodoxy. In particular, Rawls drew on a set of views now typically described as "personalism." These views were a conglomerate of different, often overlapping, arguments that came to the fore of Christianity in the 1930s. The starting point of such arguments was a claim that God was a person—an entity with its own traits that expressed themselves in action. Politically, this idea was extended to claim that human beings too are persons, since they are made in the image of God. Accordingly, personalist positions held, human beings should be respected as persons. They should not be treated as merely individuals, or entities without the core aspect of personhood: their being made in the image of God and being capable of relating to God and other beings. Nor should human beings be treated as entirely communal, not having their own individuality and so their own goals. Politically, then, personalism was a double-edged criticism of both secular liberalism that was too individualistic and societies that were overly communal to the point of becoming totalitarian, such as Nazi Germany.

Personalism had origins in both Catholic and Protestant camps.[60] The most well-known representative of the Catholic camp of personalism was the French philosopher Jacques Maritain. According to Maritain, emphasizing personhood required opposing "both the idea of the totalitarian state and that of the sovereignty of the individual."[61] Maritain used these arguments to defend human rights—a novel argument in Catholicism, later also adopted by the Catholic Church.[62]

After the occupation of France, Maritain moved to the United States and began teaching at Princeton in 1941–1942. Rawls did not take courses with Maritain, and there is no evidence that the two conversed. However, given Rawls's involvement with other members of the Committee on Religious Instruction, it would be surprising if Rawls had not been aware of Maritain's importance and encountered his arguments in at least an indirect form.

Protestant visions of personalism, which were influential on the United Nations' Charter of 1945 and *Universal Declaration of Human Rights* (1948), also linked rights to the concept of persons.[63] This type of personalism traveled to the United States through key works of mainly European theologians. Indeed, what was known as "personalism" in the United States at the time was an idealist philosophy, which had no real connection to the personalism that influenced Rawls.[64] So when Rawls drew on personalism, he drew on thinkers such as Emil Brunner and Karl Barth. Unlike Maritain, Brunner and Barth were mainly concerned with claims about the nature of knowledge of God. For them, personalism was mainly a claim that God, being a person, reveals himself in personal encounters.[65]

Engaged in the philosophical debates about the nature of religious knowledge, Rawls's teachers were influenced by this European Protestant personalism. In his first book, *Spirit and Its Freedom* (1939), Thomas argued that, made in the image of God, one should "devote oneself to the welfare of all persons" because of our belief "in the potential worth of all persons as spiritual beings."[66] His beliefs on this point did not change when he arrived at Princeton. In his inaugural lecture, Thomas argued that the "*ideal,* to put it briefly, is the fulfilment of personality in a community of free men capable of taking responsibility for their own destiny."[67]

Rawls also framed his political framework around the main themes of personalism.[68] His goal, broadly conceived, was to discover the proper relationship between persons. This political vision was governed by two main commitments: the picture of God as a person and the belief that human beings are made in the image of God and thus with the capacity of being persons. This implied a stance of absolute equality: since all human beings are made in the image of God, all are capable of being persons, and so all are required to be treated as persons. This treatment of all as persons would constitute the ideal Christian community.

This central question of the thesis shows that Rawls understood ethics as an analysis of relations between persons and its task as delineating proper relations between persons. As he wrote, "Community in the full sense, that is, the heavenly community, is the end in itself."[69] According to Rawls, this vision of ethics contrasted with a view of ethics that related a person to their own highest good. As he put it, "Proper ethics is not the relating of a person to some objective 'good' for which he should strive, but is the relating of person to person and finally to God."[70] Some interpreters argue that this distinction laid the ground for Rawls's later distinction between deontological ethics, focused on the relation between persons, and teleological ethics, focused on the attainment by a person of some good.[71] It may be true that this is how Rawls's distinction between deontology and teleology developed, but this distinction was by no means explicitly or clearly drawn in the thesis. The two models—relationship between persons and the highest good of persons—were intermixed. The highest attainment of a human being was precisely a proper relation to other persons.

The core of Rawls's political vision was the concept of personhood. Rawls himself distinguished persons from "natural" things, but the thesis as a whole shows that Rawls connected the concept of personhood to the concept of "*Imago Dei*": the claim that human beings are made in the image of God. This is evident in Rawls's claim that to be a person in the highest sense of the term is to be able to relate to others as persons. As he wrote, "Man's likeness to God consists in this ability to enter into community, since God Himself is community, being the Triune God."[72] If so, Rawls concluded, "man is by nature a communal being."[73] That this communal form was the highest form of human beings was evident to Rawls also from analyzing the uses of bodies. These were, he thought, "designed, like everything else, to fit us for community with God," but also for the community with human beings.[74] As he wrote, bodies are necessary for communication: a "person must reveal his feeling to us by means of sense-data," and "whenever the sense-data of your body appear in my consciousness, then I know that you are in the vicinity and that I can establish contact with you by speech or gesture or any other means at my disposal."[75] "Communication without some sort of sign, i.e., without some sort of body," he concluded, "is to me unintelligible."[76]

Given the importance of *Imago Dei*, community involved first and foremost a proper relationship with God: "The universe in its spiritual aspect is a community of persons manifesting the glory of God."[77] However, community did not stop with God; it also involved proper relationships with other human beings: "Since it is the case that we are all related to God, by virtue of being persons in His image, it would seem to follow that an evil done to another becomes sin in our relation to God."[78] In other words, "if we were properly related to God, we would not sin against our neighbors."[79]

But what did it mean to treat another human being as a person? It meant taking seriously their potential to be persons and their capacity to have proper relations with God and other human beings. How could one do that? By integrating others into the Christian community.[80] As Rawls put it, "Salvation restores and completes man's nature" and the ideal community "supports personality."[81] This stance explains why, in his 1942 article "Christianity and the Modern World," Rawls argued that the Western world must return to Christianity. The highest potential of being a person—being able to live in communion with others—was at stake.

Rawls did not draw concrete political implications of this personalist vision. Unlike Catholic and Protestant personalists, he did not defend the notion of rights. For this reason alone, it is difficult to draw a very strong link between Rawls's early religious belief and his later liberalism. In fact, as Jeremy Waldron has argued, the notion of community is arguably too strong to allow for Rawls's later beliefs that each person should be treated as a separate person whose rights cannot be sacrificed for the welfare of society.[82] Rawls based his version of communal society on an analogy to Triune God, that "the *Imago Dei* is communal because God is communal, Three Persons in One."[83]

If interpreted literally, these statements would lead to an overly communal society, which personalists typically rejected. But in Rawls's interpretation of *Imago Dei,* the proper community was mainly a participatory community. This part of the vision was not elaborated, and it certainly differed from his teacher Thomas's explicitly stated vision of participatory democracy. As Thomas wrote, a political decision is made good mostly because people take part in making it: "It is often more essential that the different members of the community be honestly consulted and the different interests of the community carefully considered before the decision is reached than that the decision be perfectly consistent."[84] "The heart of Christianity," he continued, "is love of God and love of man as living and concrete individuals."[85] Focusing on theology, Thomas did not teach his own book in his Religious History class. Of course, Rawls had opportunities to discuss the political issues with Thomas and to read his book. So far as the bibliography of his thesis can tell, he never did. This lack of detail in the political vision shows Rawls's interest in the ethical side as opposed to institutional aspects of politics at the time.

Nonetheless, we can piece together Rawls's participatory political vision from his arguments in the thesis. First, Rawls's conception of the person seemed to require an "open" society, or a society to which everyone can belong. In particular, Rawls was critical of societies that exclude human beings based on factors over which they have no choice. Criticizing Nazi Germany, he wrote: "One cannot become an 'Aryan' by wish. One is excluded or included from birth."[86] He leveled similar criticisms against Marxisms, which excluded human beings based on their economic status, eighteenth-century Italian humanists who excluded human beings based on their cultural distinctions, and the Roman Catholic Church, which excluded others based on their religion.[87]

This rejection of exclusion depended on Rawls's stance of absolute equality of every person. One ground of this absolute equality was Luther, who is second only to the Bible in Rawls's "Chief Sources for Our Own View" in the thesis.[88] The core part of Rawls's stance was the rejection of differentiation based on merit. Like Luther, who argued in *Babylo-*

nian Captivity of the Church (1520) that grace is received "by faith alone, without any work or merits," Rawls argued that "true community does not count the merits of its members."[89] "Merit is a concept rooted in sin," he explained.[90]

Rawls gave several reasons for this rejection of merit. The first flowed from his theological framework. The most relevant aspect of the person is the fact that each is made in the image of God. In that regard, all human beings are equal. The second reason was independent of his theological framework and would reappear in *A Theory of Justice.* Each of us, Rawls claimed, has depended on others in achieving what we have achieved. Individualizing my achievement, I unjustly hide all that helped me do what I did. This is ignoring other persons, and so a sin:

> Suppose he was an upright man in the eyes of society, then he will now say to himself: "So you were an educated man, yes, but who paid for your education; so you were a good man and upright, yes, but who taught you your good manners and so provided you with good fortune that you did not need to steal; so you were a man of a loving disposition and not like the hard-hearted, yes, but who raised you in a good family, who showered you with care and affection when you were young so that you would grow up to appreciate kindness—must you not admit that what you have, you have received? Then be thankful and cease your boasting."[91]

Beyond insistence on equality, Rawls's conception of the person seemed to require a participatory vision. As he wrote, one can know another person only if that person decides to reveal himself: "All knowledge of other persons is knowledge given to us by them."[92] Necessarily, personal relations are always "active on both sides"; they always proceed on the basis of "mutual self-revelation."[93] As he put it, personal relations are "unique" in that the partners of this conversation or mutual encounter are not "readily exchangeable": an encounter with a different person would be a different encounter.[94] Thus, if political decisions are to acknowledge persons, they have to elicit their self-revelation, which implies their voluntary participation.

This participatory model of democracy is also evident in Rawls's "Spengler's Prophecy Realized." Rawls condemned the "centralization" of Roosevelt's America.[95] According to him, the Congress was "cringing" before the president, and he expected the future elections to be "plebiscites at best" in which "the federal machinery, organized as it has never been before, will see to it that the people vote the right way."[96]

Common everyday practices seemed to require personal engagement with others. This stance is apparent in Rawls's analysis of the first kind of human sin: egoism. Egoistic relationships with persons consisted of treating persons as useful objects, not acknowledging them as persons at all. Condemning egoistic relationships as sinful, Rawls gave an example of a sailor asking another to bring him coffee. In such situations, he wrote, "other people can only enter into his consciousness as means to the achievement of the desired end. The other persons do not enter as persons at all, but purely as means."[97] In *A Theory of Justice*, Rawls would give more specific reasons for the rejection of egoism, but it is worth noting that he excluded this view as incompatible with respecting human persons already in 1942.[98]

Rawls did not specify the full implications of personalism for the economic sphere. Treating persons as persons could mean the elimination of the means-ends-based labor relations, such as hiring someone solely for the sake of completing the tasks required for a business, since that would mean treating the person solely as the means to one's good. We do not know what Rawls thought about these topics. His example of a sailor clearly condemns contemporary economic structures but does not offer an alternative. The same can be said about the customer-client relations typical of contemporary economies. In Rawls's conceptual framework, treating a waiter simply as a waiter would be considered a sin. Here too, however, Rawls did not offer any particular advice for avoiding the sin of egoism in economic transactions.

Stopping at the general principles that governed it, Rawls departed from his teachers, in particular Thomas, for whom the Christian principles had clear—if not very concrete—political implications. As Thomas wrote in 1939, treating "women and children . . . as persons, with lives of their own, and slaves . . . as equal to their masters" required eliminating economic inequality, since economic hardship prevented people from focusing on their spiritual good.[99] According to Thomas, Western democracies "have permitted the most appalling economic inequality, and they have almost lost the idea of a spiritual good dominating the common life."[100] To correct this, he recommended that Western societies "learn to respect the worth of common people."[101]

Rawls did not follow Thomas in this condemnation of poverty. His focus was on the sin of egotism, which, following Leon, he defined as "that perverse desire for height and that sinister craving for self-worship."[102] An egotist acknowledges another person as a person but seeks "to set the 'thou' below itself."[103] He gave a "capitalist" as an example. In the mind of this capitalist, the employees "are inferior, while he is superior," and "the capitalist takes great pride in his wealth; he loves to show it off."[104] Rawls's vision of an equal society required an elimination of motivations that seek distinctions, not the distinctions themselves.

How does one bring about such an ideal society? Rawls's answer relied mostly on God's grace. Christians were obliged to do certain things to bring about the ideal Christian community. As Rawls wrote, one can be restored to personhood only by others: "Personality can be restored only by personality, and community only by community."[105] However, human actions could go only so far. The main human task in conversion seems to have consisted in education. Rawls believed that "few things have served to destroy Christianity today more than sheer ignorance."[106] Thus, the first step toward a Christian society "must be a Christian education."[107]

The first step was also the only step that the human beings could take by themselves. The second step would be the "conversion of the inner man," but this, as Rawls wrote, "can only come about with the aid of Grace."[108] Election would happen through conversion, or "that intense experience of lying in exposure before the Word of God."[109] Human beings had no role in this conversion: they could not affect God's grace.

In sum, by 1942 Rawls had already emphasized treating everyone equally as a person as a core part of his political framework. This emphasis was part of a theological vision and grounded in the claim that all human beings are made in the image of God. Rawls had not yet explained what treating everyone as a person required in ordinary social situations, but it was clear that the institutions of an ideal society had to prevent impersonal relations and attitudes of superiority. This theological vision was the starting grounds for Rawls's secular political vision in *A Theory of Justice,* in which the inviolability of persons was also a core element.

The Philosophical Vision of *Meaning of Sin and Faith*

If Rawls's political vision was informed by neo-orthodox themes, his early philosophical vision was importantly influenced by liberal Protestantism. In particular, the central commitment of the thesis is that a theologian's task is to analyze religious experience, and that correspondence with this religious experience is what justifies a theological conceptual framework.

Rawls's main goal in the thesis was to elaborate a conceptual framework that analyzed our experience correctly. *Meaning of Sin and Faith* begins with these words: "Every theology and every philosophy proceeds to investigate experience."[110] Rawls's goal, to put it most broadly, was to analyze Christian experience. He proposed to "outline and investigate our fundamental presuppositions."[111] It is important to emphasize these first words of Rawls's thesis. They show Rawls's view of theology as analysis of Christian experience: something that a neo-orthodox interpretation of Rawls cannot fully capture. And they show Rawls as a philosopher: he starts the thesis with philosophical claims and moves to his political vision only later.

This is not to say that Rawls's philosophical vision did not bring in neo-orthodox themes. This is particularly true of his conception of God. According to Rawls, God was a person and as such disclosed himself to human beings frequently. As all persons, God disclosed himself to others, and full knowledge of him was available only through such disclosures: "All knowledge of other persons is knowledge given to us by them."[112] As Rawls wrote, "Man must wait for God to speak to him. He must wait for His word."[113]

However, like liberal Protestants, Rawls believed that God also disclosed himself in direct, personal, and frequent encounters with human beings, rather than only once, through Christ. Archetypal of such personal encounters with God's Word was the experience of conversion, which Rawls described as "that intense experience of flatness and lying in exposure before the Word of God."[114] Rawls's conception of the Word of God—God's disclosure—was very broad: it included God's incarnation in Jesus, in the working of the Word through the chosen apostles who spread Jesus's story, and—crucially—in the personal experiences of conversion as described in the Acts of the Apostles and by Rawls in his thesis.[115] Rawls emphasized the latter: conversion, he thought, "constitutes the synthesis of Christian experience," and all doctrines of election "which do not spring straight from it are purely academic."[116]

As was true of liberal Protestants, Rawls thought that the conceptual framework he arrived at by analyzing Christian experiences needed no further support than showing that Christians actually had these experiences. As he wrote, his main commitments "have empirical meaning and are derived from experience," such as the discussed example of conversion.[117] This theme explains why, despite remarking in the bibliography that the Bible is "always the last word in matters of religion," Rawls did not think that the truth of his conclusions depended on their correspondence to statements in the Bible.[118] Like his teachers Greene and Thomas, Rawls understood the Bible as a record and analysis of Christian experiences. As such, the Bible was a source of examples, some of which—such as Peter's speechlessness or Paul's being struck dumb—Rawls used as examples of conversion similar to his own.[119] He did think that the Bible, narrating the experiences of conversion, was a complete revelation of the nature of God: "The Bible has told us all we need to know about Him."[120] He also certainly thought that his own conclusions about God coincided with those in the Bible. However, he did not think that the Bible was the standard of truth, and, in fact, appraised the Bible by this very same standard: "The Bible is right," he wrote, "when it insists that we will be resurrected in some sort of body, whatever sort it may be."[121]

To make the reliance on Christian experience good, Rawls had to show that it was actually shared. For this reason, he insisted that all Christians, although they would experience conversion in different ways—some suddenly, others in a protracted way—would agree on its content.[122] "If any of us analyze our experience, and if that experience is genuinely Christian," he wrote, "then we should all agree."[123] As he thought that all Christians had experienced conversion and that this experience provided knowledge of God, Rawls expected that they would all recognize the conceptual framework elaborated in *Meaning of Sin and Faith* as their own. In those cases when we do not have exactly the same experiences, we would still be able to recognize them, presumably because these experiences would be sufficiently like ours: "Although we may have never experienced a sudden conversion like Paul's, we can nevertheless understand Paul and agree with him."[124]

In reality, of course, not all Christians agreed on Rawls's interpretation of Christian experience. Rawls was certainly aware of this fact. In fact, he criticized Augustine and Aquinas for providing the wrong doctrines to explain the Christian experience. In *A Theory of Justice,* nearly thirty years later, Rawls would also hold that, despite the apparent disagreement, all persons in liberal societies hold the same conception of justice. So how could Rawls hold, so unproblematically, that all Christians had the same experiences? He relied on a distinction between experiences themselves and theories that analyzed them. So, while all persons could be expected to have at least some of the same experiences, not all persons might agree on theories that analyzed those experiences. This crucial distinction is present in *A Theory of Justice* as well: both justice as fairness and utilitarianism analyze the same shared experiences—considered judgments—of reasonable persons. Throughout his career Rawls believed that the presence of competing theoretical explanations was not evidence for absence of shared experiences.

This distinction between agreement in theory and shared experiences is evident in Rawls's critique of Augustine and Aquinas. Rawls argued that Augustine and Aquinas shared the Christian experiences but failed to analyze them correctly.[125] According to Rawls, Augustine and Aquinas overlooked the crucial distinction between the personal and the natural: "All naturalistic thinkers have completely missed the spiritual and personal element which forms the deep inner core of the universe."[126] To prove their analyses wrong, Rawls attempted to show that natural appetitions cannot lead to personal relations, to egotism, or to community. Since, he assumed, we all had experiences of egotism and communal relations, this argument showed that Augustine's and Aquinas's concepts did not analyze our experiences correctly. For this failure to appreciate the distinction and to describe all human relations in terms of desires, he named Augustine and Aquinas "naturalists."[127]

Rawls also pointed out the historical origin of Augustine's and Aquinas's naturalist mistake. To do so, he appealed to the historical themes of Harnackian essentialism evident also in his teacher Thomas's work. He traced Augustine's and Aquinas's mistake to the Greeks—Plato and Aristotle—who analyzed all human relations in terms of desire and appetition. Explicitly, this account drew on the Swedish theologian Anders Nygren's *Agape and Eros*.[128] Influenced by liberal Protestantism, Nygren sought to disassociate the core of Christianity from the Greek additions. He wrote a dissertation on the biblical historicist Ernst Troeltsch (1865–1923), and in his famous 1922 essay, "The Essence of Christianity," he repeated the core historicist theme that, despite the various forms Christianity took in different social contexts, the historical figure of Jesus Christ was the uniting link.[129] To recover the lost essential meaning of Christianity, Nygren looked at how it defined itself against its rivals, in particular the Greek idea of love.[130]

Appealing to Nygren, Rawls argued that the Greek—naturalist—conception of ethics is to turn human desire toward a proper object. On this mistaken interpretation, Augustine and Aquinas only changed that proper object from the Platonic good to God.[131] In doing so, he thought, they turned God into "merely a bigger and better object of . . . enjoyment."[132] To the contrary, as we have seen, Rawls believed that ethics was not about desire but about relating "of a person to person and finally to God."[133] On the whole, then, Rawls thought that his belief in the commonality of Christian experience did not require agreement in theories that explain the reasons for this common experience.

In other respects, Rawls departed from liberal Protestantism. Most importantly, he expanded the shared experience from Christians to non-Christians and even to nonbelievers. To Rawls, this step was quite self-evident: he thought that nonbelievers would have experiences typical not of faith but of sin. In particular, he wrote, sin would engender the feeling of aloneness, or "spiritual cut-offness" and "desolating closedness."[134] Nietzsche, in Rawls's mind, was a good example of suffering the consequences of egotism. Quoting Nietzsche's claim that "this world is the *Will to Power* and nothing else," Rawls concluded that Nietzsche's world "is one of aloneness" and, as aloneness is one of the experiences of sin, that his experiences are best described as experiences of the sinful.[135]

Rawls's critique of Nietzsche reveals his belief that one's experience does not depend solely on one's conceptual framework. Rawls allowed that a person who had not thought of God and did not think of his own actions as sinful would still have experiences typical of sin. He did not compare Nietzsche's experiences of sin with those of a repenting Christian who thought of himself as sinful, in effect detaching those experiences from the beliefs that typically give rise to them. If not one's beliefs, what prompted experiences of sin? Rawls's answer was the *Imago Dei* and the human relation with God. In virtue of being created in the image of God, human beings always have the capacity for community.[136] This capacity can be rejected, but the *Imago Dei* can never be abrogated. As Rawls wrote, "All men have God as Father, but not all men are His sons."[137] Because of this image, Rawls thought, humans are always in a certain relation to God, their actions can always be described as sinful or faithful, and—Rawls seems to have concluded—a repudiated relation to God creates experiences of sin: "Aloneness is aloneness because the *Imago Dei* remains."[138]

In sum, Rawls's philosophical vision was centered on the concept of experience. As a theologian, he analyzed Christian experiences and attempted to elaborate a conceptual framework that would explain them. The concept of experience was all-encompassing but mainly contained personal experiences, such as the experience of conversion or that of sin. The conceptual framework was justified insofar as it matched and explained this experience.

The Second World War and the Loss of Faith

In February 1943, having finished his thesis and undergraduate education, Rawls enrolled in the army. Engrossed in theology, Rawls planned to join the seminary but put off his plans both because he was not sure his motives were "sincere" and because of the war. As he wrote, "I felt I should serve in the armed services as so many of my friends and classmates were doing."[139] One should be cautious to not anachronistically attribute this view to the young Rawls, but the motivating reason seems to have been fairness. As a citizen, one had to fulfill one's duties as other citizens did.

Sent to the Pacific theater for two years, Rawls served in New Guinea, the Philippines, and, toward the end of the war, in Japan. Overall, he judged the army a "dismal institution," left it in January 1946, and re-entered Princeton University in the autumn of the same year, this time as a graduate student in philosophy.[140] Philosophically, he was a changed person: his arguments no longer relied on God or other Christian concepts that structured *Meaning of Sin and Faith*. As he wrote, "I started as a believing orthodox Episcopalian Christian, and abandoned it entirely by June of 1945."[141]

Since Rawls did not write on his Christian past during the war or in graduate school, we do not have any contemporaneous documents that explain this transformation. Rawls did, however, write reminiscences on his religion and the years in the army in the early 1990s; they are published together with *Meaning of Sin and Faith* and provide us with three events during the Second World War that aid in elucidating the transformation of his thinking. They all question the feasibility of his liberal Protestant conception of the personal and direct experience of God.

The first of these events is the speech of a Lutheran pastor at Kilei Ridge in December 1944. Encouraging the soldiers before battle, the priest proclaimed that God directed the American bullets at the Japanese and protected the Americans from the bullets of their enemies. Rawls judged these claims as "simply falsehoods," yet these falsehoods made him question his own understanding of God.[142] Rawls had combined neo-orthodoxy and liberal Protestantism by claiming that God reveals himself personally, and not only through Christ but also in the more direct experiences of conversion known to every Christian. Numerous deaths in the war raised doubts about this picture of God who frequently intervenes in human affairs—even if only by self-disclosure—and led Rawls to conclude that God was disengaged from the human world.

Second, the death of Rawls's tent-mate and friend Deacon must have made this conclusion very apparent. In May 1945, on the Villa Verde trail on Luzon, Deacon died entirely due to what Rawls saw as the chance of circumstances. When the first sergeant asked for two volunteers, one to reconnoiter the Japanese position and the other to give blood to a wounded soldier, Rawls's blood type was appropriate while Deacon's was not; Deacon went to reconnoiter and, hit with a mortar shell, died.[143]

Rawls could not give this death a higher purpose, and God appeared more and more withdrawn from details of human life.

The third event, the news about the Holocaust from the first American troops to reach the German concentration camps, strengthened this conclusion. While, on his own account, Rawls had gone along with Lincoln's attempt to give the Civil War purpose and paint God as acting justly, the Holocaust, Rawls wrote, "can't be interpreted in that way."[144] Realizing that God would not intervene to save millions of Jews, he concluded that he could not expect God's response to prayer or any intervention into human affairs.[145] As his conception of God's personal self-disclosure in the experiences of conversion implied an active God that disclosed himself to particular persons, Rawls must have rejected it for the same reasons.

Rawls's war experiences by no means necessitated the abandonment of religion: he could have simply modified his understanding of God as well as the accompanying notions of sin, faith, and revelation. In fact, like many struggling liberal Protestants during the First World War, he could have turned to neo-orthodoxy's conception of revelation as God's disclosure through Jesus, rejecting his account of personal contact with God's Word in conversion. Yet, he did not. In his later writings Rawls abandoned all of these concepts.

Why did Rawls think that his experiences during the war were sufficient to abandon his religious beliefs? Perhaps he could not conceive of a God who was simultaneously just and who allowed the Holocaust to happen. Lacking this concrete picture of God, Rawls did not have a criterion to distinguish between the just and the unjust. This dilemma would explain part of Rawls's criticism of Paul Ramsey's *Basic Christian Ethics*, which is faulted for not providing a criterion for distinguishing right from wrong.[146] Alternatively, perhaps different cultures of the Pacific theater made Rawls realize that Christianity could not explain the experiences of all human beings, and, as a result, made him seek another basis for his reliance on experiences.

It is not clear just when this conversion came about. Rawls's first graduate school essay (1946) does not make use of religious concepts, leading to the conclusion that it happened before graduate school. However, in his February 1947 recommendation of Rawls, Scoon described him as religious. "He is not only vitally interested in philosophy," Scoon wrote, "but is also a religious man."[147] Moreover, explaining his changing beliefs, Rawls himself wrote that during "the following months and years" he rejected many Christian doctrines but that his "fideism remained firm against all worries about the existence of God."[148] This memory suggests that he continued to believe in the existence of God.

Some have suggested that we should view Rawls as a liberal Protestant who held on to his religious beliefs but tried to justify them in secular ways.[149] Others have asked if Rawls's later liberalism does not in fact rely on unstated religious grounds.[150] Evidence for such claims is scant and doubtful. At best, we can find occasions in which Rawls discussed religious positions in his post-1945 writings. For example, in 1947 he discussed the figure of a saint: "A man may be a friend, or a husband, or a statesman, or a saint—according to whom he serves and what purpose he serves."[151] And: "What is impious is for a man as a man to make a counter claim. Our Faith in Providence, if we have it, and our allegiance to its goal can only be because it embodies the right, not by definition, but by its nature. . . . It is not by definition that St Francis could do no wrong; but because he was the kind of person he was."[152] Although here Rawls discussed the figure of a saint as an ordinary part of our ontology, it is possible that he was merely explaining the religious point of view. The context does not make it clear. Aside from such occasional remarks, we do not have evidence that Rawls retained his religious beliefs. This distinguishes him from figures who were open about their Christianity. For these reasons, I treat Rawls as someone who, for the practical purpose that concerns us—elaborating a political and philosophical view—lost belief in God and turned away from theological concepts as grounds for his political and philosophical claims.

Despite this transformation, both political and philosophical continuities between Rawls's early work and his later work would remain. Politically, Rawls would continue taking the stance of equality and analyze the role—or lack thereof—of moral desert. Indeed, as he wrote in the 1953 lectures on Christian ethics, Christian ethical commitments overlap with what he called "philosophical ethics." According to Rawls, philosophical ethics "doesn't upset current practical moral conceptions." For this reason, he expected that "philosophical ethics and Christian ethics would in the end fit together somehow; but this [is] a question we can leave to consider at another time."[153] Philosophically, continuities remained as well. In particular, believing that the task of theology is analysis of experience, he would later argue that philosophy had the same task. Similarly, just as he argued that Christians and non-Christians had common experiences, he would make the same claim about reasonable persons in general. And finally, just as he argued that a theological theory is justified if one only shows that it analyzed shared experience correctly, he would say the same about a secular theory in ethics. In these broad themes, Rawls's early Protestant years left a mark that would be visible—though in different forms—throughout his career.

2

Drawing on Logical Positivism

WHEN RAWLS RETURNED to the Princeton philosophy department as a graduate student in the spring of 1946, he was a different person. His earliest graduate writings showed the influence of analytic philosophy and in particular logical positivism. Even the title of his first graduate essay—"A Brief Inquiry into the Nature and Function of Ethical Theory" (1946)—highlights the transformation from religious to secular. The essay contained central references to Neurath's *Foundations of the Social Sciences*, Carnap's *Philosophy and Logical Syntax* and *Introduction to Semantics and Formalization of Logic*, Hans Reichenbach's *Experience and Prediction*, and Popper's *Logic of Scientific Discovery*.[1] Moreover, Rawls consciously emphasized his debts to the tradition, describing the essay as an attempt to follow the "physicalist" example of Rudolf Carnap and Otto Neurath. Heavily relying on C. J. Ducasse for the details of his philosophical vision, Rawls modeled ethical inquiry after scientific inquiry and presented a scientific vision of ethics.

Rawls's engagement with logical positivism is surprising for a variety of reasons. To begin with, folk narratives still portray the revival of ethical inquiry in the 1950s and 1960s as a liberation from logical positivism.[2] Rawls is one of the principal actors in this popular narrative; he is shown to have brought back a more classic and also more fruitful approach to moral and political philosophy. It turns out, however, that Rawls's contribution to philosophy and ethics was actually inspired by logical positivism. This influence is not appreciated in the literature on Rawls. Yet it was important, even if Rawls did not become a logical positivist and this initial secular influence wore off as the years went on.

Second, Rawls joined the same department that had led him to write a religious thesis just five years earlier. How could the same department develop such a different thinker? And third, logical positivism was dismissive of religious thought, classifying it as "nonsensical" or without meaning.[3] Even if Rawls had lost his faith, surely a tradition that treated religious claims as having no meaning would have been difficult to accept in light of his earlier religious commitments.

This chapter explains Rawls's transition to analytic philosophy and the nature of his borrowing from logical positivism. Focusing on Rawls's philosophical vision, it shows the influence of his teachers in prompting him to read analytic texts, traces the influence of C. J. Ducasse, and gives an account of Rawls's first secular conception of ethics. Logical positivism's emphasis on analysis and especially analysis of experience undoubtedly made this tradition appealing to Rawls. Thus, while discarding his theological framework, Rawls continued to think of philosophy—now no longer theology—as analysis of experience. Philosophy was to elaborate a conceptual framework that explained human experience. If correct, this analysis would also justify the philosophical framework. Step by step, Rawls was moving in the direction of reflective equilibrium.

Rawls's Path to Analytic Philosophy

When Rawls returned to Princeton in the spring of 1946, the department had begun to change. With the exception of Greene, who was on sabbatical and would leave for Yale in 1946 after his wife's death, Rawls took courses with familiar faces: Philosophy of Plato with Scoon, Logic with Ushenko, and Problems of Philosophy with Malcolm. In the summer of that year, he took Systematic Ethics with James Ward Smith, Princeton's new hire. Smith, a Princeton BA and PhD, joined the philosophy department as assistant professor after the war, having served in the navy. Though he also had an interest in religion—he coedited the four-volume study *Religion in American Life* in 1961—most of his early writing was on analytic philosophy and ethics.[4] In 1947 he published an article on the general theory of value, arguing against the logical positivist A. J. Ayer.[5] In a 1948 article, he distinguished between different senses of subjectivism to tackle the positivist claim that all value judgments are subjective.[6] Although the syllabus from Smith's Systematic Ethics does not remain, he undoubtedly taught on logical positivism and its conception of philosophy.

Rawls also spent much of his academic time with visiting professors. Norman Malcolm, who returned to Princeton in 1946, was critically engaged with logical positivism. A student with G. E. Moore in Cambridge and an interlocutor of Ludwig Wittgenstein before the war, Malcolm was well versed in logical positivism and its shortcomings. Before the war, Malcolm had published two articles discussing the nature of necessity and was preparing to write "Defending Common Sense."[7] Both of these topics—necessary connections between facts and value judgments and reliance on common sense—would become relevant as Rawls would formulate his conception of ethical theory. The emphasis in Malcolm's course was on a Wittgensteinian approach to such topics. According to Rawls, in his course Malcolm "applied to some of the problems of epistemology and metaphysics some of the techniques developed by Cambridge group ie., Wittgenstein etc."[8]

In the fall of 1946, Rawls also took a course with Wolfgang Köhler, a founder of the Gestalt school of psychology, who taught Conception of Consciousness. By the time Köhler taught this course, he was interested in the nature of value as well. In 1944 he published "Value and Fact," which attempted to explain the nature of value in naturalistic terms and argued that value resides in the objects themselves and is perceived by observers.[9] Rawls described this course as focusing on "concepts of psychology, criterias [sic] of their meaning, and the methodology of that science."[10]

In the spring of 1947, Rawls took a course on pragmatism with Lewis Edwin Hahn, the future author of *The Library of Living Philosophers*. Given pragmatism's engagement with logical positivism, it is not surprising that Rawls would learn of Carnap and Otto Neurath in that course.[11] Rawls described this course as a study of "American pragmatism . . . stressing James, Dewey, Peirce, Lewis and others."[12] Finally, Rawls audited a seminar on "learning theory, social psychology, and math logic" with the logician Alonzo Church.[13]

The rest of the academic year was spent in the more traditional courses: Philosophy of Kant with Edgar Herbert Henderson, Philosophy of Aristotle with Scoon, and Pre-Kantian Rationalism with Ledger Wood. The summer of that year involved preparations with Ushenko for the general examinations and included the history of philosophy, metaphysics, epistemology, logic and scientific method, ethics and theory of value, and philosophy of mind. It is clear, however, that Rawls began to rely on visiting professors to pursue interests that began departing from the original members of Princeton's philosophy department.

The only essay that remains from 1946 is "A Brief Inquiry into the Nature of Ethics." In it, Rawls developed his own "physicalist" theory of ethics. Its core idea was to model ethical inquiry on scientific inquiry and then claim that it differed from scientific inquiry only in its subject matter. Thus, if observational statements were the subject matter of a scientific theory, ethical judgments played this role for an ethical theory. In other respects, the two types of inquiry were the same. Both aimed at building a deductive structure consisting of axioms and the basic observational statements deduced from these axioms. Theories in both types of inquiry were justified by the ability of their axioms to deduce observational statements (OS_D) that matched the actual observational statements (OS_A) made by the scientific community. And neither scientific nor ethical theories could be justified in a more foundational way.

The essay clearly departs from anything Rawls's teachers were writing. Even though Rawls's 1946 essay drew very obviously on C. J. Ducasse and the general logical positivist conception of science, it reflects a clear sense of independence that Rawls gained first from his teachers and then also from the texts he considered. He started with the basics, asking what ethical theory should be: what questions it should raise, and how it should answer them. The birth of Rawls the philosopher really started in these early years of graduate school.

Logical Positivist Conception of Scientific Inquiry

In our popular narratives, logical positivism is associated with foundationalist interpretations of experience. Its early works argued that basic or elementary experiences are not permeated by the conceptual frameworks of the people who have them.[14] Not depending on any conceptual framework, such experiences could be used to justify these frameworks. To justify a proposition, we must in the end resort to nonlinguistic "pointings, in exhibiting what is meant."[15] But this is not the form of logical positivism that Rawls studied and referenced in his essay. By the mid-1930s, logical positivism already interpreted all experience in linguistic terms: all experience was now thought to depend on conceptual schemes or "descriptions" and "classifications."[16] Logical positivists now thought that, lacking a rock-bottom foundation in nonlinguistic experiences, all propositions were justifiable only by other propositions of the same kind. This changed the nature of justification drastically: in principle, it went on forever, and when it stopped, it stopped in a tentative manner and for pragmatic reasons. Karl Popper (1902–1994), one of the key figures of the movement and—we will see—a direct influence on Rawls, made it clear that justification stopped when the scientific community agreed on a sufficient number of observations to declare any one scientific theory correct. In one of his most eloquent passages, Popper compared the construction of scientific theories to building on swamps:

> The empirical basis of objective science has thus nothing "absolute" about it. Science does not rest upon rock-bottom. The bold structure of its theories rises, as it were, above a swamp. It is like a building erected on piles. The piles are driven down from above into the swamp, but not down to any natural or "given" base; and when we cease our attempts to drive our piles into a deeper layer, it is not because we have reached firm ground. We simply stop when we are satisfied that they are firm enough to carry the structure, at least for the time being.[17]

While logical positivism changed significantly owing to this shift to nonfoundationalism, it nonetheless preserved some of its earlier features. Importantly for the young Rawls, logical positivists maintained the belief that some experiences are basic—not merely more basic than other experiences, but basic tout court. The notion of "observational statements" (also called "basic statements" or "protocol statements"), for which logical positivism is known, is directly tied to these basic experiences.[18] Observational statements were typically thought of as records

of these simple experiences: they were "self-consistent singular statements" of fact that reported "observable events" occurring at a given
time and a given place.[19] The notion of basic experience led logical
positivists to the belief that, as long as typical scientific observers were
appropriately placed with regard to the object of observation, they
would agree in their reports. Popper took agreement among scientific
observers as a matter of course: his notion of "observation," albeit not
elaborated, required only that the observers be "suitably placed in
space and time."[20] Indeed, Popper was so convinced of this agreement
that he concluded that, should it prove impossible, it would indicate
not a weakness in his view but a "failure of language as a means of
universal communication."[21]

In that regard, the new logical positivism retained its earlier belief
that at least some observation is basic. This shows a certain discrepancy
in its position: while claiming that, in a nonfoundational world, all beliefs and judgments are susceptible to being tested and rejected, logical
positivists continued to believe that some experiences are so basic that
it is unimaginable that they be shown wrong. This suggested that, from
their point of view, some experience was simply not affected by the rest
of scientific observers' system of beliefs.

The notion of basic statements shaped logical positivism's account
of justification. According to the tradition, a scientific theory is justified
insofar as its axioms, also known as "postulates" or "primitive propositions," yield deduced observational statements (OS_D, or deduced observational statements) that correspond to the actual observational statements made by the scientific community (OS_A, or actual observational
statements). This process is therefore that of both discovery and justification. It is a process of discovery because the actual judgments of the
scientific community have to be analyzed to determine which theory best
explains them. And it is a process of justification because, once the theory
yields deduced judgments that match the actual basic statements, it has
accounted for all the evidence there is.

On this picture of justification, the actual observational statements
(OS_A) of normal observers form the subject matter of a scientific theory.
Clearly, then, scientific theories depend on the agreement in the judgments of all normal observers: without such agreement, scientific
theory would lack the subject matter. It is crucial for the understanding

of Rawls's early ethical theory—and his "reflective equilibrium" in *A Theory of Justice*—that overlap in the judgments of scientific observers is critical for justifying a scientific theory.

When Rawls drew on logical positivism, he used this conception of scientific theory. Although this was an unusual move among logical positivists, other thinkers had done so already. They skirted one problematic part of the tradition—the analytic-synthetic distinction—and tried to make ethics into an empirical inquiry instead. This new type of argument was developed by Curt John Ducasse (1881–1969), but except for shaping the thought of its most famous follower, John Rawls, this view did not draw followers.[22] Its core idea to model ethical inquiry on scientific inquiry was simple and worn in the broader modernist movement of which logical positivism was part.[23] The French economist Jacques Rueff (1896–1978), whose *From the Physical to the Social Sciences* (1929) inspired Ducasse, had also proposed introducing the method of the physical science to ethics and constructing "a system of initial propositions, axioms and definitions capable of serving as premises to reasoning."[24] Nonetheless, fashioning ethics as a scientific inquiry was a new and unusual proposal among logical positivists who generally assumed that ethical judgments were fundamentally different from scientific judgments.

Ducasse set out to model ethics after the logical positivist conception of science while ignoring the analytic-synthetic distinction. To do so, he had to show that it had a subject matter of its own and that this subject matter was susceptible to being treated by the scientific method. Ducasse's formulation of these two notions showed logical positivism's influence. He first defined the "primitive subject matter of ethics," or those facts that are "beyond question" and "about which . . . questions [are] asked by ethical science."[25] This subject matter consisted of ethical judgments and included both particular judgments such as "This is wrong" and empirical generalizations such as "Stealing is wrong."[26] Ducasse set two conditions to these ethical judgments: they were to be "most confident" and spontaneous, or made without deliberate application of any ethical theory.[27] Rawls would draw on this picture of ethical judgments, and even his eventual account of "considered judgments" in *A Theory of Justice* would retain these aspects of Ducasse's influence.[28]

Ducasse's conception of the scientific method was typical of logical positivism. He thought that the aim of a theorist both in the natural sciences and in ethics was to formulate axioms or "premises from which could have been deduced . . . empirically discovered generalizations [such as 'stealing is wrong'] and . . . others empirically discoverable."[29] These deduced generalizations G_D were subsequently to be tested by actual ethical judgments J_A, and the theory was to be considered justified insofar as the deduced generalizations G_D matched, or predicted, actual ethical judgments J_A.[30] Ducasse did not specify the extent to which the axioms had to predict actual ethical judgments, but, given that he included only confident judgments in the subject matter of ethical theory, he must have thought that the axioms had to predict actual ethical judgments with complete or nearly complete accuracy.

Although simple and, in the broader philosophical landscape, worn, Ducasse's theory opened the possibility of a truly normative logical positivist ethics. If ethical inquiry was successful, it would result in ethical principles that all normal persons acknowledged as true of at least their most confident judgments. Assuming a human wish to be consistent, these principles would become a powerful normative force. On the individual level, the principles could reveal inconsistency between the judgments and the principles, thereby also informing us "of the alterations to be made in [these divergent judgments]."[31] Given the assumption that all observers agree in their judgments, ethical inquiry was meant to function in exactly the same manner on the social level. The principles were part of an internal critique, informing us of the alterations to be made in order to resolve inconsistencies among these judgments—in this case disagreements between different persons.[32] To fulfill this normative promise of the scientific ethics position, one had to show that ethical judgments of all persons converged sufficiently to permit the formulation of ethical principles.

Ducasse's proposal, while promising, was unfinished. He did not attempt to show that all persons would actually agree in their ethical judgments, and, most importantly, he did not explain why he thought all persons would agree. Impressed by the scientific edifice of which ethics was thought to be capable, Rawls would undertake to show that all persons would agree in their ethical judgments. Taking on this task, he would also be forced to engage the more difficult question that Ducasse ignored: why reasonable persons might agree in their judgments. His independent and creative mind would be evident in these attempts.

A "Physicalist" Approach to Ethical Theory

The shaping influence of Popper and Ducasse is reflected in "A Brief Inquiry into the Nature and Function of Ethical Theory," Rawls's earliest and only surviving essay from that year.[33] Finished in August 1946, it was most likely written for the Systematic Ethics course with James Ward Smith. It was certainly written before the spring 1947 semester, since in his application to Cornell, Rawls describes it as a finished essay.[34] It is important that Rawls saw himself as following the later evolution of logical positivism, as described here. Rawls himself made a distinction between "positivism" and "physicalism." According to him, any work that was concerned with "notational arguments" about conceptual schemes was a positivist work.[35] He included Carnap and Ayer in this category. As he put it,

> It is clear that such people are quarrelling about what sort of a notation they shall use to talk about such things as bent sticks in water, swimming pools in the desert, and Greta Garbo in a dream. . . . They are not disputing about facts, but about alternative languages with which to talk about the facts. They are not proposing genuine scientific theories which have predictive value, but linguistic conventions.[36]

Such discussions, Rawls thought, were useful only for "clarifying and stipulating rules for linguistic expression."[37] They do not solve any actual ethical problems, only problems in theory construction.

"Physicalists," on the contrary, were concerned with the facts. Rawls described his theory as "physicalist in the same sense as this term was understood by the Vienna Circle ([in] essays in *Erkenntnis* by Carnap [and] Neurath)."[38] Noting the novelty of his approach within the tradition, he portrayed his theory as an extension of the physicalist theory to ethics:

It is the business of philosophers to begin an inquiry, to break the ground, to so formulate and clarify the domain of investigation that it can become an exact science. Philosophers have already performed this duty for physics, astronomy, psychology and other sciences. The task remains to be done for ethics, and this essay is such an attempt.[39]

Extending the "physicalist" theory, Rawls drew mostly on Ducasse, whose essay he praised as "excellent throughout on many points discussed here."[40] Even the title of his essay is an acknowledgment of Ducasse's influence: Rawls essentially only added "A Brief Inquiry into" to Ducasse's title.[41] Rawls thought that ethics diverged from other scientific disciplines only in its subject matter. As he wrote, "The technique of theory construction is the same in ethics as it is in physics. The only difference concerns subject matter."[42] The subject matter "peculiar to ethics," according to Rawls, "is the facts of ethical judgment."[43]

Rawls's conception of scientific theory was typical of logical positivists. He thought that the scientist aimed at elaborating axioms from which the predicted particular ethical judgments (J_D for "judgments deduced") would be deduced and then tested against actual ethical judgments (J_A for "judgments actual"). Quoting Rueff, Rawls wrote that the philosopher's task in ethics was to formulate principles that can "predict [these] judgments":

> The following quotation from Rueff, cited by Ducasse . . . , expresses perfectly the viewpoint here presented in slightly different words: the task of ethical theory is to ". . . enunciate a system of initial propositions, axioms, and definitions which, when fed into the reasoning machine, will produce theorems coinciding with the rules of practical morals."[44]

In "Nature of Ethical Theory," Rawls took it as his task to construct and justify such a theory: "We propose to construct a theory, to make deductions from it, and to test these deductions against the subject matter of ethical theory, namely, the actual moral judgments made by the class of people whose judgments constitute the reference of the theory."[45]

Logical positivist themes that shaped the skeleton of Rawls's conception of ethical theory also influenced its central features. The key notion of ethical judgments was designed with Popper's basic statements in mind.[46] Modeling ethical inquiry after the image of empirical theories, Rawls fashioned ethical judgments as the data against which theories are tested:

> The physical sciences have as their subject matter certain processes which might be termed "thing" processes. And every physical theory is testable in that it denies that certain "thing" processes ever occur. Now ethical theory is essentially the same. Its subject matter, however, is not a "thing" process, but a "word" process, and every ethical theory is testable in that it denies that certain specified "word" processes ever occur.[47]

In other words, if ethical theory was to have a subject matter, no ethical agent would utter some word sequences, such as "having a slave is just"; and, conversely, all ethical agents would utter at least some common word sequence, such as "having a slave is unjust."

Of course, not just any utterance counted. Rawls imposed a variety of restrictions on them. First, they had to be actually uttered, not just conceived of in one's mind. As he wrote, "We discover what a person means to assert by observing his subsequent <u>behavior</u>. And so it is in ethics. To determine what people mean to assert by ethical statements, we observe how they use the word, and how they act within the 'sign-context.'"[48]

These utterances had to be made by what Rawls called "normal observers." While possibly a restrictive condition, in practice it played no role: a universalist in the scope of his theory, Rawls included in the group of "normal observers" "all animals which are capable of using, understanding, and acting on such word processes as 'this is right (wrong)' etc in whatever word-language they may be uttered."[49] Nationalities, cultures, or time periods did not exclude people from being considered "normal observers."

Second, the utterances were separated from the reasons for which they were made. Although Rawls's explanation suggested that the philosopher was interested in "what people mean to assert," his examples indicated otherwise: ethical judgments were of the type "this act is right (wrong)."[50] The reasons for which the judgments were made were not relevant for ethical theory. Indeed, he argued that these "individual mental contents" were impossible to observe and hence unsuitable for an empirical theory: "Statements about mental contents cannot be asserted and supported by any adequate technique."[51]

Why? Part of the reason was the difficulty of learning the mental contents of ethical agents in the absence of such utterance. More importantly for Rawls's later theory, however, he thought that ethical theory should not be interested in the social and historical contexts in which the utterances were made. In making this argument, Rawls appealed to the legal philosopher Hans Kelsen and his "pure theory" of law, which suggests that, according to law, ethical judgments could be detached from other kinds of beliefs. As Rawls drew the comparison: "Ethical theory <u>as such</u> must mean pure theory. In the same way as Kelsen attempted to theorize about the system of law as such, apart from historical, sociological, and historical considerations, so do we attempt to free ethics from other sciences, and yet at the same time to show its relation to them."[52] Rawls's theory was to be "pure" in the sense that it aimed "to find a schema of its use applicable to <u>all</u> ethical systems."[53] These passages do not indicate whether Rawls believed that normal observers in different cultures make the same judgments because the reasons behind these judgments are the same or because these judgments can be somehow abstracted from the reasons for which they are made. But they do explain why Rawls's theory excluded such reasons: for an ethical theory, they were not relevant.

Rawls's references to Kelsen and his "pure theory" of law may suggest a Kantian influence of Rawls. This is true, in a way—and I will point to other influences of Kant in this and later chapters. However, explaining the importance of the independence from historical and social contexts, Rawls made a different argument from that in the later years. In *A Theory of Justice,* he argued that such independence was a condition of being autonomous or self-ruling. As he wrote there, principles of justice were to be chosen as "the most adequate possible expression of [a person's] nature as a free and equal rational being." That meant that these principles could not be "adopted because of his social position or natural endowments, or in view of the particular kind of society in which he lives or the specific things that he happens to want."[54] In 1946, however, Rawls was concerned not with freedom understood as independence of the contingent facts about ourselves and the societies in which we live, but with showing how ethics was distinctive from other sciences. As he wrote, in the absence of the independence of ethics from other sciences, ethical theory "becomes anthropology, psychology, and so on."[55] This reasoning did not draw on Kantianism's main themes. Indeed, it is one of the interesting facts about Rawls's intellectual development that the classic influences were always there, but they took different forms and different emphases in different periods of his life.

The third condition of appropriate ethical judgments was that they express persons' "deep seated convictions" and "deepest feelings," for which reason those who uttered the words were also "most certain of" these judgments.[56] Rawls was not specific about what made some judgments certain or at least more certain than others. His analogy to basic statements suggests that the experience of the ethical agent was basic.

Ethical theory was meant to produce generalized statements that interpreted such confident utterances. Making this argument, Rawls drew an analogy between these "generalized statements" and "basic statements," which, following Popper, he called "basissatze." As he wrote, "A 'Basissatz' is really a probability statement claiming a very high, though not exactly specified, frequency of 'Erlebnissatze' [perceptual judgments] of the form 'I see such and such at such and such' etc."[57] Thus, "'There is a tree' is an assertion to the effect that all, or most all, of a class of normal observers will assert, under specified conditions, 'I see a tree at such and such etc.'"[58]

By analogy, the idea was to show that a sufficiently high proportion of "normal observers" agreed in judgments such as "x is just." Achieving this would provide the subject matter for a scientific ethical theory. Like the positivists who inspired his work, Rawls took the existence of this agreement for granted. Showing that this agreement exists would become Rawls's main goal between 1946 and 1951. He started this task in 1946 by proposing his own ethical theory, "imperative utilitarianism."[59]

Imperative Utilitarianism

A reader even slightly familiar with *A Theory of Justice* will be surprised to find that Rawls's first ethical theory was self-avowedly utilitarian. However, much as with the Kantian influence discussed above, we should take this label with caution. Rawls did not elaborate a standard utilitarian political vision, nor was he concerned with defending any particular ethical view. Imperative utilitarianism was instead focused on the semantic meaning of ethical utterances: the function or purposes that the terms "right" and "wrong" have in human life.

Nonetheless, utilitarian influences there were, and, indeed, they partly explain Rawls's focus on the role of ethical utterances in human life. Rawls followed Henry Sidgwick's arguments in *The Methods of Ethics* as well as G. E. Moore's recapitulation of them in *Principia Ethica*.[60] As Rawls wrote quoting Sidgwick, "In distributing our praise on human qualities, on utilitarian principles, we have to consider primarily not the usefulness of the quality, but the usefulness of praise."

It is also worth noting that this emphasis on the effect of ethical utterances was shared by logical positivists as well, especially the ethical emotivists among them. Emotivists claimed that ethical utterances, insofar as they are meaningful, should be understood as imperatives or commands meant to incite appropriate feelings or induce desired behavior. Rawls was aware of this overlap in arguments and tried to distinguish himself from emotivists. This is telling, because Rawls openly endorsed the "physicalism" of logical positivists but not their preferred ethical position. Also calling ethical terms "imperatives," which functioned "to increase or decrease, as the case may be, [the frequency of the mentioned actions]," he quibbled with the emotivist Ayer, claiming that ethical statements were in fact like imperatives, similar to them in some respects but different in others.[61] Rawls did not detail the ways in which ethical statements differed from imperatives while being like them, but it is worth noting that Rawls wanted to draw an explicit contrast between his theory and emotivism.[62]

It is also worth noting that, while Sidgwick's accounts of ethical theory and justification were broadly similar to those of logical positivism, Rawls described himself as a "physicalist" and not utilitarian in that regard. Like Rawls, Sidgwick held that the goal of ethics is "to systematize and free from error the apparent cognitions that most men have of the rightness or reasonableness of conduct."[63] Moreover, Sidgwick was also committed to nonfoundationalist justification, writing that it is not possible to prove a principle "if by proof we mean a process which exhibits the principle in question as an inference from premises upon which it remains dependent for its certainty."[64] The only possible proof was showing how that principle

> sustains the general validity of the current moral judgments, and thus supplements the defects which reflection finds in the intuitive recognition of their stringency; and at the same time affords a principle of synthesis, and a method of binding the unconnected and occasionally conflicting principles of common moral reasoning into a complete and harmonious system.[65]

If such a justification of a principle can be given, then the proof "seems as complete as can be made."[66]

Rawls's core task in the theory was understanding the semantic meaning of "right" and "wrong."[67] To defend the theory, he first had to argue that there is a common semantic meaning to these terms. He did so answering Ludwig Wittgenstein's argument to the effect that the search for regularities in the meanings of words was unlikely to succeed because the word has different uses in different contexts in which it is used.[68] Rawls acknowledged the force of this objection, agreeing that, in phrases "a good race horse," "a good work horse," and "a good horse for children to ride," "'good' means something different according to the context, according to the 'thing' to which it is applied."[69] However, he thought that Wittgenstein's objection was irrelevant because ethical theory was interested not in the criteria for ethical terms but in their semantic meaning: the use of the ethical expression to do something else, or "a certain operation of selection in terms of the characteristics of the things referred to" that the word "means to perform."[70] Thus, while "good" did not have a common intentional meaning, it still had a common semantic meaning—to direct the interlocutor's attention to qualities that make particular things good:

> In applying the word "good" to a thing in the attributive sense we are directing the hearer to perform an operation of <u>selection</u> on the qualities of the subject of the attribution according to certain definite principles such as the principles of successful fulfillment of purpose involved in the usual use of the thing.[71]

Some of Rawls's statements lead us to believe that he endorsed other aspects of utilitarianism as well. For example, Rawls's ultimate argument was that "right" and "wrong" are used to encourage rare actions that the speaker thinks "will lead to the greatest amount of good" (in the case of "right") and to discourage frequent actions that the speaker thinks diminish the amount of good (in the case of "wrong").[72] Thus, the use of "right" and "wrong" seemed utilitarian to Rawls. Like utilitarians, he wanted to show that, despite the different virtues encouraged by different societies, there was a common function to the use of ethical words. In other, more important respects, he did not take on the utilitarian commitments. For example, unlike the classical utilitarian John Stuart Mill, he did not identify the "greatest amount of good" with happiness.[73] He did not follow Sidgwick in his definition of utilitarianism as "the ethical theory, that the conduct which, under any given circumstances, is objectively right, is that which will produce the greatest amount of happiness on the whole."[74] And he certainly did not equate happiness with pleasure, following Sidgwick in the rejection of psychological hedonism that adopted this equation.[75] Nor did he appeal to Sidgwick's self-evident principle that "the good of any one individual is of no more importance, from the point of view (if I may say so) of the Universe, than the good of any other."[76] Nonetheless, this period of Rawls's life marks the beginning of Rawls's continued descriptions of himself as someone who works within the utilitarian tradition.

Rawls used his theory to explain the cultural variation in ethical judgments. He did so by noting that the "contextual occurrence" of different activities, or the "frequency with which [they] are met with in social life," differed among societies. Thus, a nation surrounded by hostile neighbors and frequently engaged in war will praise "the virtues of the soldier," such as bravery, obedience, endurance, devotion, and loyalty.[77] On the contrary, a nation that spends most of its efforts on commerce will praise the virtues of industriousness, thrift, cunning in dealing with foreigners, and the like.[78] In this way, contextual occurrence explained the change in appraisals in the same society over time. This explanation itself was formalistic: Rawls was interested not in the reasons for which different societies made their decisions but in contextual factors, such as proximity to warlike neighbors.

Political Theory, Political Practice

Rawls's conception of scientific ethics also influenced his political vision. Rawls thought that political theory would guide political practice by serving as an immanent critique. In this argument, he followed Ducasse's reasoning. Assuming the truth of the key positivist hypothesis that a "very high, though not exactly specified" proportion of "normal observers" agree in their judgments—the truth that Rawls claimed to have exhibited in imperative utilitarianism—ethical principles would represent a stable point in the swamp from which other arguments would follow. In case of disagreement, one could use these principles to draw deductions and see what judgments they require in particular cases:

> We require a theory whose predictions correspond to our "deepest intuitions." Once we have such a theory, it can function as a mediator in cases of conflict. We can say to the disputants that the theory in question explains what their moral judgments really are. If our theory is adequate to forecast their "deepest feelings" they will be convinced, and assuming they wish to be consistent, they will agree to resolve the conflict by applying the moral imperative according to the dictates of the theory.[79]

Rawls did not go into the particulars of how the principles would function to recommend any particular actions, but we can make some conjectures. For instance, it is possible to turn contextual factors into reasons when deliberating about practical politics. Thus, if Rawls's theory claimed that a society most highly values valor because it is surrounded by warlike neighbors, "being surrounded by warlike neighbors" could become a reason in deliberation. While by itself this reason would not be sufficient to lead all reasonable persons to agree on a course of action, it may have significant force, especially if, prior to the consideration of Rawls's theory, this reason was unduly neglected. Admittedly, the exact nature of the connection between theory and practice is a matter of speculation, and it is evident that in this regard Rawls's early secular ethical theory differed sharply from that of *A Theory of Justice*.

Nonetheless, the central idea that ethical theory should guide ethical practice was already there.

In sum, Rawls's approach to philosophy in 1946 was shaped by logical positivist themes. In the context of the tradition's typical positions on ethics, his approach was novel: it was centered on the claim that ethical theory, like all scientific theories, is an empirical theory. Adopting the "physicalist" picture of scientific inquiry, Rawls took up other features of logical positivism, in particular their nonfoundationalism. His theory clashed with logical positivism and emotivism in countless other ways. In particular, he set aside the emotivist objection that ethical judgments are simply expressions of emotion. He thought that this objection rested on the failure to find commonality in our ethical judgments.[80] Thinking that this impossibility of finding agreement in our judgments was yet to be shown, he offered his own theory as an example that such agreement was indeed possible. He did not engage emotivists' broader point that ethical judgments cannot be true or false, reasonable or unreasonable—in brief, objective—because they are expressions of emotion. Some relation between emotion and human agreement had to be drawn to avoid the impression that Rawls was building a scientific theory of ethics despite the emotivist objection. Between 1947 and 1951, Rawls would become aware of the need to respond to this broader emotivist claim. In 1947, he would do so by elaborating a conception of objectivity that still skirted this objection, but did so explicitly, explaining why ethics did not need to address it.

3

Engagement with Wittgensteinian Philosophy

IN THE FALL OF 1947, Rawls left Princeton for Cornell. He had been accepted there as a full-time PhD student but intended to stay for only a year.[1] Likely seeing Rawls's engagement with visiting professors, Princeton's philosophy department recognized his need to engage with different philosophical approaches. Rawls "is at present applying at Cornell with my full approval," Robert Scoon wrote in his letter of recommendation. "This is done in spite of the fact that all our department would like to keep him here, but because we believe that he ought to get the stimulus of another set of Professors, and we would particularly like to have him go to Cornell."[2]

Why Cornell? Scoon's letter implies that Rawls's advisers at Princeton prompted the process of transferring and suggested where he should apply. Their high opinion of Arthur Edward Murphy (1901–1962), at Cornell since 1945, would have been an important reason. Murphy had visited Princeton as a guest speaker and engaged in a philosophical exchange with Walter Stace, who also wrote a letter of recommendation for Rawls.[3] Murphy's intellectual background was also different from those of Princeton faculty members. He started out in the pragmatist tradition, insisting on the importance of the variety of contexts in which reason is used. By that time, he had already published *The Uses of Reason,* which also discussed the proper uses of reason in ethical contexts. To follow Ernest Nagel's incisive summary, Murphy argued that "the conditions of reasonableness which have been discovered to be characteristic of the use of ideas in one type of context should [not] be adopted as ultimate for every other type."[4] Whether because of the advice of his professors, Rawls took a yearlong course with Murphy, which consisted of informal conversations about ethics and the nature of value.

Murphy became chair of Cornell's philosophy department in 1946 and immediately started reshaping it. If there was a commonality to the department's new hires, it was that they were in one way or another influenced by Wittgenstein. This is not altogether surprising. Murphy spent the 1936–1937 academic year in England, in which he studied Wittgenstein's *Blue Book*. With the exception of the mentioned contextualist claim that different criteria of reasonableness should be applied to different activities, Murphy's work did not show Wittgenstein's influence by 1946. However, the affinity to Wittgenstein's philosophy and understanding of his importance must have already been there because his next two hires were Wittgensteinians Norman Malcolm and Max Black.

Malcolm's decision to join Cornell in 1947 would have also been a good reason both for Rawls to go there and for his professors to place him there. It is difficult to know how important that reason was. On the one hand, Rawls's letter of application mentions Malcolm in a familiar way, describing Malcolm's course on religious ethics fondly. On the other hand, Rawls did not take a single course with Malcolm while at Cornell. The two may have had conversations, but it is evident that Rawls's reason for the transfer was not solely to continue studies with Malcolm.

Malcolm and likely the Princeton philosophers would have known about Max Black's decision to join Cornell, also in the fall of 1947. Influenced by Wittgenstein, Black focused mainly on the nature of philosophical analysis. Rawls, of course, was also engaged in philosophical analysis of ethical judgments, and his faculty advisers may have seen the usefulness of Rawls's studying with Black. Rawls took a yearlong course on probability and induction with Black.

Rawls also took a yearlong course with the historian of science Henry Guerlac, who was hired by Cornell in 1947 to start instruction in the history of science. Rawls attended lectures three times a week on topics ranging from Babylonian science to Lavoisier and Hobbes. He seems to have been interested in the topics since in the first year he wrote his own independent essay instead of taking the final exam.[5]

Whatever reasons Rawls may have had for transferring to Cornell, it is clear that there he intended to continue his exploration of ethics understood as science. With Guerlac, he studied different conceptions of science, and with Black, he studied justification of science understood as using inductive logic. These first encounters with Wittgenstein's ideas would make Rawls receptive to Wittgensteinian philosophy. But the circumstances of his transfer to Cornell lead us to believe that this Wittgensteinian direction was not preplanned or deliberately sought in his first years of graduate school. This theme of unintended directions to which one is led by exploring an idea reoccurs throughout Rawls's intellectual history.

And so the year at Cornell prompted changes in Rawls's thought. Until then, he had examined the nature of ethical theory and concluded that philosophers in ethics analyzed ethical judgments. They had the task of elaborating a conceptual framework, which could be tested against these judgments by deducing from it the expected judgments and comparing them with the judgments that were actually made. If the predicted judgments matched the actual judgments, one could consider the conceptual framework correct. In 1946, Rawls did not ask why the support of the actual judgments was sufficient. As we saw, already in his religious years he took a theory's coincidence with the actual Christian experience as sufficient justification.

By 1947, however, Rawls felt the need to defend this model of justification. This need is likely to have arisen through his discussions with both Murphy and Black. If we can take Murphy's 1952 article as giving at least weak evidence to his ideas in 1947, he was skeptical of justification of ethics such as C. J. Ducasse's. Murphy criticized Ducasse's ethical theory as noncritical but merely descriptive—a criticism that Rawls, as we know, would have rejected. But Murphy also argued that ethical inquiry differed from scientific inquiry in that one could change the actual ethical judgments of persons, but one could not change scientific facts in the same way. Had Rawls discussed his scientific theory with Murphy, such criticisms would likely have arisen.

The Cornell philosophers could offer something more positive as well. Both Murphy and Black dealt with skepticism about the scientific method that, broadly conceived, Rawls tried to bring to ethics. In effect, their argument was that once all the concrete criticisms of the scientific approach have been answered, we no longer had reasons for doubting that approach. Further doubts, and so further requests for justification, were absurd. In his *Uses of Reason,* Murphy defended perceptual observation so long as it provided a "factual basis for inquiry and for the rational organization of beliefs."[6] Once it did so, Murphy argued, "it lacks nothing necessary to its validity, and needs no further warrant than can be provided by its confirmation in the inquiry through which its factual authenticity is discovered."[7]

Black defended inductive logic in a similar way in the two courses Rawls attended. In a seminar summarized by Rawls, Black argued that the skeptic of induction is making an unreasonable demand. "To make the asking of a justification sensible," Black proceeded, "we must have a standard in terms of which the justification is given." However, he continued, the questioning of inductive logic as a whole takes as such a standard the rules of deductive logic. Inductive logic is asked to meet the same standards as deductive logic. In short, the skeptic is asking to show "that induction is deduction."[8] Behind this request, Black thought, is the skeptic's fear that things "might" be otherwise—that one's explanation is incorrect. But this fear rests on an equivocation of the term "might," implying that there might be an empirical rather than logical possibility of things being otherwise. However, the logical possibility of things being otherwise does not entail the actual possibility that our explanation is not complete, and so the skeptic's fears are not justified.[9]

Debates about the nature and justification of induction expose the differences between Rawls's Wittgensteinian teachers at Cornell and his earlier guides, including Karl Popper. Unlike Black, Popper simply brushed away David Hume's worries about induction. As Popper explained late in his career, once we understand that the accumulation of knowledge can be explained "in terms of the method of trial and the elimination of error," we also see that we do not need to engage Hume's worries about induction. As Popper wrote, "The place of the problem of induction is usurped by the problem of the comparative goodness or badness of the rival conjectures or theories that have been proposed."[10]

As we will see, Rawls began to describe his ethical theory as an inductive theory of ethics. However, he would draw on debates about induction for his own purposes. For this reason, it would be a mistake to describe this period as Rawls's transition from a deductive theorist to an inductive theorist. Rawls never aimed to derive ethical principles deductively. His goal, like Popper's, was to elaborate from our intuitions a series of ethical principles (deductive axioms), which can then be tested against the body of evidence (actual ethical judgments). Moreover, as we will see, Rawls drew inspiration from Black's argument not to reject requests for deductive justifications of ethics, but to explain why we are allowed to stop our arguments at some point. These explorations, different from those of his teachers, will lead Rawls to make creative and useful discoveries.

Scientific Objectivity

Participating in conversations about induction, Rawls started looking for reasons to defend his own conception of ethics as science. This concern is evident in his 1947 essay "Remarks on Ethics."[11] The essay is interesting because it shows the continuities with his earlier thinking and the changes prompted by such discussions. The more remarkable is the continuity. Despite participating in discussions about induction, Rawls likened ethical judgment to perception and justified appeals to ethical judgments because they show the ethical object at hand.

Attempting to formulate an account of objectivity in ethics, Rawls modeled ethical objectivity on scientific objectivity. He argued that ethical judgments were objective insofar as they satisfied appropriate tests: "The objectivity of science does not depend upon how it is learned, or how it is arrived at, but rather upon its satisfaction of certain tests which we apply to statements once they have been formulated."[12] He assigned three such tests: ethical judgments had to gain agreement of all reasonable persons, this agreement had to be correlated with the occurrence of a relevant objective quality, and any disagreement had to be explained as a result of failure, or "a certain definable illness or peculiarity."[13] So, agreement about a claim did not constitute the objectivity of that claim, but it was evidence for it. The crucial part of the equation, it seems, was the "relevant objective quality," which was to be the object of agreement. Physics provided Rawls with an example of how such tests are satisfied.

In physics, he argued, there is a general agreement on the use of terms for color, this agreement is correlated with the occurrence of "physical properties" (namely, the wavelengths of the light emitted), and failure to discern a proper color is "paralleled with defects in [one's] organs of vision."[14] To be objective, ethical judgments had to satisfy the three tests in an equivalent way.

Rawls argued that ethical judgments did satisfy these tests. Doing so, he developed the first version of the concept "reasonable person." As he proposed to show, all reasonable persons agreed in their ethical judgments. This agreement was correlated with proper motivation to do the right thing: "When we study when and where they agree, we find that we can correlate the quality spoken of as the property of a greater and less tendency to do the right 'of itself' on the part of human character."[15] And disagreement in ethical judgments was explained by lack of education and disagreement in beliefs about the world: "Disagreement can be correlated with inability to learn what right and wrong are, lack of training and education, but most often in common life, with variability of beliefs, ie., people are not even examining the same situation when they believe differently."[16]

Rawls spent most of his efforts on showing that ethical judgments satisfied the first test: that all reasonable persons agreed in their ethical judgments. Between 1947 and 1950, he devised ways to limit the range of ethical judgments that an ethical theory had to explain. As Rawls wrote in his 1950 dissertation, "Many judgments which we make are not meant to be taken seriously, and many others, we readily admit, do not deserve to be conscientiously considered."[17] To eliminate such judgments, he developed the notions of the "reasonable man" and "rational" or "reasonable" judgments, which would play an important role in the concept of "reflective equilibrium" in *A Theory of Justice*.

These notions originated in Rawls's attempt to build an empirical theory of ethics. So far as it is possible to tell, he continued the "physicalist" project. Indeed, the concept of "reasonable man" carried a functional resemblance to the concept of "normal observers." Both were meant to exclude certain persons, but in particular their judgments, from being considered as evidence to be explicated. Although the concept of both a reasonable person and a reasonable judgment had had a long history in legal philosophy and practice, Rawls did not formulate his concepts around the legal counterparts. He was aware of the "reasonable person" and "reasonable" in law, but the content of these notions was shaped by the demands of an empirical ethical theory.[18] In law, the "reasonable person" functions as a standard to evaluate the reasonableness of the defendant's actions. It draws an intuitive limit to actions that are permissible and specifies actions that are required. But "reasonable person" and "rational judgments" could not play this role in an empirical theory because they constituted too strong of an ethical standard.[19] For its justification, a "physicalist" theory such as Rawls's relied on its ability to explain the protocol statements of a universal, or nearly universal, scientific community. Introducing a strong ethical standard in the selection of judgments to be explained would beg the question. The same was true for an empirical ethical theory: it could not introduce a strong ethical standard to tamper with its subject matter. Therefore, "reasonable person" and "rational judgments" could not be defined by a strong ethical standard "without making the basis of moral principles tautological."[20] By the same reasoning, the weaker the conditions imposed on the notions of the "reasonable man" and "rational judgments," the wider the range of admissible judgments, and the stronger the support for the claim that ethical judgments are objective.[21] Both in 1947 and in 1950 Rawls's ambition was to make the theory universal.[22] The role of these notions was therefore to restrict the data pool for ethical theory to trustworthy judgments without damaging the empirical basis of the theory.

Rawls defined the notions of "reasonable man" and "rational judgments" with the purposes of empirical theory in mind. A reasonable man had three characteristics: (1) the "ability to understand and to use [the] canons of evidence" by which he "may justify his right to hold an opinion," (2) knowledge of these canons, and (3) willingness to "submit to judgment of these canons to determine what opinions, beliefs, and propositions he shall assert to be true."[23] It is debatable how much normative weight these restrictions actually carried. For example, the ability to judge which evidence is appropriate to ethical questions arguably presupposes some very weighty standards. However, it was not Rawls's intention to define the reasonable man in contestable terms.

Indeed, his ambition was to make the theory universal: the reasonable man was said to be any person of reasonable intelligence and moral sensitivity.[24]

The notion of the "rational" or "reasonable" judgments, developed only in Rawls's dissertation, "A Study in the Grounds of Ethical Knowledge" (1950), was also meant to sift off judgments unsuitable for serving as evidence to be explained.[25] To avoid begging the question, Rawls defined judgments as spontaneous or—tellingly—"empirical," rendered after a "direct and instantaneous" contemplation of the ethical situation and not after a conscious application of some moral rule or theory.[26] They were also to be stable, or "reflecting an enduring disposition to judge in the same way"; impartial, or based on knowledge of relevant interests and not hastily made or favoring unjustly one interest over another; and, finally, certain, or expressing "deep-seated intuitive convictions which remain on reflection."[27] The idea was to exclude judgments based not on their content but on the way they were rendered. These restrictions were meant to be weak enough to permit unresolvable disagreements among reasonable persons.

The 1947 essay introduced another important change. Rawls was now interested in the intentional meaning of ethical terms—the content of ethical judgments. He focused on "the kinds of actions to which guilt [for instance] is attributed, and the conditions under which such actions occur."[28] His earlier formal interest in the function of ethical terms was from then on a thing of the past. This change of interest is intelligible as a response to Wittgensteinian philosophy that sought to find criteria for the right use of words.

This change made the task of showing agreement of all reasonable persons much more difficult. Moreover, in comparison with his later self in *A Theory of Justice*, Rawls was strikingly pessimistic about the range of agreement one could expect on ethical issues. In 1947, Rawls thought that pervasive ethical disagreement was an inevitable result of people's diverging opinions about the world. Since the content of beliefs about the world "provides the character of the situation to be examined and judged," Rawls expected the ethical judgments of reasonable persons to differ as long as they were based on different beliefs about the world.[29] To attain agreement on ethical issues, all reasonable persons had to share these broader beliefs about the world:

As long as there are people duped by fantastic magical ideas, and as long as there are those who share a more sophisticated form of it in some kind of Hegelian idealism or its invert, dialectical materialism, and the like, the agreement which would be made known by sharing the truth, is hopelessly covered by distortion.[30]

One of the interesting parts of Rawls's intellectual development is seeing how he dealt with this fact of "meaning holism": the fact that the meaning of one concept at least sometimes affects the meaning of another concept.[31] Believing something about one area of life, such as the nature of the universe, might affect what one thinks about another area of life, such as the human place in nature. Meaning holism is at the core of historicists' criticism of Rawls. According to them, Rawls's theory of justice wants to depart from the historical and social contexts, but ethical judgments are made in historical and social contexts. If the beliefs of one culture or intellectual tradition are different from those of another, then so will be their ethical judgments.[32] To assess these criticisms of Rawls, it is important to acknowledge that Rawls accepted the thesis of meaning holism throughout his career—at least in his own ways, perhaps unsatisfying ways for the historicists—and tried to elaborate a universalist ethics despite it. In *A Theory of Justice,* as we will see, Rawls's goal was to set aside those facts about ourselves that lead to disagreement. But in that book the problem of the totality of our experiences affecting the content of our judgments was not discussed explicitly. In *Political Liberalism,* published in 1993, Rawls turned to this problem explicitly. Introducing the concept of "burdens of judgment," or those characteristics of human reasoning and judgment that make agreement difficult to achieve, he virtually recapitulated the 1947 position:

> To some extent (how great we cannot tell) the way we assess evidence and weigh moral and political values is shaped by our total experience, our whole course of life up to now; and our total experiences must always differ. Thus, in a modern society with its numerous offices and positions, its various divisions of labor, its many social groups and their ethnic variety, citizens' total experiences are disparate enough for their judgments to diverge, at least to some degree, on many if not most cases of any significant complexity.[33]

In 1947, meaning holism potentially compromised Rawls's notion of the basic statements. If the totality of our experiences affected the content of our ethical judgments, can there be situations so basic that all reasonable persons would understand them in the same way? Rawls effectively deflected this question in his first years of graduate school. In 1946, he thought that ethical theory was not interested in the reasons behind ethical judgments because it focuses on the function of ethical utterances. Since meaning holism matters precisely when we explain such reasons, Rawls was able to go around the problem. In 1947, however, he was already interested in the intentional meaning of ethical utterances. He thus had to deal with the reasons behind judgments and therefore meaning holism.

Here again Rawls did not tackle the problem, writing that his goal in the essay was to show objectivity of ethical judgments. For that, he argued, it sufficed to show that all reasonable persons agree if they hold the same beliefs about the world: "Before instability [of ethical judgments] can be demonstrated it is required that the conflict exists when there is agreement in relation to all relevant beliefs."[34] This response was a sufficient argument against the emotivists who claimed that agreement in belief cannot guarantee agreement in attitude (ethical judgment).[35] Showing that such agreement actually exists was more difficult: it would have required redefining the "reasonable person" in terms of scientific beliefs. This would have been a way to get "at the truth [about the world] and . . . [adopt] an objective standpoint."[36] This objective standpoint was offered by the presumably "physicalist" scientific temper: "The firm adoption of the scientific temper of mind will show the underlying convergence of judgment which exists. Only as such a temper spreads throughout the world will this convergence be known."[37]

Judging from the several paragraphs in which it was discussed, the "scientific temper" was a very restrictive notion and resembled logical positivists' rejection of metaphysics. The "scientific temper" excluded Marxists because of their reliance on the dialectic method. As Rawls wrote, "A Marxist justifies the totalitarian methods he uses [as] an essential part of the dialectical process. . . . By scientific standards, there is simply nothing in these opinions at all."[38] Hegelians were excluded for their reliance on metaphysics, which did not meet scientific standards either: "Metaphysics is the last resort of the sophisticated thinker who wishes to defy the accepted moral judgments. By metaphysics he lays claim to a superior kind of knowledge, or presents to himself his own world, all of which serves the purpose of rationalizing his escape from the moral judgments he would otherwise have to make."[39] And so, "Hegel's 'Phenomenology,' Schopenhauer's 'World as Will and Idea' etc are useless as serious cognitive investigations, and the explanation of their origins lies elsewhere."[40]

It is not obvious how compatible the two notions—"reasonable persons" and "scientific temper"—were in Rawls's theory. On the one hand, "scientific temper" is discussed in the closing pages of the essay, after the argument has been completed. Moreover, when Rawls tried to show that all reasonable persons agree, he never qualified this statement by saying that reasonable persons hold the "scientific temper." On the other hand, reasonable persons of course exhibit the "scientific temper" in some ways. As we have seen, they possess the ability to understand and use canons of evidence as well as the willingness to submit their judgments to these canons. Moreover, it is plausible to say that, according to Rawls, Hegel failed to exhibit this willingness to submit his judgments to scientific canons of evidence. By this argument, it is precisely because Hegel wanted to hold on to his judgments that he turned to metaphysics. So it is possible to argue that Hegel was excluded from the list of reasonable persons.

However, it seems that Rawls left the notion of reasonable persons inclusive. This is seen from his stated goal: Rawls wanted to show that all reasonable persons agree on at least some ethical judgments "irrespective of [their] other beliefs."[41] So, again, although Rawls clearly acknowledged the thesis of meaning holism, his goal was nonetheless to try to detach ethical judgments from some other background beliefs. His assumption must have been that ethical judgments were detachable from at least some beliefs in the person's wider framework of beliefs. In this case—if we follow Rawls's arguments against Hegel—he may have thought that some of these other beliefs should be detached, since they were accepted for the wrong, psychological, reasons. So the goal was to detach ethical judgments from such supposedly mistaken beliefs.

Although Rawls's 1947 idea calls to mind the notion of the "overlapping consensus" that Rawls would develop in *Political Liberalism,* the two should not be confused.[42] In 1993, Rawls would claim that all reasonable persons would agree on reasons that decide controversial political questions.[43] In 1947 and 1950, however, he thought of these higher-order principles as background presuppositions to our ethical thinking. The rejection of these, he argued, was unimaginable—absurd—because it would require the rejection of other beliefs and practices we take for granted. Rawls's list of such principles speaks for itself. For example, the first principle required that only acts over which we have control should be judged as indicative of our moral character: "An act is not to be considered as indicative of the moral worth of the agent's character, unless, in the circumstances under which it was performed, the agent could have done otherwise if he had chosen."[44] The remaining five principles were similarly general. The second principle, for instance, claimed that the character of a person contemplating an evil action without doing it "is not to be judged as bad as the character of an agent who not only contemplates [an evil action], but does it."[45]

Rawls insisted that these principles help solve some practical ethical problems. For instance, the first principle ruled "as wrong the various forms of political discrimination against racial groups . . . [which punish] a man or a group for attributes which he or it cannot choose to have or not to have."[46] Despite such practical applications, Rawls acknowledged that "a good number of indeterminate ethical questions will remain."[47] These principles listed "the kinds of actions" to which the term "indicative of moral worth" is attributed, but for the most part they left off the discussions about the kinds of actions that are morally worthy. In comparison with A Theory of Justice, which would raise precisely these latter kinds of questions, the practical relevance of the 1947 principles was markedly limited.

Rawls justified these principles by showing that the entire tradition of philosophy affirmed them. He did so in broad strokes, writing that these principles are affirmed by "all ethical theorists as far as I know," are "widely recognized," and reflect "the moral opinion of men generally" and that there is no one in his knowledge "who has ever denied these principles."[48] When the proposed principles seemed to go against the tradition of ethical thought, he took pains to show that it was a wrong impression.[49] This type of justification was consistent with his conception of ethical inquiry: principles, he thought, were justified by showing that their implications are affirmed by reasonable persons.

Thus in its overall character, "Remarks on Ethics" continued the scientific project started in his 1946 "Nature of Ethical Theory." Rawls's conception of objectivity was based on the analogy between reasoning in ethics and reasoning in science, and it required that the philosopher show the actual overlap in the judgments of reasonable persons. The "reasonable person" and "rational judgments" were two important steps in that direction, following the earlier notions of "normal observers" and "basic statements."

Absurd Requests for Further Justification

Despite retaining the earlier shape, "Remarks on Ethics" already showed signs of his Cornell teachers' influence. Rawls drew on the notion of "absurdity" to draw a boundary between questions that the skeptic could legitimately ask and those he could not. He used the notion of "absurdity" to justify ethical principles by showing that their denial requires living a life so odd that it is nowhere to be found. As Rawls wrote:

> One appeals to the voluntary agreement of reasonable men throughout the tradition to mark off the point where one need no longer feel obligated to answer the request for a justification. By carrying our justification this far we have done all that can be done; and the moral skeptic is using the word "justification" in such a way that it is logically impossible to satisfy him.[50]

The notion of absurdity helped Rawls show that the decision to stop the argument on these particular principles, far from being arbitrary, was in some sense natural because the denial of these principles was odd and incomprehensible. Calling this argument "justification by reason," he now claimed that "one ought to show that the principles are reasonable; and that the denial of them either leads to absurdity or promotes a situation which reasonable men cannot accept."[51]

Of course, arguments such as Murphy's and Black's could silence the skeptic only if a position did not have any concrete criticisms against it. So long as reasonable criticism against a position could be raised, the skeptic raised his doubts legitimately. That is why Black's defense was of induction in general, not of any particular inductive inference. The same was true for Rawls. It may well be absurd to question ethical judgments in general, but it is not absurd to question a particular ethical judgment unless legitimate concerns about it are really lacking. This is what Rawls had to show: that some ethical judgments are so basic—to use his 1946 term—that no reasonable person could have reasons to question them.

This is what Rawls did. He showed that there are principles so ingrained in our thought that their rejection would be absurd. To be so crucial to our thought that their rejection is absurd, ethical principles had to be very general.[52] To exhibit the absurdity of denying his ethical principles, Rawls resorted to an example of a person who "<u>lives</u> nonsense": a person who, rejecting the commonsense principles, is also forced to abandon our commonsense judgments and ways of living.[53] He took the example from conversations with Malcolm, who, in turn, gleaned it from Samuel Butler's *Erewhon*.[54] The idea was to show that some of our beliefs are so crucial that a society that rejected them would be so incomprehensible that it is nowhere to be found (hence perhaps the novel's title, which, apart from the misplaced "w" and "h," reads "nowhere" in reverse). Rawls used Butler's argument to provide further justification for his first principle, that involuntary actions should not be treated as indicative of the moral worth of our character. Butler depicted a society that acted against this principle: people were put in prison for being sick and sent to the hospital for committing a crime.[55] Other interpersonal relations changed accordingly: for example, sick people were met with moral indignation. As Malcolm had argued in conversation with Rawls at Cornell, we cannot correctly call the judge morally indignant of the defendant's illness, because one of our key criteria for moral indignation is voluntariness of action.[56] Adding that this conclusion reflects our stable attitudes, Rawls implied that to reject these attitudes would be to live nonsense.[57]

Although this "justification by reason" was undoubtedly a new argument, Rawls portrayed it as part of the scientific framework of ethics. It is a remarkable part of Rawls's history that he weaved together the themes from his early physicalist conception of ethical theory and the new Wittgensteinian strand of reasoning. This is seen in Rawls's claim that the appeal to absurdity was not an appeal to a standard. "It is not such an appeal at all," he wrote. Whether something is absurd is "a question of fact," and this fact was established by seeing whether the quality of absurdity is agreed on by "the voluntary agreement of reasonable men."[58] This quote follows Rawls's 1946 statement about the basic statements: "A 'Basissatz' is really a probability statement claiming a very high . . . frequency of 'Erlebnissatze' [perceptual judgments] of the form 'I see such and such at such and such' etc."[59] Like the notions of the "reasonable person" and "rational judgments," "absurdity" was defined in such a way that it left the assumptions of an empirical theory very broad and inclusive. In 1947, Rawls's theory was meant to be thoroughly empirical.

Objective Moral Facts

This continued analogy between ethics and science pulled Rawls into specifically positivist problems. In particular, the analogy drew Rawls closer to moral realism, the claim that ethical entities exist in the ethical situation itself and are perceived by the mind.

The conversations at Cornell, or perhaps his own later thoughts, forced Rawls to ask why reasonable persons would agree in their ethical judgments. He needed some kind of philosophical anthropology—something akin to the *Imago Dei* theory he held in *Meaning of Sin and Faith*. In 1947, his account of objectivity lacked this explanation. His 1947 rejection of Dewitt Parker's claim that the "world is valueless apart from man" suggests that Rawls thought of ethical qualities as not dependent on the human mind.[60] Yet he did not detail the nature of this independence, brushing aside claims that the moral quality discerned by ethical insight existed as a physical object or in the brain.[61] Indeed, it is curious that Rawls would refuse to provide this philosophical anthropology, especially because it played such a crucial role in his thinking in 1942. Now he argued that ethical theory did not need to take sides on this question as it relied on the agreement of reasonable persons and the absurdity of denying the proposed principles. As he put it as late as 1952:

It does not matter at all what the causes of prudential decisions actually are. They may be the result of intuition of non-naturalistic value qualities and so on. All that we attempt here is to explicate these choices; and if the use of the principles would lead to the same choices that competent counselors recommend, then that in itself is sufficient for our purposes, so far as we are concerned with explication.[62]

Rawls gave more detail of this philosophical anthropology in 1950, when he submitted his dissertation, "Grounds of Ethical Knowledge." Logical positivists explained agreement of normal scientific observers by claiming that protocol statements were reports of a physical reality and that normal scientific observers had sufficiently similar epistemological apparatuses. Rawls's answer was along these lines. His dissertation shows that, despite the constant claims that questions about the nature of ethical qualities are irrelevant to ethics, Rawls felt the need to posit objectively existing qualities. Now calling them "objective factor" or "objective moral fact," he argued that these qualities determined ethical judgments of reasonable persons, thereby implying that they were mind-independent.[63] The notion stemmed from his earlier analogy between perception and ethical insight: "Just as our common perceptions are caused by, and controlled by, an objective order to events, so we have some reason to think that there is a common objective moral fact which causes and controls our moral judgments."[64]

In contrast to 1947, in 1950 the notions of "reasonable person" and "rational judgment" were defined in relation to this "objective factor." The reasonable person was now more sharply modeled on knowing, and constraints imposed on this definition were interpreted as "necessary conditions for the reasonable expectation that a given person may come to know something" and essential for the "knowledge-getting process" and "finding the truth."[65] The rational judgments were also modeled around the objective factor, which was expected to "evidence itself through the complex of different cultural and personal backgrounds."[66] Analysis of ethical judgments was now not solely the search for agreement among reasonable persons but also the grasping of this objective factor: "We cannot locate this factor unless we go directly to spontaneous judgments as defined above."[67]

As in 1947, Rawls chose to not detail the nature of the objective factor: "I leave aside the question as to how this common objective moral fact is to be interpreted."[68] Yet given his repeated appeals to this notion, by 1950 it was becoming evident that Rawls felt the need to elaborate this concept in order to explain the agreement of reasonable persons. Modeling ethics on science and ethical judgment on perception, he was forced into a vision of ethical qualities that drew their objectivity from an "objective factor" residing in an ethical situation.

The Nature of Ethical Judgment

Rawls's scientific theory of ethics led Rawls to a mechanical conception of ethical judgment, which stemmed from the uneasy combination of two claims: that the correct principles of a theory predict its subject matter, and that the principles can and should replace the currently used intuitive judgments. The key commitment leading to this dilemma was the logical positivist conception of analysis, or its requirement that ethical principles predict the judgments they explain. As Rawls wrote in as late as 1952, "Principles are like functions in mathematics: just as functions applied to numbers, say, yield other numbers; so principles applied to circumstances yield a decision."[69] Combined with the "necessary rules of application," the principles had to predict the actual judgments of reasonable persons: "A person who fully understands [both the principles and the rules of application], will be led, by their use, to employ the term expressing the concept on exactly the same occasions, and in exactly the same way, as that term is used in the data with which the explication is concerned."[70] Rawls specified that the principles were to be so precise that they are "mechanically followed," or used by consciously applying the rules without appeal to intuition.[71]

But it was always a question of how these mechanical rules uncovered by philosophical analysis are related to reasonable persons' judgment. Rawls always held that ethical principles were in some way implicit in our judgments, and that the philosopher had to formalize these implicit "rules and principles."[72] Yet the nature of this implicitness needed clarification. Do these rules determine the judgments of reasonable persons? If so, is it because reasonable persons explicitly follow these rules in their judgments? If the judgments of reasonable persons are actually made for other reasons, how are the rules uncovered by the analysis related to these other reasons? These are the questions that would surface again and again, until the publication of *A Theory of Justice.*

Rawls's answer to these questions changed. Between 1947 and 1950, the understanding of implicitness was formalistic and consistent with logical positivism's commitments: Rawls did not require that the principles be explicitly used by reasonable persons in their judgments. As he specified in his dissertation, in formulating the principles we are not looking into "what people intend to assert" or "what is before their minds when making an assertion."[73] Inquiry into this intentional meaning, he thought, was "an unnecessary inquiry which it is possible and helpful to avoid."[74] Indeed, he went so far as to argue that "an explication may be successful even if it can be established with certainty that everyone would reject it as a statement of what they intend to assert."[75] This view implied that reasonable persons did not have to recognize these principles as their own for these principles to be deemed correct. In theory, as long as reasonable persons could understand them, the principles could be mathematical formulas employing no intentional notions. Appropriately, referring to Neurath's, Carnap's, and Popper's works as examples of such explications, Rawls called his view a "logical physicalism so far as it may be applied to ethical theory."[76]

As we can see from these examples, Rawls continued to develop his "physicalist" conception of ethics even while at Cornell, taught by Wittgensteinian professors, and in his dissertation. On the one hand, Rawls developed concepts that were independent of Wittgensteinian themes: "reasonable person" and "considered judgment" allowed him to delineate the subject matter of ethical theory. On the other hand, he developed new arguments that fit with the old. Drawing on his Wittgensteinian teachers, he introduced the notion of absurdity and claimed that some requests for further justification were absurd: if put in practice, they would require absurd ways of life. Even this concept, however, resembled his earlier concepts of basic statements. These two sets of ideas led to a consistent view of ethical inquiry. A theorist had a goal of analyzing the judgments of reasonable persons and outlining the principles that lie behind these judgments. These principles were so ingrained in human thought that questioning them was absurd. Therefore, showing the agreement of reasonable persons was the only thing a theorist could do to justify the theory. In the later years, Rawls would draw on the Wittgensteinian tradition to replace aspects of his "physicalist" vision. For now, however, borrowing from his Wittgensteinian teachers supplemented his early creative act of drawing the analogy between ethics and science.

This period also saw an emerging concern and struggle to explain why reasonable persons would agree in their judgments, even if these judgments were so obvious that no one would question them. Rawls did not live up to the directness of his 1942 vision that relied on *Imago Dei*. For much of the time he denied the need to give such an explanation, and when he gave an answer—an "objective factor" residing in an ethical situation—he did not give it further detail. In the later years, this struggle with an account of justification in ethics would make Wittgenstein's thought especially appealing to Rawls.

4

The Fair Games of Autonomous Persons

R AWLS'S POLITICAL VISION underwent significant developments during his graduate school career. In effect, he had to outline a new philosophical anthropology, explaining what features of human personhood were morally salient. Unable to draw on his earlier image of *Imago Dei,* Rawls had to build his theory from the ground up. He outlined his first substantive secular political vision in the 1947 "Remarks on Ethics," most likely written at Cornell. In this essay, we see Rawls drawing inspiration from Kant. While he explicitly rejected Kantian metaphysics, Rawls made use of Kant's idea that the ability to follow moral laws is the most important feature of personhood. We also see Rawls discussing his political vision in terms of rights, a concept that was alien to his theological vision of 1942.

Why Kant? For a start, Rawls knew Kant's thought well, having studied it in numerous courses. In the fall of 1941, he took Kant and the Philosophy of the Nineteenth Century. Taught by David F. Bowers, it analyzed the time period placing "particular emphasis" on "the Critical Philosophy of Kant and upon Kant's influence on nineteenth century thinkers."[1] As a graduate student, he took The Philosophy of Kant, taught by Edgar Herbert Henderson in the fall of 1946, and Pre-Kantian Rationalism, taught by Ledger Wood in the spring of 1947. Rawls must have also encountered Kant through Sidgwick's *The Methods of Ethics*.[2] Rawls would refer to the book in his analysis of justice throughout his career, and, according J. B. Schneewind, it already played an important part in Rawls's thinking in 1951. At that time, Rawls was back at Princeton. He had returned in 1948, and, appreciated by the philosophy department professors as "brilliant—the most brilliant student we have here now [1947], and one of the most brilliant we ever had," he was offered a job as instructor of philosophy after filing his dissertation in 1950.[3] As Schneewind wrote reminiscing about an encounter with Rawls in 1951,

> John Rawls had finished his dissertation just before I arrived but was still there, as an instructor for undergraduates. Despite his great personal modesty, he already had an awe-inspiring reputation. He urged me one day to read Sidgwick, and I took his advice the next semester, with long-term consequences.[4]

In terms of ideas, Kant's insistence on treating others as ends and not as means fit well with Rawls's earlier religious arguments to the same effect. Rawls himself did not explain this shift. He simply began his 1947 essay with explicitly Kantian ideas.

The second important influence on Rawls's early secular political vision was game theory. After filing his dissertation in 1950, Rawls found inspiration in a reading group on economics and game theory during the 1950–1951 academic year. As chance would have it, he studied at Princeton when it was a home of the nascent game-theoretical revolution in economics. In 1944, John von Neumann, a fellow at the Institute of Advanced Studies, and Oskar Morgenstern, a professor in the Princeton economics department, published the landmark *Theory of Games*.[5] Rawls would draw on this theory to suggest the analogy between society and games, which would in turn make him more receptive to the analogy between ethical reasoning and games. Employing these analogies, Rawls would create model situations—games of ethical reasoning—to bring out the principles behind our thinking about justice. This was a crucial step in Rawls's explication of our judgments of justice. From that point onward, the basic idea of the experiment was already developed, and it only remained for Rawls to find a more efficient and elegant way of deriving his conclusions.

The Early Kantianism

What happened to Rawls's political vision as he lost faith after the war? Rawls's 1947 essay "Remarks on Ethics" shows new developments in his thinking. Rawls continued to use the term "personhood," now connecting this concept to rights. As he wrote explaining the structure of his political argument, "Certain characteristics and properties of human nature, which, if present in an individual, are understood to create moral claims, or to be the grounds of certain rights."[6] According to Rawls, moral claims were expressed in terms of moral principles: "Persons and groups, and the State, have whatever rights they have on the basis of what rights they ought to have in light of the moral principles."[7] His goal in the political part of "Remarks of Ethics" was to "state what properties of human nature form the grounds of a moral right."[8]

This very claim that features of human nature gave grounds to rights led Rawls to the principle of equality. One's status in the moral context was based on one's having or failing to have this characteristic. As Rawls wrote, "Whatever person, regardless of his other characteristics, possesses the properties which constitute the grounds of a right, has that right." To treat persons equally was to "appraise their claims only in terms of their claims to right" and to treat them as having rights if they had the properties of human nature that were considered as grounds for these rights.[9]

The important task was to delineate the features of human personhood that could serve as grounds for rights and argue for their fittingness to serve this role. Rawls framed the conversation around needs, outlining a variety of them that seemed part of leading a human life. It is important to note this variety. Rawls emphasized needs that drew on Kant's theory, and while those needs were the most important ones, they were not the only ones. A need, according to Rawls, was a "demand of [human] nature such that a man will die, or be sick, or languish unless it is fulfilled" but also one that "must be met to achieve the higher life, which is the working out of the capacities and excellences."[10] While Rawls listed the relevant excellences as those skills and virtues required to be an inquirer, artist, friend, husband, statesman, saint, and simply a person, eventually his argument focused on the excellence of human freedom.[11] As he wrote,

> To discuss this excellenc[e] [the most general, as well as being a precondition for the others], it is desirable to consider the person from the standpoint of freedom. Freedom is one of the basic concepts of the person, and to discuss what freedom of the person is will clarify the meaning of the person as an excellency of human nature.[12]

Although he discussed political freedom, it is clear he thought moral freedom was more important. Rawls's initial discussion showed that moral freedom was constituted at least in part by having proper goals in life:

> To be a person is one capacity and excellency of human nature; and to be a person means to be free—to have purposes and aims worthy of a man, to have one's character properly disciplined about these goals, and to be situated in life so that these ends can be worked out without external hindrance.[13]

The second aspect of moral freedom was the capacity to formulate and obey moral laws. This, he thought, was a requirement for the highest human life. "A man is born as a 'mass of protoplasm,'" he wrote, "and some men, somewhere along in life, acquire the ability to follow principles. When they acquire this capacity they achieve the final stamp of a free and reasonable man." As Rawls put it yet more clearly, "When a man's actions are caused by his own character deciding according to the principles of right then that man is free."[14]

Rawls freely acknowledged that this understanding of human beings was Kantian. As he wrote,

> The ideal state of affairs is, in this view, similar to Kant's idea of the "Kingdom of Ends", since it postulates as reasonable the presumption that the moral community is a community of agents, capable of exer-

cising their rights according to moral principles which they can all impose, without violating their rational nature, upon their own will.[15]

Despite following Kant in the description of moral freedom, Rawls distinguished his argument from Kant's in two respects. First, Rawls phrased the discussion in terms of rights, not maxims. As he wrote, "Reference is made naturally to Kant's maxim, yet I wish to state it in the terminology of rights."[16] Phrased in this political way, Kant's requirement to treat others as ends and not as means meant attributing to them rights when the relevant grounds for them were present. As Rawls wrote,

> To treat a person as a means only means to deal with him solely with respect to one's own purposes and to ignore whatever claims the other person can rightly make. To consider a person also as an end, means to call upon his service only wherein his service is morally compatible with his rights.[17]

In the political context, this meant treating persons as "bearer[s] of rights which can never be counterbalanced except by a stronger claim on the part of another; and never, under any conditions, can these rights be overlooked, or ignored."[18]

The second difference lay in Rawls's rejection of metaphysics. Perhaps following his Cornell teachers' interest in analyzing the actual uses of ethical terms, Rawls brought Kant's argument to the everyday life. As he wrote, "I wish to avoid [the] problems of metaphysics if possible."[19] Rawls's main reason for rejecting Kant's metaphysics was its alleged lack of real connection to the everyday notion of freedom. Rawls wanted "to discuss freedom as an everyday notion, used of everyday things and actions, and thereby to make clear its properties as applied to the person."[20] Kant's metaphysical distinction between the noumenal and the phenomenal realms was not part of this everyday notion of freedom:

> Whatever may be the merit of discussions modelled after those in Kant's *Critique*, it is evident, to me at least, that they have nothing to do with the kind of thing one talks about when one talks about political freedom, or freedom of the press, or freedom from one's passions and the like.[21]

Rawls supplemented this Kantian vision with elements that are intelligible as remnants of his earlier neo-orthodox political framework and its emphasis on human sin. Most notably, while he held the ability to follow moral principles as the highest part of human nature, he did not believe that most human beings were capable of doing this without the external help of the state. Thus, the state had the task of protecting the rights of individuals: the state is a "legal corporation, existing only in the contemplation of the Law of the Land, which endows it with certain powers and rights, and which allows it to have certain personal agents to exercise those powers and rights."[22] Since the state was composed of individual human beings who were also far from the highest human nature, its extent was to be minimal. "If history teaches us nothing else," Rawls wrote, "it certainly teaches us this: all power corrupts, and absolute power corrupts absolutely (Acton)." Given this, he concluded, it is "sheer folly of granting to its agents extensive and unified powers."[23]

Drawing the Boundaries of Justice

In the early 1950s Rawls turned toward analyses of justice. The precise date is difficult to pinpoint because the documents are undated. Since the problem of justice was a new problem for Rawls (his dissertation deals with considered judgments about the moral worth of character, not justice), he must have begun working on these themes after the dissertation was finished. Some of the documents are clearly lecture notes for courses Rawls taught as instructor of philosophy at Princeton during the 1950–1952 academic years. Judging by the overlap of themes, another important document, "Delimitation of the Problem of Justice," was written in the same period. These documents cover the 1950–1952 academic period, and in particular the 1950–1951 academic year.[24]

In "Delimitation of Justice," Rawls set out to draw the boundaries of the concept of justice, thereby also explicating precisely what question his studies of justice would answer. Clearly, not all issues were issues of justice, and at least rough boundaries of the problem at hand had to be demarcated.[25] According to Rawls, the subject matter of justice was defined by three main features. Some of them contained Kantian features, showing that even as Rawls turned to the more economic understanding of autonomy, Kantian elements persisted. For instance, the individuals concerned had to be capable of "grasping the sense . . . of moral precepts and ethical principles" as well as "applying them to the conditions at hand to determine the course of action appropriate to the case."[26] Moreover, the case at hand had to affect the interests of at least two persons, and these interests had to be "especially important," such as "life, liberty and the pursuit of happiness." "The problem of justice arises," he wrote, "whenever these are substantially interfered with." And last, not specified further, these interests had to be interfered with in a "substantial" way.[27]

The task from here was to give an account of judgments that reasonable persons make about cases of justice. The specific task of this explication still drew on the physicalist account of analysis. As Rawls wrote, the task was to "discover and formulate a set of principles such that, when applied to those cases wherein the problem of justice arises, will yield exactly the same decisions, case by case, as those decisions which are made intuitively by competent judges as these are known by their considered judgments."[28]

"Delimitation" provided only a very beginning of such analysis of justice. It imagined a "model situation"—an imaginary "forum"—in which persons made claims for their interests. The persons were provided with a sufficient amount of time to consider these claims, and they had to give reasons for refusing claims.[29] While a precursor to the "original position" of *A Theory of Justice,* this scenario did not significantly simplify the problem in 1947, and Rawls struggled to derive an account of the principles of justice using the experiment. Clearly, he needed a breakthrough in his analysis of justice.

Societies and Games

This breakthrough came as Rawls considered game theory, which offered a new way of studying societies' economic patterns. Von Neumann and Morgenstern's *Theory of Games* offered an explanation of economic behavior "from an altogether different angle; this is, from the perspective of a 'game of strategy.'"[30] Von Neumann and Morgenstern analyzed society as a multitude of strategic games and defended this analogy by citing its ability to explain actual economic behavior.[31] They assumed that economic agents have all-embracing and complete systems of preferences and full knowledge of their own preferences and those of other players.[32] The goal of the individuals was to discover a strategy that would maximize the satisfaction of their preference functions. The goal of the analyst was to find equilibria: states of affairs to which those actions that were individually most effective would lead.[33]

In 1951, Rawls drew on *Theory of Games*. As he did, the Kantian language began to lose its limelight in his political arguments. As he wrote in the 1951–1952 lectures, "It is profitable to view society as a game, even as a number of games."[34] Attributing this analogy to *Theory of Games*, he nonetheless departed from von Neumann and Morgenstern's uses of it. Much like with Kant, Rawls proposed to bring the analogy to the everyday life. He wanted to "move on a more primitive level" and to look at the analogy "from a purely common sense point of view."[35] This change in viewpoint led to a difference in emphasis. Rawls was interested not in the rational strategies of individuals, but in the aspects of society and the people that the analogy illuminates.

While this difference in emphasis may have been prompted by Rawls's Wittgensteinian teachers' emphasis on the actual uses of ethical terms, the economist Frank Knight's influence was likely another source. Rawls read and annotated Knight's *Ethics of Competition* (1935) by 1952 at the latest. However, since the influence can already be seen in his 1951–1952 lectures, Rawls likely had read the book earlier.[36] Knight saw himself as part of a liberal tradition and analyzed people's motivations in business and politics through the analogy of a game. "Liberal economics and liberal politics," Knight wrote, "are at bottom the same kind of 'game.'" In both, Knight thought, "the fundamental fact . . . is the moral fact of rivalry, competitiveness, and the interest in power."[37]

For Rawls, this analogy reemphasized the importance of autonomy. However, in this context, he understood autonomy as the ability to choose one's own plan of life, thereby departing from his earlier Kantian interpretation of the concept as the ability to follow the moral law. Rawls did not reject the Kantian interpretation of autonomy. Rather, he placed the emphasis on another aspect of one's personhood: the capacity to determine one's goals in life. This is seen in his explanation of the term "person," which was now defined by the ability to decide on "what is good and right."[38] In *A Theory of Justice,* Rawls would explicitly combine these two notions of autonomy—the right to choose one's good and to exercise one's moral capacity—into one, naming them the two "moral powers."[39] In 1947, however, he used the two notions simultaneously in different contexts, and only quotes such as the one above indicate that they were part of one conception of personhood.

To the extent that the right to make decisions by oneself needed defense, Rawls stressed the pluralism of the good, or the plurality of reasons for which people play games. If goods were plural, it would be more difficult to argue that the state could impose one conception of the good on its citizens. So, Rawls argued that there is no dominant end, understood as the end that trumps all others: "We recognize in ordinary life that there are literally thousands of ends; . . . Nobody knows what the end is: there is no such thing."[40] This argument was further elaborated in "Delimitation." Defining the "absolute" good as a good that, "in all cases of conflict, . . . is rightly preferred" from both an individual's and a society's points of view, Rawls argued that it does not exist.[41] Even security, the only good that came close to being absolute in this sense, would not be rightly preferred if all other goods had to be sacrificed for it. Moreover, the absence of the absolute good meant for Rawls the absence of ordering of goods. "We do not say that being an inquirer is better than being an artist. What we do say is that any full human life must mix them together to a certain extent and realize them all to a certain degree." In sum, he concluded, "there is a plurality of distinct highest goods, and the task is always to so arrange one's character and social conditions so that they may all be achieved to at least a certain degree."[42]

Interestingly in light of realist criticisms of Rawls, Rawls's second argument for respecting persons' right to decide was the political impossibility of changing people's minds. Even if there were one dominant end, or if it were possible to rank the plurality of goods, politically it is impossible to impose the good on people. Seeking one's own good, Rawls wrote, should be accepted as "the basic motivation of the basic social groups," and "moralizing and preaching won't change it."[43] Rawls was at least in part accepting politics as it is.

The conclusion of these considerations was that political philosophy and the state should take the right to choose one's good in life as a central value. Political philosophers were to accept the players' motives, so long as the players followed the rules of the game.[44] As Rawls wrote, "Persons are capable of deciding, and ought to have the <u>right</u> to decide what they want . . . ; and therefore there is never a question of forcing a good on a person, or forcing on him more than he puts in a claim for."[45] Respecting autonomy, political philosophy was to direct this self-interest through social institutions toward socially beneficial ends. Here the game analogy was helpful as well. Rawls distinguished between the motivations of the players (to win the game) and the objective of "the game itself as a group activity."[46] As he wrote, "The point is that we can achieve an objective by getting people to follow certain rules—even an objective of <u>justice</u> when they are all <u>egoistic</u>—provided we <u>design</u> the <u>rules correctly</u>."[47] The wise legislator—and political philosopher—is therefore someone who "so arranges the rules, so preserves conditions, that this result comes about."[48]

For Rawls, the group objective was the continuation of the game. Analyzing what this requires, he concluded that society should allow as much autonomy—misleadingly called self-interest in the following quote—as is consistent with order. "The game analogy warns us," he wrote, "that we must not oppress self-interest—it's a poor game in which nobody wants to play." Liberty and order could be achieved by setting up rules that "guide," "enlighten," but do not "stamp out" self-interest, which is the "motor of society."[49] "Under certain conditions," Rawls wrote, referring to Adam Smith, "'the <u>free</u> play' of self-interest achieves a rational order."[50] A proper society left people's decisions to themselves as much as possible.

Moreover, the analogy brought out a key feature of justice: it had a crucial connection to fairness, an important aspect of games. Rawls's spring 1953 Oxford notes show attempts to distinguish justice from fairness by applying the two terms to nouns such as "wages."[51] The 1953 Cornell course, entitled Justice as Fairness, clarified the distinction: "The notion of <u>fairness</u> has its home in games; when we must play the 'game,' the notion of justice enters."[52] Since we must play the game "which our social institutions impose upon us," the notion of justice is appropriate to describe society.[53] Following the analogy, Rawls began to view justice as fairness. A society organized in a just manner was for Rawls like a fairly set-up game.

Reasoning Games

The analogy between society and games thus helped Rawls specify some features of justice. A year later, however, it also prompted him to consider another analogy. This time, Rawls drew the analogy between ethical reasoning and games.[54] In fundamental respects, ethical reasoning was like a game. The analogy—the first influence of Stephen Toulmin's *The Place of Reason in Ethics*—would have more significant implications in the later years, but in the 1950-1951 academic year Rawls used it to set up a heuristic device—a game of ethical reasoning—to bring out the principles of justice. As he wrote, "Reasoning is in many respects like a game where winning consists in presenting a decisive case for a conclusion by adducing good reasons."[55] The strategy was to construct a thought experiment in such a way that individual players would bring out the group objective—finding out what justice requires: the "finding out the right answer is the group objective of reasoning games."[56]

Rawls explored the analogy between ethical reasoning and social games in his 1951-1952 lectures at Princeton and would continue this task at Oxford as a Fulbright scholar the following year.[57] His strategy, developed most fully in the 1953 Oxford notes, was to impose restrictions on the kind of reasons the players can give to one another. As Rawls wrote, a "fundamental strategy is to get the sides to state the forms of reasons which they will accept <u>before</u> the actual play begins; i.e., to compel sides to commit themselves to forms of reasons before the facts of the case are clearly ascertained."[58] As we will see, this strategy of excluding certain reasons as improper for the question at hand will be a key feature of the "original position" in *A Theory of Justice*. There, certain knowledge would be placed behind the "veil of ignorance"—and so reference to that knowledge would be excluded before the deliberation would even begin.[59]

Constructing the thought experiment was the tricky part. Much of Rawls's writing in the early 1950s is concerned with this rather technical task. His early thought experiments state the desired conclusions but do not provide an argument for them. The first such experiment, elaborated in Rawls's 1951-1952 lectures on justice and coined as the "pure case" experiment a year later, outlined a reasoning game that would reflect the considered judgments of reasonable persons.[60] To model the commitment to autonomy, persons were given the right to seek the goods of their choice. One person divided fixed goods among the others; if someone objected to the division, there would be a hearing in which the person objecting would present his case and the person dividing the goods would defend the division.[61] Analysis of the pure case consisted of making explicit the reasons these rational persons would use for dividing fixed goods. These reasons would be the reasons of justice.

The experiment yielded general but powerful principles. For instance, every claim was to be evaluated by the same principles, and no claim denied without a reason.[62] The conclusion was significant, as justice was shown to involve formal equality: the same laws applied to everyone equally. Moreover, Rawls thought, when applied to actual cases of justice, this formal equality led to substantive equality. Since there were no relevant differences between persons in the pure case, the distribution of goods among them was to be equal. To respect persons equally was to treat them equally unless good reasons required exceptions.

Analysis of more complicated cases of justice, where departures from the standard of equality were expected, required using new and unrelated concepts.[63] In particular, Rawls argued that inequalities are justified if they are "functional,"–if they can serve some other purposes.[64] As Rawls wrote, institutions are justified as long as the inequalities they engender are "functional or effective, in increasing the amount produced at such a rate that it is reasonable for each man to prefer the benefits of the expected increase rather than to take the benefits of equal distribution now."[65] While this argument may seem permissive, given that there is always some good that results from inequalities, Rawls's intentions were actually quite radical: his focus was set on persons who least benefit from inequalities. In the 1953 lectures at Cornell, Rawls defended what he called the "principle of assuring subsistence"; namely, the demand that no person should fall below a minimum level of subsistence, determined "by the average level of wealth prevailing in the society."[66]

While the "pure case" experiment allowed Rawls to arrive at the principles of equality and functional inequality, it did not provide an argument by which this could be done. Rawls still had to show how rational persons convinced each other to accept the principle of functional inequalities. The subsequent experiment, developed in 1952–1953, did not fare much better. In this game, players proposed principles of justice independently, to avoid the illegitimate use of force and persuasion.[67] These proposals were moderated by an official body.[68] Not knowing which principles this body would select, the parties were expected to propose principles advantageous to themselves and fair to others.[69] If the parties proposed different principles for new cases, the official body would fine them if it decided that the new principle was inconsistent with the previous principle. This ensured that, from the beginning, participants would propose general principles that would cover all possible cases and would therefore give no "special advantage" to their authors and their special circumstances.[70] This was a promising idea, but its particular descriptions were too difficult to defend from an ethical point of view. As Rawls recognized in a 1991 interview, this thought experiment was "just too complicated." "There were certain seemingly insoluble problems; for example, how great we make the pressure to agree—how much time we allow, and things of that sort." As a result, Rawls "couldn't work it out."[71]

In sum, the value of autonomy became the core of an ethical vision that replaced Rawls's religious commitments. Accordingly, the concept of personhood acquired a different content. Respect for persons now required respecting their autonomy, in a twofold way. Influenced by Kant, Rawls stressed the human capacity to determine and follow the moral law. Prompted by von Neumann and Morgenstern's analogy between society and games, he emphasized the importance of another aspect of personhood: the capacity to determine the direction of one's own life.

Rawls's engagement with game theory also produced his first formulation of the principles of justice, according to which every person was to be treated equally in the eyes of the law and any inequality was to be justified on functional grounds. Rawls's subsequent formulations of the thought experiment and its conclusions became more complex. By 1958, when he published "Justice as Fairness," Rawls had already arrived at the two principles of justice. They would reflect the conclusions of the early thought experiments: the first principle of justice granted equal liberty to all those participating in a practice or affected by it, while the second declared all inequalities arbitrary unless "it is reasonable to expect that they will work out for everyone's advantage" and that offices remained open to all.[72] The beginning of these conclusions is to be found in Rawls's exploration of the analogy between society and games.

5

Practices of Reasoning

RAWLS'S CONCEPTION of philosophy underwent significant changes in the early 1950s, during his last year as instructor of philosophy at Princeton and a subsequent year as a Fulbright Scholar at Christ Church, Oxford. The influence stemmed from philosophers working within the tradition of Ludwig Wittgenstein. To Rawls, the most convincing current of Wittgensteinian inquiry was the thought of Wittgenstein's student Stephen Toulmin. In light of Rawls's intellectual trajectory up to that point, it was not surprising that he should favor this current. Focusing on the notion of practice or human activity governed by socially accepted rules, Toulmin's Wittgensteinianism overlapped with Rawls's vision of ethics as a search for regularities in normative judgments and his newfound interest in analogies with games. Understanding language and reasoning as practices, Wittgensteinian philosophers such as Toulmin saw these rules as constitutive of what counted as an appropriate use of a word, and took explication of these rules as the main task of philosophy.

Early linguistic philosophers, including Wittgenstein himself, were not primarily concerned with ethics or political philosophy. However, by the early 1950s their students had extended Wittgenstein's novel approaches to these disciplines. Seeing ethical reasoning as a practice governed by rules, Toulmin sought to spell out its logic and specify what reasons count as good reasons in ethical arguments.[1] Hence the name by which it is known, the "good reasons" approach.[2] Much as Rawls did when drawing on his teachers at Cornell, these Wittgensteinians argued that "good reasons" are all we can give in favor of our views. If these are accepted and no concrete doubts can be raised, the claim in question should be considered justified.

By the 1951–1952 academic year, Rawls had worked with Wittgenstein's ideas for several years, first in his 1946 course with Malcolm and then via his teachers at Cornell. However, up until then he had used these ideas to complement his vision of ethics as scientific inquiry. That changed in the early 1950s, as he read works of linguistic philosophers, especially Stephen Toulmin, Stuart Hampshire, and Herbert Hart, and discussed Wittgenstein's philosophy with Oxford's J. O. Urmson, who worked as visiting professor at Princeton in 1950–1951.[3] Already conceiving ethics as a study of ethical judgments, Rawls found many themes from Wittgensteinians' philosophy convincing. Indeed, he soon adopted their central views, regarding ethical reasoning as a practice and ethical theory as an attempt to elaborate the rules of this practice. Philosophically, understanding ethical reasoning as a practice helped sever any links with moral realism. Human beings agreed in their ethical judgments because judging was a practice, not because there was an objective factor residing in an ethical situation. Politically, the notion of practice restricted the subject matter of justice to the major institutions or practices of human society.

Rawls's reception of Wittgensteinian currents reveals the landscape from which Rawls borrowed and the character of Rawls's own thought. Wittgenstein himself attempted to show the many different meanings of the same words. This concern with difference was later reemphasized by Rawls's future Harvard colleague Stanley Cavell as well as Rawls's lifelong friend and interlocutor Hampshire, whom Rawls met during the year at Oxford.[4] Rawls, however, drew on Wittgensteinians, who emphasized commonality rather than difference. These philosophers looked for beliefs that characterized practices and, in the case of Toulmin, a goal of ethical reasoning as a whole.[5] This emphasis on commonality appealed to Rawls. It fit into the framework of his theory, which sought to uncover the empirical regularities in the judgments of reasonable persons. In this way, although Rawls took another step away from his earlier physicalist vision of ethical theory by redescribing it in Wittgensteinian terms, this vision shaped the way Rawls understood Wittgenstein's arguments and the reasons for which he found them appealing.

Themes from Linguistic Philosophy in the Early 1950s

Rawls's engagement with the thought of Oxford Wittgensteinians started before he left for Oxford. Rawls reviewed Toulmin's *Reason in Ethics* in 1951, only a year after it was published. He described it as "the first book to consider [the subject of ethics] from the standpoint of the kind of analysis now being practiced at Cambridge and Oxford."[6] Toulmin's work was distinctive in its drawing on the notion of "practice." This idea was implicit in Wittgenstein's arguments. Wittgenstein viewed language as a practice, or an activity governed by shared understandings or what he called "conventions." These activities played a role in human activities; they were used to do certain things, achieve certain purposes.[7] The shared understandings constituted what counted as the right use of a word: as certain moves in games count as "false moves," or moves that violate the rules of the game, so certain uses of words count as improper uses.[8] Whether a particular use of a word was appropriate depended on shared understandings or conventions. According to Wittgenstein, these conventions were implicit, often imprecise, but, for them to be conventions, they had to be shared.[9] Even though he allowed that human beings can disagree about particular statements, Wittgenstein expected human beings to share these conventions, or "agree in the *language* they use."[10]

Moreover, Wittgenstein thought that words had a variety of functions in human life. To emphasize this diversity, Wittgenstein coined the term "language-game," which was "meant to bring into prominence the fact that the *speaking* of language is part of an activity, or of a form of life."[11] He insisted that "there are different *kinds of word*"—words that have different functions—and his examples of practices reflected these different uses of words: giving orders, reporting events, forming and testing a hypothesis, playacting, and making a joke were all considered practices.[12] Other practices were broader and included academic disciplines, such as chemistry and calculus.[13]

Toulmin's innovation was to argue that ethical reasoning as a whole is a practice. As such, it had to have a logic of its own—inferences that were "peculiar to ethical arguments"—irreducible to deductive and inductive logic. Describing such inferences as those "by which we pass from factual reasons to an ethical conclusion," Toulmin called them "evaluative" inferences.[14] Of course, ethical reasoning made use of deductive and inductive inferences as well, but the evaluative inference was distinctive of ethical reasoning. As such, ethical reasoning had its own rules and, therefore, criteria for distinguishing between good and bad reasons: "Good reasons and bad reasons, correct and incorrect inferences, sound and unsound arguments, all are decided in this case by the rule of the game."[15] The content of the sound and unsound arguments was determined by the larger function of ethical reasoning in human activities, which, Toulmin thought, was "correlat[ing] our feelings and behavior in such a way as to make the fulfillment of everyone's aims and desires as far as possible compatible."[16] Ethical reasons were therefore classified as good or bad by how well they managed to adjudicate between everyone's conflicting aims and desires.

It is remarkable how liberal—and political—Toulmin's ethical vision was and how compatible it was with Rawls's political vision described in the previous chapters. According to Toulmin, the task of ethics was to take the aims and desires of persons for granted—at least initially—and then bring them into coherence (presumably understood as the lack of conflict) as much as possible. The task of ethics was not, for example, to deliberate about the goals of life. Thus, it could overlap seamlessly with Rawls's economic conception of autonomy, or the right to determine one's good. In Rawls's political vision, citizens' aims were also taken for granted.

Like the preceding linguistic philosophers, Toulmin denied that one could justify ethical reasoning in any stronger way than showing that it actually fulfills its function and adjudicates conflicts between incompatible desires. He distinguished between justifying within a practice and justifying the practice itself. Thus, he thought, ethical reasoning, having a logic of its own, provided a way to justify actions and, to a limited extent, practices of a society. One could justify individual actions by appealing to reasons set by a practice: an institution of promising, for example, gives us a reason—though not necessarily a sufficient reason—to do what we promised.[17] One could also justify practices that fall under the purview of ethical reasoning, although such justification, Toulmin thought, was much more limited: one could argue for one practice over another if the proposed new practice could be shown to eliminate the problems of the previous practice without changing anything else, or if it could be shown that a new practice would be more congenial to other practices of our society.[18]

However, Toulmin emphasized that ethical reasoning itself could not be given further foundations. Once we have considered all the good reasons for fulfilling our promise and have decided that doing so is the right thing to do, he argued, we have all the reasons to fulfill our promise. The further question, But why should I do what I promised? or, more broadly, But why should I do what is right? could no longer be asked because ethical reasoning could provide reasons that stem only from the inside of the practice.[19] Reasons that go beyond the practice of ethics, such as expediency or authority, were not appropriate for justifying ethics as a whole.[20] In a Wittgensteinian manner, he argued that requests for further foundations extend ethical reasoning beyond its original home: "As a consequence of the ways in which we employ the words concerned, and of the purpose which [ethical] questions . . . serve, there is logically no place in such a situation for this question—taken literally."[21] Since these unanswerable questions revealed the limits of ethical reasoning, Toulmin called them "limiting questions."[22] The best way to deal with them, he thought, was to address the motives and doubts from which these confused questions arise and to try to dispel the question by explaining to the questioner that the origins of the notions "right" and "obligation" are "such as to make the sentence 'One ought to do what is right', a truism."[23] Thus, Toulmin regarded it an impossible task to give a "*general* answer to the question, 'What makes some ethical reasoning "good" and some ethical arguments "valid"?'" Like other linguistic philosophers, he refused to provide further foundations for all reasons in ethics.[24]

The express refusal to ground ethics as a whole became a common commitment of many philosophers at Cambridge and Oxford. Toulmin's book played an important part in this trend. Naming his approach the "toulminian conception of the logic of justification," some of his followers similarly argued that ethics could only provide reasons that are generally accepted as good, that it could not give any further foundations for these reasons, and that such requests for further reasons were confusions of "logical cupboards."[25] Others arrived at nonfoundationalism independently. Gilbert Ryle's student Kurt Baier, for example, argued that one could provide paradigmatic examples of good reasons in ethics, but that, apart from showing how "irrational" it would be to reject these reasons, philosophers could not give any stronger argument in ethics.[26] Urmson, about to visit Princeton as professor in 1950–1951, remarked even more strongly: if we cannot generate agreement around the criteria for good horses, "I do not know what one can do about it. All co-operative activities, all uses of language, must start from some agreed point."[27]

Of course, there was disagreement among Wittgensteinians on how much agreement on the rules of a game one could expect. Toulmin and Baier held that these reasons would be shared, but not everyone agreed. Hampshire claimed that "no argument can show that B *must* use the criteria which A uses and so must attach the same meaning (in this sense) to moral terms as A." Hampshire allowed for disagreement in ethical arguments even after all reasons have been given. In such cases, he argued, one has to make a decision: "Between two consistently applied terminologies, whether in theoretical science or in moral decision, ultimately we must simply choose; we can give reasons for our choice, but not reasons for reasons for . . . *ad infinitum*."[28]

In addition to its nonfoundationalism, linguistic philosophers in the 1950s adamantly rejected constructions of theories in ethics and politics. In their stead, they put forth a philosophy of example. This opposition to theories stemmed from its view of ethical judgment: resting their case on examples, linguistic philosophers argued that we make decisions about justice (for instance) by appealing to different reasons. For example, Hampshire wrote that concepts such as "justice" could not be defined in terms of one or several reasons, since such formulations wrongly assumed that there must be a "single sufficient reason from which I always and necessarily derive my judgment."[29] This argument was echoed by Hart, eventually Oxford chair of jurisprudence and a participant in the Saturday morning discussions with J. L. Austin.

Hart also concentrated on the ordinary uses of words and, relying on this usage, argued that statements of necessary and sufficient conditions for the correct application of words were usually flawed. Concepts, Hart argued, were "defeasible," as "any set of conditions [for the correct use of a word] may be adequate in some cases but not in others." This conception of ethical reasoning had radical implications for philosophy's usefulness to the practice of politics: both Hampshire and Hart argued that a philosopher burdened with the task of explaining "justice" could refer only to the "leading cases on the subject, coupled with the use of the word 'etcetera,'" and that these paradigmatic examples would be useful in practice by "direct[ing] attention to further known facts as relevant to a judgment."[30] This conception of ethics and its relation to practice stood in sharp contrast to Rawls's goal of arriving at a determinate list of principles that explained the concept of justice precisely and from which one could deduce particular practical judgments.

Rawls's Embracement of Wittgensteinian Philosophy

Rawls's vision of ethics as an empirical inquiry led him to appreciate Wittgensteinians' views of ethics. Undoubtedly, Urmson's visiting professorship at Princeton in the academic year 1950–1951 also played an important part. While at Princeton, Urmson lectured on ethics "with a view to determining the nature of ethical problems and the criteria for their adequate solution."[31] A year later, when Rawls taught the same course to Princeton undergraduates, his views were already significantly influenced by Wittgensteinian ideas. Between 1950 and 1952, three important developments took place in Rawls's thought: he elaborated a new conception of justification, modified his account of ethical principles, and employed the concept of a practice to restrict the subject of justice to the basic institutions of our society.

Three sets of writings are helpful in exploring the changes that took place between 1950 and 1952: Rawls's 1951 review of Toulmin's *The Place of Reason in Ethics;* "On Values," a paper written most likely in 1951; and the mentioned 1952 Princeton lectures that consist of two files, "Ethics and Its Reasoning" and "Diseases of Ethical Reasoning."[32] By the time Rawls left for Oxford in 1952, the most important changes in his thought had already taken place, and the yearlong stay, together with the first years at Cornell, by which Rawls was hired in 1953, brought developments but no sweeping changes. For this reason, if the reformulation of the same idea does not hide an important conceptual advance, I sometimes use Rawls's later writings—1953 notes "On Explication" and "Oxford Notes: Spring 1953" (hereafter "Oxford Notes")—to explain the earliest changes in Rawls's thought.[33]

Rawls's new way of looking at justification was centered on viewing ethical reasoning as a practice. This time, his analogy between ethics and reasoning brought out conclusions different from the ones described in Chapter 4. Rawls now emphasized the agreement on rules that must obtain for the game to be played. As he wrote in "Ethics and Its Reasoning," "reasoning is an activity. It is something that men do." To bring to light the implications of this comparison, he introduced the analogy of reasoning to a game. While reasoning is not a game, he wrote, it is nonetheless "instructive to look at it like a game and to see where the points of likeness are."[34] One such instructive likeness was that "reasoning, like most games, is a social activity. That is, 'reasoning' is always an answer to the question, 'What are they doing.'"[35] As such, Rawls thought, it is carried out in accordance with certain generally accepted rules that create the possibility of moves and positions within the game. Rawls did not call these rules "constitutive," but his understanding of them in 1952 contained everything but the name. He listed several types of such rules, including those defining players and rules of etiquette, but he emphasized that the most important among them were principles, which "form the logical structure of reasoning . . . [by] govern[ing] what is to be accepted as a good reason, and rejected as a bad reason."[36]

Much like Wittgensteinians, Rawls began to view philosophical activity as an attempt to uncover the constitutive rules of ethical reasoning. This new view fit in well with his earlier vision of ethical inquiry: Rawls could still view the philosopher as an analyst who tries to produce a theory, or an account of the constitutive principles that govern our reasoning. Thus, in his 1954 seminar on Christian ethics, he wrote that "to speak roughly the aim of the moral philosopher is to give a logical account of a good moral argument in much the same way that a logician attempts to give a logical account of a good deductive and a good inductive argument."[37] But in 1952, he stated that any particular ethical theory is a hypothesis about such criteria, and that a hypothesis of this kind is confirmed or refuted by reference to the actual ethical judgments.[38] Thus he continued to believe that the existence of ethical reasoning depended on one of such hypotheses being correct. Despite this change in overall outlook, then, Rawls still thought of ethics as an empirical inquiry, since it was "a question of empirical fact whether there is moral reasoning or not."[39] He set out to determine "the sort of criteria which are used [in ethical reasoning] to distinguish good reasons from bad reasons."[40]

How to go about discovering these criteria was a different question. As Rawls acknowledged, unlike many games, ethical reasoning did not have explicit, written rules created by particular people at a particular time; in fact, the rules of reasoning were implicit and its rule-making body is everyone. As he wrote in "On Explication" (1953), "The striking thing about the constitution making body of reasoning is that its constitutional making body is everybody. It is part of its constitution that it has no official body."[41] Since there was no rule-making body in reasoning and no explicit rules, Rawls concluded that philosophers interested in discovering criteria for good reasons in ethics had to begin by analyzing the judgments of its informal constitution-making body: everybody. In that regard, he explicitly agreed with Toulmin's suggestion that we can discover criteria for good reasons by examining actual reasoning, or "various instances of the sort of reasoning in question and noticing how we actually distinguish between good and bad reasoning."[42]

Conceiving of ethical reasoning as a practice did not prevent Rawls from remaining a universalist. He did not think that all instances of reasoning were useful for a philosopher tasked with giving an account of ethical reasoning.[43] Toulmin, he wrote, failed to specify just which instances of actual reasoning we should examine.[44] To correct this flaw in Toulmin's account, Rawls suggested that we restrict the range of relevant case studies. Although in his review Rawls did not explicitly limit relevant judgments to those that were considered and made only by reasonable persons, the reference to his own "Decision Procedure for Ethics," where these notions are central, indicates precisely that.[45]

Despite this restriction, Rawls remained as much a universalist as Toulmin: he thought that ethical judgments of all reasonable persons should be part of the subject matter of ethical theory. As he wrote in 1952,

> The question whether there can <u>be</u> reasoning about a certain kind of question turns on whether or not that part of the constitutional body which sits in England agrees with that part of it which sits in India; or whether that part of it which sits in America agrees with that part of it which sits in Central Africa. Or if they do not <u>now</u> agree, can they upon mutual discussion and reflection come to an agreement on what the rules should be.[46]

Thus, while Rawls disagreed with Toulmin about the kinds of ethical judgments that may serve as the subject matter of an ethical theory, he nonetheless agreed that an ethical theory is a universalist theory.

Toulmin's arguments also helped Rawls specify aspects of his philosophical vision. As Rawls wrote in the review of *The Place of Reason in Ethics*, Toulmin was right to stress "the finite character of all reasoning, how in rational discussion it must be permissible to rest one's case at some point, how senseless it is to keep asking for a reason indefinitely."[47] Toulmin's example allowed Rawls to clarify just what requests for further justification would be senseless. In his 1952 Princeton notes, he introduced the notion of intuitive judgments, or judgments for which "no further reason can be given, or at least no one knows how to give one, and when no further reason seems necessary."[48] This was a new term, but it did not depart from the concepts he had used earlier—the "basic statements" of 1946 and statements that are absurd to reject of 1947.

In 1954, calling intuitive judgments "inescapable," Rawls related them to his previous notions of competent judges and considered judgments: intuitive judgments were such that "competent persons in their considered opinion find . . . [them] inescapable, and they can't imagine how an argument against them would go."[49] Rawls elaborated on this inability to raise sensible objections against intuitive judgments in his Cornell lectures. Inviting his students to imagine themselves sailing and spotting a floating lifeboat without people in sight, he argued that we all would turn our boat in its direction. If a fellow sailor, unaware of the lifeboat, asked us why we changed direction, we would give him a reason: namely, that we spotted a boat with no people in sight. His further question "Why go there?" would, in this context, be difficult to grasp: "We can't clearly get straight what we would say if you still said: that's no reason for going off our course (in this case). We might think you were joking; but it wouldn't be funny."[50] Although this example contains no references to Toulmin, the intellectual link is evident: in Rawls's example, we provide a reason to a fellow sailor, but—much like in *The Place of Reason in Ethics*—the sailor raises an undefined question, "Why?" or "Yes, but why should we turn our boat?" Rawls emphasized that the sailor no longer even provides reasons: he does not, for instance, say that changing course in these circumstances is dangerous, or give any other such reason that we would typically consider as a good reason in normal circumstances. As a result, we do not know what the fellow sailor finds objectionable in our decision: we do not know what reasons against our proposal we should consider. Thus, Rawls asked—now almost rhetorically—"what can be proposed as an alternative statement [to our decision] and what would be the form of reason involved in this alternative statement?"[51] He did not answer this question. Instead, he concluded that the sailor's "Why?" rested on doubts that did not stem from an actual rival set of commitments. Having reached this point, Rawls thought, reason giving can be allowed to stop.

In his "Oxford Notes," Rawls made a second, much broader, argument against the further request for reasons. It relied on another theme from Toulmin: the function of ethical reasoning. Toulmin claimed that the function of ethical reasoning was "to correlate our feelings and behavior in such a way as to make the fulfillment of everyone's aims and desires as far as possible compatible."[52] In retrospect, considering contemporary realist criticisms of "high liberalism," Toulmin's idea that ethical reasoning as a whole should have one common goal seems odd. For example, exploring one's own commitments, trying to understand the place of human beings in the world, seeking intellectual fun—all these can be good reasons for engaging in ethical inquiries. But the fact that the search for the constitutive goal of ethical reasoning seemed natural to Toulmin shows well the intellectual milieu in which Wittgenstein's writings were debated and the arguments against which Rawls's thought developed.

Rawls too now started relying on the concept of the function of ethics. As he wrote in 1954 at Cornell, the function of arguments about justice in particular was to decide between competing claims.[53] Requests for further reasons arise, Rawls thought, only in special circumstances—namely, when people disagree. Thus, even if further reasons can be given, they need not be given as long as there is a general consensus on reasons already provided: "We only need to show that . . . [our account of the principles of justice is] such that a competent person is <u>willing</u> to <u>admit</u> that he stands on it without <u>further</u> reasons, whether or not further reasons <u>can</u> be given."[54] That this is so, Rawls wrote, is an important point about the concept of justification: "If there is <u>general</u> willingness to stand on [our account of principles] there is no (general) obligation to give any further reasons, for the obligation to give reasons only <u>arises</u> where there is not general agreement."[55] Insofar as the function of ethical reasoning was completed, there was nothing else for an ethical argument to do. Thus, justification, as Rawls now understood it, was a passing of the burden of proof: if an objection is made, there is an obligation to respond to it; once it is dealt with, the burden of proof is passed on to an imaginary objector, and one need not give further reasons.[56]

Summarizing this new conception of justification, Rawls now explicitly rejected his earlier views on the topic and their accompanying dilemmas. If in graduate school he was repeatedly led to ask whether human agreement was justified because of an objective moral fact or whether the moral fact was made objective by the human agreement, in 1953 he rejected this formulation of the question altogether. "This recognition and acceptance [by competent judges] isn't what makes the principles exist," he wrote; "for to talk this way is nonsensical."[57] In his Cornell lectures a year later, Rawls made the point more forcefully, contrasting two different notions of justification: "We don't offer the general opinion of competent persons as a further reason for the judgment, or as justification of it, but we do offer it as justification for putting the burden upon him who would doubt."[58]

Rawls's argument also clarifies the relationship between agreement of reasonable observers and the status of the claim in question. He began viewing debates about justice as debates about a reconciliation of competing claims rather than an inquiry into truth. If in 1950 Rawls was trying to establish the "objectivity" of ethical statements, where "objectivity" could be associated with "truth"—an ethical statement expressed a truth of some kind—by 1952 the appropriate label for an agreed-upon ethical principle was something like "reasonable." For example, it was reasonable to stop the ethical debate at a certain point, and it was reasonable to use some principles but not others to solve disagreement. Rawls himself did not use the term "reasonable" in this context, but it seems most adequate to express his ideas given his other commitments. The function of ethics was to solve disagreement. If a principle of ethics can do that, it does not make it true of something, but it does make it reasonable for us to use that principle to achieve our sought goal.

At this point, Rawls did not clarify the conditions that were imposed on a proper agreement. In *Political Liberalism*, he would distinguish between "modus vivendi," an agreement forced on us by necessity, and an agreement by which its object—the conception of justice—is endorsed for moral reasons.[59] Nor did Rawls specify that a proper agreement had to be consistent with the main values of the parties to the agreement, such as self-respect, equality, or authenticity. Yet, although Rawls did not make these distinctions and qualifications in the early 1950s, the core idea of his political vision was already there. Agreement about justice is a practical step toward a common life in which everyone's main values are respected.

Rawls's remarks on the nature of objectivity in ethics also help us understand why Rawls argued for his political vision—"justice as fairness"—by considering alternative conceptions of justice instead of deriving "justice as fairness" from some other agreed-upon assumptions. If we are looking for principles that have a role—to solve disagreement—then likely more than one principle could serve this role. In that case, we need to show that one or several of these alternatives are better at solving disagreement than their rivals. The chosen principles of justice might not clarify all difficult moral cases and so dissolve all disagreements, but at least they will do so better than the available alternatives. Having reached the point where alternatives have been shown lacking in more important ways than the chosen set of principles, the argument can provisionally stop—until another, better, alternative is elaborated.

Philosophy and Politics: The Basic Structure, Justice as Fairness

The notion of "practice" prompted a second important development in Rawls's thought: it allowed Rawls to draw limits of his inquiry to the major social institutions of a society. As we saw, Rawls started drawing the boundaries of the concept of justice in the early 1950s. However, his later steps were markedly influenced by Toulmin. If in "Delimitation of the Problem of Justice" he concluded that the subject of justice was situations in which important interests, such as those in life, liberty, and the pursuit of happiness, conflicted substantially, by 1953–1954 he had confined the subject of justice to the institutions and the constitutional structure of society.[60] This evolution took place in two steps, both inspired by the new conception of ethical reasoning as a human practice.

The first step was to restrict the application of "justice" to institutions or practices, which Rawls did in the 1952 lectures at Princeton. It is important to note—as Rawls did—that one had to provide a further argument for the move from understanding ethical reasoning as a practice to claiming that ethical reasoning was a second-order practice that regulates other practices.[61] One could as well, he thought, have analyzed the justice of individual acts.[62] Rawls's main argument for this step was influenced by Toulmin's account of justification, which distinguished between justifying individual acts and justifying practices or institutions. Toulmin thought that reason giving within a practice consisted in appeals to principles: once the act was shown to be justifiable by the rules of the institution, one could criticize it only by criticizing the institution itself.[63] In that regard, he treated justification of institutions as primary.

Toulmin's distinction struck Rawls as very useful, and, in fact, in 1955 he published "Two Concepts of Rules," suggesting a defense of utilitarianism based on this very distinction.[64] Meanwhile, in 1952 he used it to restrict the subject of justice. Actions, Rawls wrote, are justifiable by appeals to rules, most of which fall in the context of some institution.[65] To evaluate an action or a rule, we must, therefore, consider the relevant institution: "Thus we ask: do these rules, as directives to be followed, accomplish in the best possible manner, the purpose of the institution of which they are a part?"[66] Although Rawls did not explicitly conclude that, therefore, a philosopher in ethics should concentrate on the justice of institutions, given the reasoning so far this step seems natural. In his 1953–1954 lectures at Cornell, Rawls experimented with a stronger argument: appealing to the use of the word "just," he claimed that we do not apply this label to particular actions but, rather, to the institutions of which they are part. For example, he wrote, breaches of legal rules have their own labels, such as "murder, theft, assault" and so on; but we do not say of these actions that they are unjust, restricting the use of this label to the corresponding institutions: "Particular actions so covered are not said to be just or unjust; it is the institution itself which may be just or unjust."[67] Later in the same lectures, however, Rawls brought to light cases in which particular actions were in fact called just or unjust. His eventual decision to restrict the subject of justice to practices must have therefore rested not on the argument that the term "just" is not actually applied elsewhere, but—as he argued in *A Theory of Justice*—on the judgment that the justice of practices is a more important subject owing to its long-term effects on people's prospects in life. In 1953–1954 his reasoning may have been similar, but it was not stated in print.[68]

Theory and Practice

Wittgensteinian philosophy required more problematic changes in Rawls's conception of ethical principles. In 1946, following Ducasse, Rawls thought that it was possible to discover principles that underlie all of our judgments of justice. This view rested on two independent expectations: that of universality, or the claim that we would all decide questions of justice for the same reasons, and that of homogeneity of judgment, or the claim that we would decide all questions of justice for the same reasons. Until about 1951, Rawls had not discussed these expectations in great detail. He thought that the deduction of particular judgments from principles would be mechanical, but did not explain how this deduction would take place in practice. Linguistic philosophers such as Hampshire and Hart questioned the homogeneity assumption and, together with it, the ability to use ethical principles as premises for deduction. Rawls acknowledged the force of their objections already in 1951 and, in fact, used them against Toulmin in his review of *The Place of Reason in Ethics,* criticizing him for assuming that ethical judgments are homogenous. First, Rawls reiterated Hart's argument that ethical rules or principles are "defeasible": "Certain standard exceptions are allowed for, and also openings are left for the entirely unexpected."[69] Second, he claimed that principles highlight reasons that are relevant in the subject matter discussed. However, Rawls argued, the weight of these reasons cannot be determined in advance, and so any one reason cannot be said to prevail over all other relevant reasons in all circumstances: "[While] it is true that if there is a recognized rule then appeal to it always has *some* force . . . the force of the appeal varies from one kind of case to the next."[70] Summarizing his discontent with an account such as Toulmin's, in his 1952 lectures Rawls explicitly sided with Hampshire, arguing that "a search for definitions or verbal equivalences is often done under the assumption that there must be some single sufficient reason from which one must always and necessarily base one's judgment; and further that this is a mistake."[71]

Given Rawls's insistence that ethical reasoning is a search for agreement, this emphasis on heterogeneity might appear as an inconsistency in his thought. In fact, however, it indicates a change in his view of what kind of agreement among reasonable persons one might expect. At best, he thought, the agreement would be "loose." Indicative of this change, Rawls started understanding principles of justice not as axioms from which particular judgments can be mechanically deduced, but as guides that highlight relevant but not necessarily decisive reasons. Principles should be understood as "logically loose" guides to judgment. As he put it on the margins of the 1952 lectures at Princeton, the principles act not as premises for deduction but as "bins, boxes of reasons."[72] "It is characteristic of moral arguments," Rawls wrote explaining this new conception of ethical theory, "that the principles always constitute a form of good reasons; but the application of no single principle need be conclusive. There is no conclusion at all in the sense of there being a conclusion to deductive and inductive arguments." Ethics was a different kind of reasoning. So, instead of looking at the principles as the premises for deduction, he wrote, we should view them as indicating "reasons supporting a certain course of action."[73] In the 1952 paper "On Values," Rawls incisively called the principles "rules of relevance," or "instructions as to what aspects of a situation are relevant."[74] The boxes will contain many reasons, but not all of them will be relevant in any one particular case. In addition, the weight of these reasons cannot, he thought, "be precisely determined" in practice.[75] So, instead of being a straightforward deduction from the principles given by an ethical theory, our decision "depends upon what other reasons there are and how the reasons taken as good support one another or fend one another off."[76] As Rawls wrote in a summary, "No valid account of ethical reasoning about justice can take the form of a cook-book code. It may be precise and clear, as I hope my account is; but it will remain <u>logically loose</u>: a way of patterning, arranging and testing for valid argument, but not a mechanical way of grinding them out."[77]

This change in the conception of principles affected the role the principles could play in philosophic or democratic debates about justice. They now became akin to loose guides to discussion. In 1950, as Rawls defended principles as mediators in cases of disagreement, he understood them as premises for deduction, sufficient to lead all reasonable persons to the same judgments about particular circumstances. Depicting the principles as "bins of reasons" weakened that possibility. If the principles were "logically loose" guides to decisions, it was no longer evident that the same ethical principles would determine the decisions of reasonable persons in the same direction.

Of course, it was still possible that all reasonable persons would use the relevant reasons in precisely the same ways. However, the 1951–1952 lectures and the later writings exclude this possibility. Rawls clearly had in mind that principles applied to people who reasoned from different conceptual frameworks (how different is a question to be dealt with later). As he wrote discussing typical cases of ethical reasoning, we are dealing with "people whose theoretical ideals differ, or seem to differ." Such people may nonetheless agree on broader goals, just as "Catholics and Protestants in America can agree upon the necessity of social order and national defense."[78] The principles then try to organize these broad objectives under one umbrella.

It is also clear that Rawls intended the principles to be used in addressing disagreement. As he wrote in the 1953 Cornell seminar, "It is in cases of conflict that we resort to <u>principles</u>: principles are the sorts of things proposed to do this sort of job. They are ... designed to straighten out difficulties in a coherent way <u>wherever</u> difficulties may appear."[79] Now, however, Rawls thought that the principles would be able to solve many—but not all—disagreements. As he wrote, "We would expect anyone to be able to assent to [the principles], and then use these principles in such a way that they do straighten out many controversial particular matters."[80] The 1952 lectures also mention for the first time

that even the people who reason appropriately may not agree on particular courses of action, since, given their varied backgrounds and experiences, they may assign different weights to the same reasons.[81] As we will
see, in 1952 Rawls came closest to *Political Liberalism* in his understanding
of the practical reach of the principles of justice. Hampered by the "burdens of judgment," citizens disagree about which reasons were relevant
in which situations and about the weights of these reasons. However,
they use the same principles—the same bins of reasons—to solve their
conflicts. Although Rawls did not state this explicitly in 1952, one can
infer that, to respect a person's autonomy, it was sufficient to discuss political questions using these "bins of reasons."

Such was the first truly shaping influence of Wittgensteinian philosophy on Rawls. When Wittgenstein's *Philosophical Investigations* was
published in 1953, this influence took another and arguably even more
fundamental form. Influenced by the book, Rawls offered a ground-
breaking seminar on moral feelings at Cornell, in which he attempted
to draw necessary connections between moral emotions and moral
principles. On this account, our judgments of justice had natural bases
in natural and moral feelings. Prompted by Wittgenstein, Rawls would
begin formulating a naturalistic ethics.

6

Natural Bases of Justice

ANALYTIC MORAL AND POLITICAL philosophy underwent a naturalist turn in the 1950s and the 1960s, as philosophers appealed to facts about human nature to argue for ethical and political views. This transformation owed a large debt to Ludwig Wittgenstein and his focus on "forms of life": the various human practices and capacities required to engage in them. It is fair to say with Stanley Cavell that, bringing to light such human capacities, Wittgenstein "put the human animal . . . back into philosophy."[1] Wittgenstein wrote little on moral and political philosophy, but others brought his approach to these fields. Analyzing the capacities of the human animal, they asked how they are relevant in arguing for any particular moral or political view.

Rawls was at the forefront of such philosophers. He read Wittgenstein's *Philosophical Investigations* shortly after its publication in 1953, studying the book intensely, making summaries, dividing it into themes, and even creating its index.[2] As we have seen, by that time Rawls had already used Toulmin's analogy between ethical reasoning and games. However, reading *Philosophical Investigations* marked the beginning of a new and perhaps the most creative period of Rawls's philosophical thinking. Although he drew on Wittgenstein, Rawls raised his own questions; these questions were about the nature of ethical thinking, and the paths he tried out in answering them were refreshingly original and explorative.

Rawls's naturalist approach to ethics was prompted by Wittgenstein's idea. Rawls started viewing morality as "a form of life, or as an aspect of a form of life," which meant understanding it as "a natural phenomenon, as a complex of thought, feeling and action continuous with other aspects of human life."[3] This way of thinking about morality had a variety of implications on Rawls's political thought. First, we see the return of the term "person" to Rawls's philosophical vocabulary. This time, however, the term is understood in the broadest possible way, to fall in line with Wittgenstein's investigation of human life, not any particular human life. Accordingly, Rawls defined a "person" as a being with emotions, interests, and goals. This was a departure from the Kantian and economic autonomy that was central to Rawls in the early 1950s, but, as we will see in the later chapters, it did not mean the abandonment of Kantian autonomy. Second, Rawls used naturalism to explain the expected agreement of reasonable persons. As he argued, natural feelings, if only given free expression, would lead human beings to converge on the same principles of justice. They needed only to look at the world from a particular point of view: the moral point of view.

Third, early in these naturalistic investigations Rawls thought he might be able to arrive at the principles of justice by considering what it means to recognize a person as a person. Justice, as Rawls put it, "is the reciprocal recognition of persons as persons."[4] So, if prior to 1958 Rawls's only way of deriving principles of justice was the "pure case" thought experiment, now the naturalistic argument offered itself as an alternative way of deriving these principles. As Rawls elaborated in "Twofold Basis of Justice," written most likely in 1958, principles of justice could be derived from a "conventional basis," or by showing that they can be agreed upon when reasoning from an egoistic perspective in the situation of justice. But they can also be derived from a "natural basis," or by showing what follows from recognizing persons as persons equally.[5] Rawls was not sure how the ways of deriving the principles related to one another. As he asked, "If limits on content [of morality] follow from both Justice as Fairness arg[ument] and nat[ural] feelings, how are these two derivations related?"[6]

We see some remnants of these exciting naturalistic explorations in *A Theory of Justice*. For example, Rawls briefly describes a theory of justice as a "theory of moral sentiments," and two sections of the book summarize some of the novel questions and arguments.[7] We do not see more, because Rawls's attempts to derive the principles of justice from their natural bases were unsuccessful. Describing personhood in such a broad way, Rawls could not even show that a consistent sadist—someone who recognized a person's aims and took pleasure precisely in preventing their completion—recognized persons as persons inappropriately. Consequently, Rawls abandoned this naturalistic way of deriving principles of justice, and the moral psychology from this time period began serving another purpose by 1964: it was used to show that the most defensible conception of justice can be psychologically more stable than its rivals.

Drawing on Wittgenstein's *Investigations*

Rawls's inspiration for a naturalistic approach to political philosophy came at least partly from Wittgenstein's *Philosophical Investigations* and partly from philosophers who were already using his ideas. Wittgenstein's concept of the "form of life" meant to bring attention to capacities presupposed in even the most mundane practices. For example, *Philosophical Investigations* opens with a discussion of St. Augustine's conception of language, in which names stand for objects and new words are taught by pointing to the objects. According to Wittgenstein, even such a seemingly basic way of teaching presupposes the capacity to understand that extending one's arm and directing a finger at an object is pointing at it.[8] Wittgenstein wanted to bring to light such presupposed capacities. Discussing the capacity to raise the question, for instance, he wrote: "One has already to know (or be able to do) something in order to be capable of asking a thing's name. But what does one have to know?"[9]

One of the conclusions that flow from these considerations is that these capacities are part of the biological constitution of being human. At a little over a year, a child already has the capacity to understand that extending one's arm and directing a finger at an object is pointing to it, and that doing so is an attempt to focus the child's attention on the object. Other capacities develop similarly, such as the capacity to understand that another human being is in pain. This capacity is learned in the simplest interactions with the world. As Cavell argued, "To want to know why the baby is crying is to want to know why it is in pain. If you don't know in general that crying means pain, psychological theories aren't going to teach you."[10]

This interpretation of human life, as Cavell argued, depends on the notion of "normalcy." Cavell asks, How do we know that a person is screaming in pain and not actually singing? We do not know with full certainty, but if the person in front of us is a typical example of a human being, we can conclude with certainty that the person is screaming in pain. That's just how human beings behave: "It isn't that people normally (on the whole, statistically) don't sing that way; but that *normal people don't,* people don't."[11] Similarly, it is possible that a person expresses affection by screaming in pain or attacking us. Such people may live in some world. But, Cavell writes, they "do not live in *our* world."[12]

Cavell's comment on normalcy brings out Wittgenstein's insight that human practices depend on human biological capacities. Were a human constitution to change, new concepts and practices would open up. As Wittgenstein wrote, "Let [someone] imagine certain very general facts of nature to be different from, what we are used to, and the formation of concepts different from the usual ones will become intelligible to him."[13] For the same reasons, different biological constitutions might prevent understanding the practices of other species. Even if lions could speak, Wittgenstein wrote, we could not understand them: not sharing many of their biological features, we could not overcome the alien nature of their practices.[14]

Natural and Moral Feelings

Wittgenstein himself did not analyze human capacities required for moral life or moral practices dependent on these capacities. Followers of Wittgenstein, however, engaged in these explorations.[15] Wittgenstein's approach and the inquiries of his followers led Rawls to analyze morality as a form of life. This influence became most apparent in 1958, when Rawls offered a seminar on moral feelings. Rawls's guiding principle was to look at "having morality as a form of life, or as an <u>aspect</u> of a form of life" and to treat morality "as a whole, as a natural phenomenon, as a complex of thought, feeling and action continuous with other aspects of human life."[16] Of all the capacities assumed in moral behavior, Rawls chose to focus on the capacity to have feelings. "With Wittgenstein I shall assume," he wrote in his seminar notes, "that <u>having a concept</u> is essentially mastering the use of a word in its proper background of thought and feeling."[17] His goal was to outline connections between moral views and the complex of feelings that makes these views intelligible.

Why feelings? In part, this was the legacy of the emotivist philosophy in analytic ethics in the 1930s and 1940s. Philosophers in the 1950s drew on Wittgenstein's ideas to criticize the emotivist claim that feelings do not have a necessary relation to reasons.[18] According to emotivists, any reason could call forth any emotion. Wittgensteinians countered this claim by showing necessary connections between reasons and feelings. Philippa Foot and J. N. Findlay opened this field of inquiry in 1954, arguing that not every moral belief can call forth moral emotions.[19] Foot's argument about the attitude of pride seems to have impressed Rawls the most. Pride, she argued, can be called forth only with respect to objects that can be related to us. While it is possible to be proud of one's child, work, or countrymen, it is typically not possible to be proud of a sea.[20] To call forth the emotion of pride with respect to the sea, we need to provide some special story, such as this sea being the cleanest sea due to our countrymen's efforts. In short, we need to provide a background of beliefs in which having this emotion makes sense.

Elizabeth Anscombe, the translator of Wittgenstein's *Philosophical Investigations* and an Oxford professor whose lectures Rawls attended in 1953, also left an impression on Rawls. Anscombe argued that human beings cannot want just anything. There are limits to what one can want. She appealed to the human capacity to find things valuable, and assumed that this capacity is at least to some degree defined naturally, not by human beliefs but by the human constitution. Adopting Wittgenstein's approach, she drew connections between wanting and related concepts. In particular, she argued that wanting an object has to express itself in trying to get that object.[21] For instance, if a person expresses a want for a pin, is given the pin, and yet does nothing with it, we cannot intelligibly say that the person truly wanted the pin.[22] Without special backgrounds, then, some actions are unintelligible as human actions.[23] These kinds of examples gave Rawls some assurance that there is value in exploring the moral relevance of the capacity to have feelings.

While Rawls may have started his inquiries prompted by Foot's and Findlay's articles, his interests soon departed from theirs. He started focusing on the natural feelings involved in recognizing another human being as a person. In this way, the concept of "person" returned to the forefront of Rawls's philosophical vocabulary. However, the meaning of "person" changed, this time to fit the Wittgensteinian inquiry into the human form of life. Rawls described a human being broadly, as someone "who has wants and interests, who experiences emotions like fear, grief, etc; . . . [who] is rational, is able to deliberate and decide; is able to state intentions and has memories."[24] This definition is noticeably broader than Rawls's earlier definitions of the person, lacking the focus both on Kantian and on economic autonomy. This is not to say that Rawls rejected his earlier understandings of the person, but they played no role in his naturalistic arguments. Moreover, Rawls's definition of a person was broad enough to focus on different aspects of being human. For example, while Elizabeth Anscombe chose to examine the implications of having intentions, Rawls focused on feelings. His goal in the seminar was to explore how this recognition of others as persons expresses itself in the form of what he called natural and moral feelings.

It is noteworthy that Rawls attributed the origin of his emphasis on the recognition of another as a person to Wittgenstein and his discussion of pain. Summarizing this argument in "Justice as Fairness," Rawls wrote that his idea that "the response of compassion, under appropriate circumstances, is part of the criterion for whether or not a person understands what 'pain' means is, I think, in the *Philosophical Investigations*."[25] His own argument, Rawls thought, was "simply an extension of this idea."[26] Thus Wittgenstein's remark, "Pity, one may say, is a form of conviction that someone else is in pain," and his argument that the word "pain" is applied to human beings but not to dolls or stones led Rawls to develop his own version of naturalism.[27]

Focusing on feelings, Rawls divided them into natural and moral. The former, unlike the latter, did not have to presuppose moral concepts. He listed natural feelings by enumeration: joy, grief, anger, fear, love, hatred, sympathy, pity, compassion, envy, jealousy.[28] In his accounts of the development of the moral view, also from 1958, Rawls stressed reciprocity. Of these natural responses, Rawls treated sympathy, compassion, and reciprocity as core, in the sense that other responses could be prompted by them. He defined sympathy as "a certain concord of feeling and approval of a person's stand," which results from thinking oneself "into the reasonings and conceptions of another" and feeling "the force of or the reasonableness of the position."[29] Compassion—the importance of which would soon decline in Rawls's theory—was understood much like pity: as concern with the situation of the person regardless of the fact that the observer does not identify with his point of view.[30] Finally, as in *A Theory of Justice*, reciprocity was understood broadly as a tendency to respond in kind.[31] So, in these early explorations of natural feelings, Rawls acknowledged the importance of both sympathy, which has traditionally been important for utilitarians, and reciprocity, which drew its origin from Jean Piaget, a Kantian thinker. As we will see in Chapter 8, Rawls saw himself drawing on both traditions until 1962, and, indeed, he acknowledged the importance of sympathy even in *A Theory of Justice*, having rejected utilitarianism definitively.

Natural feelings were natural in another sense as well: they were characteristic of typical human beings because they were acquired without specific training. As Rawls put it, "One does not have to be taught this behavior; and any other response would be astonishing."[32] In all explanations of morality, we could take these tendencies for granted. In particular, Rawls emphasized compassion:

> Thus we might say, as a sort of philosophical remark, that compassion is the basis of morality. The point of saying this would be to call attention to the fact that teaching morality, as opposed to insuring obedience to punishment, begins with this natural expression of the recognition of some one else suffering, or of some one's deprivation.[33]

Further, Rawls thought that the more particular expressions of compassion are also natural, in that they do not require specific training. They develop given normal human conditions:

> This development [of natural emotions] is perfectly natural: that is, their affection and liking for companionship will occur if it is given only that minimum of environmental invitation found in the simplest conditions of group life, and so under the natural and normal conditions under which men have lived. The liking and capacity for friendship and affection is natural in that it develops under normal conditions.[34]

Finally, natural feelings were natural in the sense that one did not need to justify them. They were part of being human. As Rawls wrote, "This form of life is as natural as the capacity to perceive and distinguish colors or speech: whatever the explanation of the capacity, and the liking, it is there. We need not, for our purposes, derive it from anything simpler."[35] Natural feelings, for Rawls, became the basic starting points for moral philosophy.

Unlike natural feelings, moral feelings did "presuppose moral standards of some kind." That is, they were explained with reference to moral concepts, such as "justice."[36] For example, the feeling of guilt can typically be explained by citing a rule or an obligation that was broken. Rawls started by listing the moral feelings by enumeration: guilt, shame, remorse, indignation, resentment.[37]

The crux of Rawls's argument was the claim that moral feelings are logically connected to natural feelings. A person with natural attitudes would "necessarily exhibit . . . certain forms of moral behavior."[38] Thus, Rawls wrote, "it is part of the definition for a person's being proud of something, or of viewing him as holding a certain position, and considering certain things below him, that he feels shame in certain circumstances."[39] Similarly, "shame is connected with [natural attitudes of] self-esteem and self-respect," and remorse is connected to compassion: "For we may think of remorse as compassion for those who we ourselves have injured and wronged."[40] Since moral feelings are implied by natural feelings, they too are by extension natural.

Yet Rawls wanted to argue that moral feelings were natural in another sense as well: in typical circumstances, they developed from natural feelings. Rawls thus needed a story of psychological development, in which the typical natural feelings would develop into the typical moral feelings. He developed this story appealing to the writings of the Kantian moral psychologist Jean Piaget. Piaget's story of moral development relied on the concepts of both autonomy and reciprocity. He argued that children achieve autonomy only when they see the rules as arising not from the decisions of adults but "as the outcome of [their own] free decision."[41] The rules seemed worthy of respect to children because the origin of these rules was in reciprocal respect of persons. Reciprocal respect was required because otherwise a law would apply to, or be made by, someone who was not respected. Thus, as Piaget wrote, "any relation with other persons, in which unilateral respect takes place, leads to heteronomy. Autonomy therefore appears only with reciprocity, when mutual respect is strong enough to make the individual feel from within the desire to treat others as he himself would wish to be treated."[42]

Drawing on Piaget's account of moral development in 1958, Rawls emphasized only reciprocity in his arguments. He developed the first laws of moral development already in 1958, but they seemed to play only a small role in Rawls's overall naturalistic endeavor: to show how moral feelings develop out of natural feelings. The first law of moral development claimed that an infant's natural tendency to love her parents is developed by the love shown toward the baby by her parents. As Rawls wrote,

> I want to say that it is a basic psychological fact about human nature that love is created in another by love, compassion by compassion etc. That is to say, the child learns to love and feel for others, has his capacity for this developed, by others loving and caring for him; and having this capacity developed in this way is the precondition for subsequent moral conduct.[43]

Young children, of course, do not yet have a morality, since their tendency to love is not based on reasons and because the only persons they love are immediately present. Their sense of guilt also stems from having broken a command of the person they love, as opposed to a reason or a principle that is independent of the parents. That is why Rawls called children's guilt "authority guilt."[44]

The second law of moral development explains how this limited love expands to include people in voluntary associations or even the voluntary associations themselves. Since we are talking about children, voluntary associations are typically games, and, as with most games, they depend on rules. Since in games everyone follows a rule for everyone's benefit, the attitude of fairness becomes of primary importance. This attitude is developed by seeing the benefits that the association brings about, and the dependence of the benefit on the attitude of fairness. A breach of fairness will be followed by what Rawls called "association guilt." These feelings are moral in some respects but not others. On the one hand, the attitude of fairness takes into account others' interests, and the feeling of guilt arises from having injured the persons in the association. On the other hand, the persons in the association are known, and so in typical circumstances the sense of fairness does not extend to persons unknown. Fairness remains, at least initially, within the boundaries of the game that the children actually play.

The third law of moral development describes the emergence of the sense of justice out of participation in such voluntary associations. The sense of justice, while it involves fairness, arises without the direct presence or knowledge of the persons injured. In that regard, the sense of justice is the most abstract state of the natural attitudes from which it started. The sense of guilt arises from breaching rules of justice or failure to work for the establishment of rules.[45] Knowledge that someone was injured as a result of this failure is not required. Knowledge that no one was in fact injured may bring us relief, but not necessarily the end of the feeling of guilt.

Finally, Rawls took for granted the logical connections between moral views and moral feelings. One's moral views determine whether one's moral feelings are called forth. For example, an account of civil disobedience greatly affects whether the person holding these views will feel guilty for breaking the laws. As Rawls himself would argue later, though in normal circumstances the breaking of the laws would be accompanied by the feeling of guilt, under the circumstances of severe injustice in which the laws are implicated, the feeling of guilt would not arise. Similarly, Ajax felt such shame for slaying the field of sheep in a mental craze that he deemed it to warrant suicide. In a morality less influenced by warrior virtues, such acts, though perhaps they might be thought shameful, would not be thought to require ending one's life.

Natural Morality

Analyzing connections between natural and moral feelings helped Rawls draw moral and political conclusions. Most immediately, this connection allowed Rawls to show that morality is a natural phenomenon. The consequence of the logical connection was that a person without moral feelings would also lack natural feelings. Given that moral feelings were a natural extension of moral feelings, "one could not be <u>without</u> moral feelings without also being [without] certain natural feelings."[46]

Rawls did not argue that persons without at least some of the natural feelings did not exist. But he did want to say that if they did exist, they were abnormal human beings. For example, he allowed that "systematic sadists" may exist on this earth. Initially, Rawls described such sadists as not persons, since they failed to recognize others as such.[47] This argument depended on the notion of "normalcy," which played a key role in Wittgenstein's arguments as well. As Rawls emphasized discussing reciprocity in *A Theory of Justice*:

> This tendency is a deep psychological fact. Without it our nature would be very different and fruitful social cooperation fragile if not impossible.... If we answered love with hate, or came to dislike those who acted fairly toward us, or were averse to activities that furthered our good, a community would soon dissolve.[48]

The conclusion that a human being without moral feelings would be an abnormal human being was, Rawls concluded, "a <u>kind</u> of grounds of morality."[49] This argument seems to have been primarily directed against the skeptical question: Why be moral? As we saw, following Toulmin five years earlier, Rawls rejected the need to justify morality as a whole. So long as particular moral doubts were answered, we did all we could do. Rawls's reengagement with this skeptical worry about the grounds of morality shows that he had some lingering doubts. Now he could use his naturalist background to answer these doubts. If the argument above is correct, he wrote, then we realize that a skeptic of morality would have to view nonmoral human beings in a very different biological light:

> For when a person reflects on the grounds of morality or asks himself why he should <u>be</u> moral, he may be tempted to think that one could be without a morality and everything <u>else</u> be the same; but there are obviously connections of <u>some</u> kind between the moral and the natural feelings.[50]

In other words, the human being without the capacity to be moral would also lack other capacities that make us human. And this, Rawls thought, is an argument-ending realization. For beings such as ourselves, morality is unavoidable. As Rawls put it, seeing that a person without morality is not fully human makes "the having of morality and moral behavior rational and intelligible."[51] He would repeat this argument in *A Theory of Justice* as well, writing that "by understanding what it would be like not to have a sense of justice—that it would be to lack part of our humanity too—we are led to accept our having this sentiment."[52]

Boundaries of Morality

From the beginning, Rawls's inquiries into natural and moral feelings were meant to shed light on moral views (theories). Foot's argument that not every principle can be a moral principle was, after all, one of the most important causes of Rawls's decision to study moral feelings. So, breaching this new area of inquiry, Rawls also asked if natural feelings impose any limits on the content of plausible moral views. Some moral views, Rawls thought, cannot plausibly evoke moral feelings. As he put it, "What cannot be connected at all with such [natural] attitudes is not really a morality."[53] Engaging in such explorations would therefore mean exploring "limits [on the] content of morality."[54]

It is noteworthy that Rawls did not make a more direct argument that natural feelings require a particular moral view, such as his own "justice as fairness," for reasons similar to those discussed in Chapter 5. Just as there could be several reasonable principles of justice, so could there be several plausible expressions of natural feelings. The more direct and ambitious line of argument from natural feelings to "justice as fairness," he thought, could soon turn into a tautological argument that defined natural feelings in an overly narrow way.[55] To take an example of joy, the direct line of argument would require showing that a moral theory privileging reciprocity and fairness is either the only view that plausibly evolves from the natural capacity of joy, or that it is the view that develops most plausibly from it, or that it so develops with the fewest problems. In the 1950s, Rawls already had the developmental story, but he did not yet think that this story privileged any one moral theory. As he put it in 1958, natural feelings allow for "many different types of moralities."[56] To solve moral disagreements, a different type of argument was needed:

> Nothing in my argument settles in advance the important moral questions of every day and politics etc in the favor of some limited and definite view. These questions, for all that I have said, are left over to be settled on their merits, and on the basis of arguments of another kind.[57]

This meant that Rawls had to carry out a more limited argument: draw limits on the range of views that could be made compatible with natural feelings. He maintained that only certain moral principles could be made compatible with moral (and therefore also natural) feelings. Yet instead of focusing on substantive moral theories, such as utilitarianism or Marxism, Rawls turned to emotivism and its claim that any principle can be a moral principle. Taking R. M. Hare's *The Language of Morals* as representative of emotivism, Rawls argued that some principles, such as "Do not walk on the sidewalk," could not be connected to typical moral feelings, such as guilt or shame. As he wrote, "What I have attempted to show, after having examined some of the moral feelings, is that the standard moral feelings could not be defined with respect to any content: that is, that these feelings require certain objects."[58] Rawls argued that only certain objects can give rise to moral emotions and reasons. Referring to the already-mentioned example of Philippa Foot, he argued that moral principles such as "Do not walk on the sidewalk" cannot evoke the moral emotion of guilt when this rule is breached. Connecting such rules with moral emotions would be "in some instances nonsensical, in others the conduct itself would be unintelligible."[59] Considering this principle a moral principle would require a "very great . . . shift" in "our whole way of viewing morality and human feelings. . . . This is [a] drastic conceptual shift."[60] Such a view would "completely unhing[e] our moral vocabulary, and further, our vocabulary of natural attitudes and personality."[61]

This argument may work against bizarre principles of justice, but it has less purchase against actual moral theories, the principles of which are more defensible. Perhaps for this reason Rawls did not evaluate the more traditional moral theories against the background of his naturalistic philosophy. The main problem with the argument was the breadth of the terms "person" and "recognizing." If one defines a "person" as someone who has interests and wishes, and "recognizing" the person as acknowledging the person's having of those wishes, then a variety of behavioral patterns could count as recognizing the person. As Rawls himself noted, "We certainly recognize others as persons in revenge and retaliation." Similarly, we may recognize persons while behaving toward them in an unjust or otherwise inappropriate manner. As Rawls wrote, we "may certainly recognize . . . others as persons when we shove them aside in the pursuit of our own interests. Cheating, or stealing from another, doesn't presuppose that we fail to recognize him as a person."[62] Such broad understandings of "person" and "recognizing" therefore allowed all kinds of behavior—and certainly Marxist and utilitarian—to count as recognizing another as a person. On the other hand, narrowing the meaning of "person" and "recognizing" would have required building in specific interpretations of moral concepts and therefore arguments beyond moral psychology. Rawls did not attempt to go in that direction, and so the achievement of this line of argument was the rejection of emotivism but not any substantive moral theory, such as utilitarianism or Marxism.

Overlap of All Moralities

Focus on natural feelings also allowed Rawls to make a third argument. He argued that all moral views compatible with natural feelings will have some shared content. This overlap between moralities and the agreement in judgments, should they obtain, would be explained by the natural attitude of recognizing persons as persons, and feelings involved in this attitude. As Rawls wrote in an undated "Essay V," "Sharing prima facie principles, there must be many types of cases on which all moralities agree."[63] In this argument, Rawls made use of Wittgenstein's notion of "family likeness" or "family resemblance": the idea that although related practices may not share any one trait in common, they will have sufficient overlapping similarities.[64] Rawls employed the same reasoning with regard to different moral conceptions, arguing that they have a point of overlap: "My hypothesis is this: that anything which we would call a morality has a certain specific set of prima facie principles. Or, all moralities resemble one another in their prima facie principles; they have this sort of family likeness. They resemble one another in their principles."[65]

Here again, Rawls did not think that this agreement on principles would produce agreement on all particular cases to which these principles apply. To use his earlier language, principles of justice were "bins of reasons," and different people might use the same reasons while weighing these values differently. Rawls held this belief in 1958 as well, despite the fact that he now conceived morality in the naturalistic light. In this case at least, the Wittgensteinian language allowed him to explain that the agreement of moralities was loose agreement. There were "family resemblances" between moralities, but not necessarily agreement on even central moral issues. As he wrote, even though moralities "have the same principles (or principles that bear a likeness to each other) they may differ by varying the emphasis and so favoring one principle over another, in a wider or narrower scope, and in using different frameworks."[66] The extent of this overlap of the reasonable persons' moral conceptions was not clear without further analysis. It was Rawls's task to discover the extent of this overlap.

Rawls's naturalist background also allowed him to partly explain why moralities would overlap, even if in limited ways. The reason lay in the fact that normal human beings have a natural tendency to recognize other human beings as persons:

> If it is true that moralities all have a certain set of prima facie principles in common (or some family resemblance to some set), as I think is the case, this finds its explanation in the fact that these principles are connected with forms of recognition of persons, and forms of acting with them. This set has itself between its members a family resemblance: to violate any of them would be to violate some kind of personal connection.[67]

Why, then, did human beings fail to recognize others as persons in real life? Rawls pointed to two reasons. The first was self-interest. If our own well-being, or the well-being of the people closest to us, was at stake, we might fail to recognize others as persons: "The natural reaction to suffering is compassion; to a breach of trust is remorse, etc. These reactions may be blocked, or inhibited by various factors: hatred of the sufferer, preoccupation with one's own affairs, belief that he deserves to suffer, and so on."[68]

Rawls also thought that sympathy was at fault. According to him, the sympathetic understanding of another's viewpoint led us to be partial toward that person. "Sympathy does incline us to be <u>partial</u>," he wrote. "That is, it inclines us to favour more than we should the claims of those with whom we sympathize, and not to favour as we should those with whom we do not sympathize." Thus, he concluded, "sympathy must be regulated and controlled, . . . we need to correct for its natural biases."[69]

These arguments affected Rawls's understanding of justice. Some notes suggest that he tried out, at least briefly, the utilitarian path of a sympathetic observer who knew and weighed each person's interests equally. He did this by tying morality to sympathy that is equally extended to all. "In what sense can we say that morality is a <u>generalization of sympathy</u>?" Rawls asked. "Is it this: that to act morally is to act as if one sympathized with the ends of all persons equally?"[70] Other notes show that he brought his own "justice as fairness" into the claim that morality starts with sympathy. How does one decide how to sympathize equally with everyone's needs? he asked. "For this one might resort to the principle of reciprocity (and of justice)," he reasoned. "Thus the principles of justice can be desired as the principles which an impartially sympathetic man would use to regulate his actions expressing his wanting what others want."[71] So, Rawls now argued, justice is an impartial treatment of persons, or impartial recognition of persons as persons. As he wrote, "The principles of justice reflect the judgments of one whose aim [is] to care for all interests equally, to pay due attention to them all, and to take them all into account." This understanding of justice rested on "the natural basis," or the equal treatment of all persons' interests.[72] Still, at that point, his description of morality was intermixed with the admission of the debt to utilitarians' conception of morality. As he wrote:

> It may be in order simply to state that I think the view which may be found in Hume and Adam Smith, and in the utilitarians generally, is certainly correct: that the moral feelings build on the natural attitudes, that they represent a kind of generalization and extension of them under the control of reason.[73]

Rawls's notes from this period show how he used the principles of justice to correct for the biases of sympathy. In Chapter 8, we will see how Rawls corrected the natural biases of sympathy to arrive at the principles of justice. This move is more interesting, because it announces that if we only employ sympathy and other natural feelings well enough, we can show how all reasonable persons can agree on principles of justice. This argument will require explaining a key idea—taking the moral point of view—and analyzing Kantian influences on it. In this chapter, it is useful simply to point out that Rawls's naturalism led him to redescribe parts of his theory, especially what would become the "original position." Considered judgments, which were earlier described in terms of the physicalist empirical theory, now acquired the connection to natural feelings. They were the judgments made spontaneously and, in particular, in circumstances in which our interests or the interests of those closest to us were not involved. This condition was required to ensure the impartiality required by justice. Once such misguiding conflicts were not present, natural feelings directed everyone's considered judgments in the same direction: "The conditions of considered judgment [are] conditions which set the stage for this reaction and remove anything which may inhibit it, or distort it. They allow free and full play for the natural reactions of recognition; and in this way, the explanation for the agreement which follows may lie."[74]

In sum, Rawls's explorations of natural feelings allowed him to draw three conclusions about morality. First, morality is an extension of the capacities possessed by the human animal: to experience joy and affection, to grieve the misfortune of another, and the like. Second, these natural feelings limit the range of moral views that human beings can reasonably possess. Some moral views are unintelligible as moral views because they cannot evoke moral feelings of shame, remorse, or the like. Third, moral views within the range of plausible moral views have shared content precisely because of their origin in natural feelings.

These are undoubtedly important conclusions. However, they were grounded in very little analysis of particular feelings or specific moral views. Rawls did not discuss the moral views that are excluded by natural feelings, the reasons for which they are excluded, or the content that different moralities share. Nor did he explain why, given the same natural feelings, different moralities emphasized different aspects of human experience. In short, the normative implications Rawls drew from the analysis of natural feelings did bring the human animal into the analysis of morality, but they analyzed that human animal in very broad terms, to draw very broad conclusions. Implications for particular moral theories, such as utilitarianism, perfectionism, or Kantianism, would still have to be drawn.

Stability as a Reason

As Rawls taught the history of political philosophy in his classes, the concern with the stability of the social system loomed larger and larger in his thinking. In the 1963 lectures on political philosophy, Rawls used Hobbes to point out two kinds of instability of a social system. The first kind of instability, he wrote, "obtains when it is to the advantage of any one person not to do his part (not to cooperate) if the others in the scheme will continue to do (or have done) their part." The second kind of instability occurs when "any one person thinks that others will not do their part."[75]

Moral psychology helped Rawls address these problems of stability and the problem of stability in general. In addition to taking the Hobbesian route and claiming that the sovereign will eliminate the feeling of uncertainty about the actions of others, Rawls argued that citizens in a just society will be motivated to follow the principles of justice internally, not solely by fear of force. The reasons that will so motivate the citizens will be provided by the very principles of justice that will govern a just society. While Rawls did not yet call this stability "stability for the right reasons," the idea was the same.[76] A conception of justice was stable if it had internal support—people going along with the main institutions of the society because they endorse them using reasons provided by that very conception.

Rawls's concern with stability shifted his interests in moral psychology. While even in *A Theory of Justice* he held some of the commitments described earlier, moral psychology now became part of his argument that "justice as fairness" is stable and the most stable conception of justice.[77] This shift took place in the early 1960s. Now, unlike before, Rawls's main concern was determining the relationship "between the correct psychological explanation and the correct moral theory" and asking whether all major ethical theories are compatible with correct psychological explanations.[78] Telling of this change in emphasis, the rival ethical view was not emotivism but utilitarianism—a moral theory with clear practical commitments. Deciding between his own theory "justice as fairness" and utilitarianism required specifying "a plausible psychological theory which explains how (rational) persons acquire the desire under normal conditions to do what is right."[79] In short, Rawls asked how compatible the two rival moral theories are with the laws of psychological development.

The core of the argument was the claim that theories relying on reciprocity, or the tendency to respond in kind, were psychologically more stable than theories relying on sympathy. Belief in the strength of reasons provided by the tendency to reciprocity helped Rawls's argument against utilitarianism. Only "justice as fairness" relied on reciprocity, the latter relying on sympathy, a "weaker and less common" inclination.[80]

Relying on reciprocity, "justice as fairness" could generate self-respect, which ensured "a sense of [citizens'] own value."[81] As Rawls argued, "By arranging inequalities for reciprocal advantage and by abstaining from the exploitation of the contingencies of nature and social circumstance within a framework of equal liberty, men express their respect for one another in the very constitution of their society."[82] Self-respect thus served as an anchor of stability: the sacrifices required of the least advantaged citizens do not hurt their conceptions of themselves.

Utilitarianism, Rawls thought, was less likely to generate the sense of self-respect and therefore of citizens' self-valuation. As Rawls wrote, the principle of utility "asks men to forego greater life-prospects for the sake of others." Surely, he continued, "it is natural to experience a loss of self-esteem, a weakening of our sense of the value of accomplishing our aims, when we accept a lesser prospect of life for the sake of others."[83]

Rawls did not deny that utilitarianism could feasibly generate such internal support, however. Perhaps the sense of self-respect could be saved by some means, such as by relying on sympathy and "altruistic sentiments." As Rawls acknowledged, "These inclinations certainly exist; the contract doctrine does not, of course, deny this."[84] Serving as a devil's advocate to utilitarianism, Rawls rewrote the second law of moral development around the principle of utility, analyzing how the utilitarian sense of justice could develop. The law now read: "Individuals tend to acquire friendly feelings towards others who with evident intention [to] do their part in cooperative schemes publicly known to maximize the total sum of advantages, or the average satisfaction per person if the contractual variant [of the principle of utility] is used."[85]

Nevertheless, Rawls believed it was difficult to imagine how "friendly feelings" toward those who benefit from our sacrifice could develop without any kind of reciprocity from those benefited. In fact, he argued, the strongest feelings of altruism presuppose acts of reciprocity. One could be sympathetic toward those benefited (one could adopt their standpoint and see it as reasonable) because of the prior reciprocal relation between those who benefit and those who are asked to sacrifice their life prospects. As Rawls wrote,

> In a well-ordered society as defined by justice as fairness, such [sympathetic] identification might be quite strong, and could perhaps be an important supplementary force making for stability. But this seems probable precisely because of the reciprocity inherent in the basic structure of society. Given the constant assurance provided by the two principles of justice, individuals will develop a sense of worth and self-esteem that makes possible a love of mankind, and its more subtle forms enlightened by sympathy.[86]

Thus, Rawls thought, the feelings of sympathy and the acts of sacrifice would be strongest in a society governed by "justice as fairness" and its principle of reciprocity. However, he argued, to require sympathy without reciprocity is to require an exceptional sacrifice: "To appeal to altruism directly as a foundation for moral behavior in the absence of reciprocity in the basic structure of society seems much less plausible. It certainly puts a much greater burden on men's capacity for sympathetic identification." For these reasons Rawls concluded that "other things equal, the conception of justice as fairness is bound to prove more stable than utilitarianism."[87]

The argument from stability allowed Rawls to believe that agreement of reasonable persons would increase as the tendency to reciprocity was given free play in a society governed by justice as fairness. At the same time, this argument was accompanied by cautious remarks. In particular, as the "other things equal" qualifier in the above quote testifies, Rawls thought that the argument from stability added some weight to "justice as fairness" but was not decisive. Even in *A Theory of Justice* he allowed that utilitarians could give a plausible story that showed its society stable for the right reasons.[88] Consequently, he could not have thought that the argument from stability gave sufficient grounds for rejecting utilitarianism.

In sum, Wittgenstein's focus on the human animal led Rawls to explore the moral "form of life." Rawls's emphasis on natural feelings allowed him to point out the necessary connections between natural feelings and moral feelings, and between moral feelings and moral views. In principle, at least, these kinds of connections allowed Rawls to draw limits on the content of acceptable moral views. Some views, he argued, are simply inconceivable against the background of natural and moral feelings.

However, when applied to existing and accepted moral theories, such as utilitarianism, Kantianism, and Marxism, these naturalist explorations into human emotions proved to be less fruitful than expected. Rawls concluded that the background of natural feelings allows for various moral theories. Moral feelings of guilt, shame, and remorse could of course be called forth by utilitarianism, Kantianism, and Marxism. Why should there not be a Marxist shame or a utilitarian guilt? To decide between political visions, Rawls argued that those relying on reciprocity were more stable than others. This was one more reason for accepting "justice as fairness."

7

No Shortcuts in Philosophy

RAWLS FIRST JOINED Harvard as a visiting professor in the 1959–1960 academic year and, after spending two years as chair of the Massachusetts Institute of Technology's philosophy department, returned there as a full professor in 1962. By the early 1960s Harvard had become a center for Wittgensteinian thought, employing David Sachs, Rogers Albritton, Burton Dreben, and Stanley Cavell. Despite Rawls's interest in Wittgenstein, his philosophical vision during the mid-1960s was most markedly influenced by W. V. O. Quine, "the greatest logical positivist."[1] Rawls met Quine during his first stay at Harvard, read his books, and discussed them with Dreben, who on Rawls's own account made "Quine's view clear" to him and with whom he worked intensely between 1962 and 1967.[2] Despite the fact that Quine wrote virtually nothing on moral subjects and seems to have had little personal interaction with Rawls, there was an intellectual affinity between the two thinkers. Both drew on the logical positivist traditions at the beginning of their careers to formulate their philosophical frameworks, and the problems the two thinkers faced in the 1960s were for that reason at least partly shared. Drawing on Quine's naturalism and nonfoundationalism, Rawls emphasized the nonfoundationalism of his own philosophical vision, introduced the notion of "fixed points" (on which we can temporarily rest our argument), specified that justification of a political vision is not absolute but rival to other political visions, and clarified that the argument for the preferred political vision rests on many arguments that are each individually not decisive. There were no shortcuts in philosophical argument. Effectively, then, drawing on Quine helped Rawls formulate the concept of reflective equilibrium, or the state of affairs in which these many fixed points in our thinking about justice were consistent with principles of justice. These concepts were not wholly new in Rawls's philosophical framework, but engaging Quine's ideas helped Rawls give them sharpness, bring them to light, and gather them all into a consistent philosophical vision.

Quine the Positivist

The intellectual affinity between Rawls and Quine stemmed from their early engagement with logical positivism and the legacy of this tradition in their thinking even in later years. As a young philosopher, Quine studied with the logical positivists Rudolf Carnap in Vienna and Alfred Tarski in Warsaw in the academic year 1932–1933. Quine never fully agreed with Carnap, but he nonetheless saw him as "the leader of the continuing developments" in philosophy from the 1930s onward.[3] Despite their disagreement, Quine thought that Carnap "was still setting the theme" and that his own "line of . . . thought was largely determined by problems that . . . [Carnap's] position presented."[4] Most broadly, Quine's approach to knowledge was empiricist in its reliance on data acquired by the senses: he held that "physical things generally, however remote, become known to us only through the effects which they help to induce at our sensory faculties."[5] Like Carnap's later position, Quine's empiricism was nonfoundational: he did not believe that knowledge gained by sensory qualities is unquestionable or necessary.[6] As his criticism of foundationalism in "Two Dogmas of Empiricism" (1951) reveals, Quine's nonfoundationalism stemmed from meaning holism, or the claim that the meaning of any one term depends on the meaning of other terms. Quine offered two arguments against foundationalism in "Two Dogmas": that the notion of analytic and necessary truths is not clearly defined, and that foundationalism's attempt to reduce all knowledge to immediate and defined experiences is flawed because knowledge is not stored in individual statements or experiences. Rather, "the unit of empirical significance is the whole of science."[7]

The key implication of meaning holism was justificatory holism, or the claim that one justifies not any single statement of a theory but the theory as a whole. Any one statement—including the allegedly necessary statements—does not have many implications by itself: "A scientific sentence cannot in general be expected to imply empirical consequences by itself. A bigger cluster [of assumptions] is usually needed."[8] As a result, by testing any one statement, we are in fact testing the "bigger cluster" of premises on which the statement relies. Theories stand the test of experience not as a collection of individual statements but as a collection of interdependent premises.[9]

While Quine's version of meaning holism was radical in its implications for positivism's analytic-synthetic distinction, it remained indebted to the tradition's key commitments. It is remarkable how much Quine's story parallels Rawls's. Quine continued to believe that meaning holism would not harm positivism's claim that all scientific observers would agree on at least some scientific statements. He followed the tradition in calling these statements "observational statements," or statements to which other beliefs are largely irrelevant. As he put it, observational statements are statements "most strongly conditioned to concurrent sensory stimulation" and least dependent on our wider web of beliefs, or "stored collateral information" or "stored information beyond what goes into understanding the sentence."[10] Being least dependent on the wider web of beliefs, observational statements were also those "on which all speakers of the language give the same verdict when given the same concurrent stimulation."[11] Thus, although Quine endorsed meaning holism, he limited its implications by allowing that some observations are little affected by the wider webs of beliefs of those who observe. This feature of Quine's thought is little emphasized: noted for his meaning holism, Quine is thought to have opened the door to contesting the existence of observational sentences. In fact, however, Quine did not take that step. In that respect, he remained indebted to his early logical positivist framework.

The extent of Quine's positivism is most apparent when contrasted to contemporary historicist approaches to the philosophy of science.

Thomas Kuhn, for instance, drew significantly more radical implications from meaning holism. Like Quine, he criticized the early logical positivist understanding of observation by arguing that individual observations took place in the context of wider scientific theories.[12] Unlike Quine, however, Kuhn objected to the notion of "observational statements" defined in terms of sensory impressions, claiming that questions about sensory impressions "presuppose a world already perceptually and conceptually subdivided in a certain way."[13] Starting from these different premises, he criticized Quine for assuming that "two men receiving the same stimulus must have the same sensation."[14] In the absence of observational statements or other shared beliefs, scientific theories cannot be judged to be better or worse by appealing to these commonly shared beliefs. Instead, Kuhn wrote, scientific theories are justified from their own point of view and with reference to their "accuracy, simplicity, [and] fruitfulness" in explaining their subject matter.[15] Similar positions were held by Michael Polanyi and Norwood Russell Hanson.[16]

Quine rejected such radical interpretations of meaning holism and defended the notion of observational sentences. Claiming that thinkers such as Kuhn, Polanyi, and Hanson "belittle the role of evidence and . . . accentuate cultural relativism," he argued that one could have observational statements that encompass the entire scientific community.[17] "What counts as an observation sentence varies with the width of community considered," he wrote. "But we can also always get an absolute standard by taking in all speakers of the language, or most."[18] Quine seemed certain that this universal standard would be met. As the contrast to historicism shows, Quine's "observation sentences" were meant to play the role of "hard" evidence. They were evidence, which, while not foundational, was little dependent on wider frameworks of beliefs and therefore capable of providing common points to adjudicate disagreements.

Quine himself did not extend this conception of justification to ethical or moral issues. When Rawls did so, he did it against Quine's judgment. Quine thought that meaning holism was so pervasive in ethics that this discipline contained no observational statements and therefore no subject matter. For Quine, ethical statements such as "that's outrageous" were not observational statements. According to him, their truth or falsity "hinge[d] on collateral information not in general shared by all witnesses of the acts."[19] Paradoxically perhaps, despite rejecting the thought of modeling ethics on scientific inquiry, Quine did not espouse ethical relativism. Rather, he thought all societies would agree on at least some ethical principles, on some "common core," because "the most basic problems of societies are bound to run to type."[20] In ethics, just as in his entire approach to philosophy, Quine did not think that competing intellectual traditions would present incommensurable webs of belief.

Reflective Equilibrium

Quine's influence started showing in Rawls's work in the early 1960s. Rawls accepted meaning holism in Quine's limited sense, although he concentrated not on the epistemological arguments but on the implications of meaning holism in ethics. In particular, Rawls emphasized justificatory holism and argued against Cartesianism that a single consideration is insufficient to deduce principles of justice. Rawls had already rejected this line of thinking by 1947 and certainly by 1952, as he drew on Toulmin's understanding of ethical arguments as giving reasons. On this account, ethical statements were not reducible to other kinds of statements: ethics had a logic of its own. This time, however, the position to be rejected was different. Rawls understood "Cartesianism" as an attempt to claim that certain premises are self-evident and necessary, and then deduce ethical conclusions from these premises alone. As Rawls explained to his students in 1966,

> There is a tradition in philosophy—let's call it Cartesianism—which thinks of justifying a proposition as <u>deducing</u> it from <u>self-evident</u> premises, from necessarily true statements. Taking statements of concept identity, logic and mathematics as such statements, we might try to justify our ethical [conclusions] from these.[21]

Rawls rejected this Cartesian foundationalism for two main reasons. First, he thought that no adequate account of necessity had yet been given. As he argued in the 1967 lectures on ethics, any account of necessity had to be placed in a larger philosophical framework that makes clear why the chosen necessary statements are significant in the context of ethical inquiry. Without such an explanation, one would not know how to use the necessary statements:

> In general I agree with Quine, or at least as I understand him, that no one has yet given a philosophically useful account of logical or mathematical necessity which distinguishes it and shows why it [is] essential philosophically to show that certain propositions are necessary in this sense. No doubt we can take as given by enumeration a class of (logical) truths and definitions and then clarify this class and its consequences as logically or mathematically necessary. But why this class, especially with its definitions, is of any particular significance has yet to be explained.[22]

Rawls therefore saw no reason to treat any definition as necessary. His discussions of the good and his naturalist explanation of morality had to be shown useful in another way than claiming it necessary. This can be best seen in his remarks in a 1965 seminar on the good. Rawls claimed that there is no good reason for including something as part of a definition:

> You want to make it part of the concept of goodness that to recognize that X is good implies being moved to some degree. I believe that in the absence of an account of necessary truths which shows why this connection is desirable from a theoretical point of view, little if anything is gained. And I don't believe that we have an adequate account of necessary truths.[23]

Rawls allowed for a theoretical possibility that such a philosophically useful account of necessity would be elaborated in the future, but he could not imagine even a rough structure of such an account. This seeming impossibility stemmed from the fact that there are always several feasible definitions to any concept used in the theory, and the choice of any particular definition needs to be supported by reasons. As Rawls wrote in 1967:

> If we specify correct moral principles as those which would be agreed to by rational men, we need a (real) definition presumably of the concept

of a rational man. But as there [are] various interpretations of rationality (as well as of other notions we would have to rely on), we might just as well take our preferred interpretation as an extra premiss, and drop the pretense that our conclusion is in any way necessary. . . . We should abandon, at least in ethics, the idea that philosophy is the analysis of concepts.[24]

As we will see, Rawls did exactly that with the concept of morality, defining it in ways that were useful for his theory and not defending it as a definition of morality fitting for all cases. As he wrote, "It might be objected that this definition of morality is either inappropriate in principle (definitions of morality beg the moral question) or that it is too restrictive." To reply, Rawls argued that all he needed to do was to defend the role of the definition of morality in the theory he was elaborating. Presumably—to follow Quine's reasoning—if the theory as a whole is justified, so will be the definition. As he wrote, "[The definition] may indeed be too restrictive for a general analysis of all moral concepts. What one has to consider is whether it is too special for the analysis of the notion of <u>justice</u> as a virtue of social <u>institutions</u>. In this instance only need it be considered."[25] Rawls would treat other pieces of his argument in the same way—as part of the defense of the entire theory. This explains in part the transformation of Rawls's approach to moral psychology, described in Chapter 6. It began as an independent exploration of the limits to moral views, but ended as part of Rawls's larger theory, showing the relative stability of "justice as fairness."

Rawls's second argument against Cartesianism was that no important conclusion can be drawn from such necessary truths even if they can be found. As Quine argued that "a scientific sentence cannot in general be expected to imply empirical consequences by itself," so Rawls claimed that the allegedly necessary ethical premises are not sufficient by themselves to yield a conception of justice:

There is no hope [to derive ethical conclusions] without complex definitions which [are] in effect further premises and not in any way necessary. (Quine on unclarity of analytic and the notion of concept identity.) There may be value in the Cartesian exercise, but it doesn't provide a Cartesian justification based upon necessary truths alone.[26]

Rawls deemed such deduction from self-evident and necessary premises unlikely mainly because arguments that proceed from self-evident principles and truths of logic do not say anything about human life:

> The truths of logic are truths <u>about</u> very general notions: propositions, individuals, properties, relations; and about certain (logical) relations given by enumeration. It is not likely that truths of <u>this</u> kind about such general notions <u>suffice</u> to determine what our <u>ethical</u> principles should be, what a rational <u>man</u> should accept.[27]

As Rawls summarized, "One doesn't <u>want</u> a justification rooted in logic <u>alone</u>. That would only show that morals had nothing to do with men."[28] While Rawls was never interested in deriving ethics from logic alone, this comment shows how far he had traveled from his early "physicalist" years. Having developed a philosophical anthropology, Rawls now thought it obvious that ethics and political philosophy should relate principles of justice to facts about being human.

To extend Cartesianism to human affairs, Rawls played devil's advocate and suggested that it take as its premises the human purposes "which would be <u>self-contradictory</u> not to have." That would be a step in the right direction, he agreed, but added that even "if there are such purposes, they will not suffice to vindicate and give content to a system of ethical principles."[29] As we will see, Rawls would make the same argument against Kantians, who emphasized Kant's formula of universality, or the claim that the principles that cannot be made universal should not be considered moral principles. There too Rawls would argue that such a requirement imposed few, if any, restrictions. Already by the early 1960s, Rawls was convinced that, devoid of substantive claims about human life, Cartesianism had little to contribute to discussions about justice. At most, self-evident claims would be part of a broader ethical argument.

Discussing the virtues and the shortcomings of foundationalism helped Rawls clarify his own approach to ethical questions. The first clarification was the claim that theories of justice have to be supported by a variety of considerations. As Rawls wrote in the 1965 draft of *A Theory of Justice,* "The justification of a conception of justice is almost certain to be cumulative and to rest on the consilience of many distinct considerations."[30] The emphasis on the scope of considerations required for ethical arguments was not new to Rawls, but he now stated this argument expressly, arguing in particular that the formal constraints on the concept of justice (universality and generality) are not sufficient by themselves to deduce principles of justice.[31] The claim that in moral philosophy "there are no shortcuts of this sort"—no appeals to special kinds of considerations—became pervasive in Rawls's approach to questions of justice. Rawls stated that even considered judgments are not sufficient by themselves for the philosopher in ethics: "We must assume that the fixed points [considered judgments] are not sufficient to eliminate all but one set of principles. Several alternatives will presumably remain."[32] Other types of considerations were not sufficient for this purpose either. Truths of logic and definition, formal conditions imposed on the concept of justice, and truths of moral psychology by themselves could not lead to a particular conception of justice. Taken singly, they provided "too slender a basis" for such a goal.[33]

The second clarification in Rawls's philosophical framework was the claim that conceptions of justice are justified as wholes. Since conceptions of justice depended on many considerations, any conception of justice was bound to be contested and possibly found wrong somewhere. Consequently, Rawls insisted, one could not fault a theory merely for being wrong somewhere. As he wrote in *A Theory of Justice*, "Objections by way of counterexamples are to be made with care, since these may tell us only what we know already, namely that our theory is wrong somewhere. The important thing is to find out how often and how far it is wrong."[34]

The third novelty in Rawls's philosophical framework was the explicit emphasis on the claim that conceptions of justice were to be justified relative to other conceptions, by showing that the preferred vision of justice has fewer weaknesses than the rival conceptions. Rawls first made this argument in his 1964 seminar on moral psychology, where, referring to William Frankena's "Obligation and Motivation," he wrote:

[Frankena] thinks that "each theory has strengths and weaknesses, and deciding between them involves determining their relative total values as accounts of morality. But such a determination calls for a very broad inquiry." . . . I should like to second this opinion: it is often possible to decide between views if one broadens the lines of investigation; or more likely perhaps each view will turn out to be inadequate in some way.[35]

In his later writings, Rawls would state explicitly his belief that justification in ethics is relative. As he told his Political and Social Philosophy class in 1965,

> Philosophy proceeds by argument against other positions in large part. In this sense it is <u>dialectical</u>. We see the weaknesses and strengths of our own position by comparing it with <u>other</u> positions. Thus our aim is to ascertain where A's position is <u>weak</u> so that we may try to go beyond it in these respects.[36]

Since justification was relative, Rawls thought, it had to involve comparison of rival theories. In turn, this comparison required an elaboration of rival theories so that their relative strengths and weaknesses were seen. As Rawls told his Ethics students in 1967, "We are not in a position to judge between ethical conceptions (that is, systems of moral principles) until we know a great deal about the substantive structure of particular views."[37] By 1964, Rawls had clarified that ethical theory had three tasks: that of explication, or the "description by <u>principles</u> of the class of considered judgments"; that of justification, or the "derivation of the <u>principles</u> of the correct explication from philosophically defensible premises"; and that of the delineation of psychological development, or an "account of how the person comes to <u>desire</u> to do and to <u>act</u> upon what is right, to the extent that he does."[38]

The primacy of the description of conceptions of justice was reflected in Rawls's syllabi. From 1960 onward, his courses discussed the concepts of liberty, equality, and the common good. In his 1960 Political and Social Philosophy course, for example, Rawls told his students that one of the tasks of political philosophy is to describe the different values, such as justice, equality, the common good, social utility, liberty, and toleration, and try to arrange them in the order of priority "so that a reasonable choice can be made when they conflict."[39] Unlike the intuitionists, Rawls was not satisfied merely discussing these values; their weights had to be outlined as well.[40] The overall goal was to elaborate a conception of justice in which these values are related to one another in such order of priority. Outlining the structure of his argument to students, he summarized the original position as a way of clarifying the conceptual connections in our reasoning: "The <u>analytic framework</u> which I shall use for the presentation of classical liberalism . . . is a rather <u>general analysis</u> of the concept of <u>justice</u>: that is, I am going to work from a certain analysis of this moral concept which is sufficiently <u>general</u> to allow a setting for the <u>three</u> notions of liberty, equality, and the common good (or, as I shall sometimes call it, social utility)."[41]

In 1962 Rawls introduced the concept of "reflective equilibrium" or the "equilibrium of reflection," which would later combine the three novelties of Rawls's philosophical framework under one umbrella.[42] Reflective equilibrium was a state of affairs in which the preferred conception of justice was deemed the best available explanation for our considered judgments of justice. "What one is trying to achieve," Rawls wrote in his lectures on political philosophy, "is a state of <u>self-conscious reflective equilibrium</u> with respect to one's own judgments on the justice and injustice of institutions (acts, and persons)."[43] In a sense, reflective equilibrium was a state of affairs in which all the pieces of the philosophical puzzle fit together well—or at least better than those of rival conceptions.

Toward the Original Position

By the mid-1960s, as Rawls made it explicit that justification of a conception of justice rests on many kinds of considerations, he also focused on the second task of political philosophy: deriving a conception of justice from the original position. Believing that a conception of justice rests on many kinds of considerations, he started viewing the original position as a way of collecting this diverse range of considerations and modeling it with a simplifying apparatus. As he put it in the 1958 article "Justice as Fairness," the original position was to present an "analysis of the concept of justice," resulting in the "principles involved in [the considered] judgments when made by competent persons upon deliberation and reflection."[44] Each aspect of the original position was to "[bring] out a feature of the notion of justice."[45] He repeated the same view in *A Theory of Justice*. The original position aimed to "collect together into one conception a number of conditions on principles that we are ready upon due consideration to recognize as reasonable" and then "establish that taken together they [impose] significant bounds on acceptable principles of justice."[46]

Rawls created four versions of this experiment: the first "pure case" of justice elaborated in the 1950–1954 notes, the second one in the 1958 article "Justice as Fairness," the third in the 1964 and 1965 drafts of *A Theory of Justice,* and the final version in *A Theory of Justice* in 1971.[47] The second version of the thought experiment departed from the earliest "pure case" scenario primarily by expanding the range of considered judgments that were to be modeled in the original position. These now included the constraints of having a morality and the circumstances of justice. The former, reflecting the conclusions of the "pure case" scenario, required that the principles apply to everyone equally and that no one is exempt merely because these principles are to one's disadvantage.[48] The circumstances of justice, on the other hand, depicted situations in which questions of justice typically arose. This restriction reflected Rawls's considerations of human behavior, as these were revealed by the analogy between society and games. According to Rawls, persons pursued goals that were in their own or their family's interests. A just arrangement considered these claims fairly. As Rawls put it, summarizing this restriction: "Conflicting claims are made upon the design of a practice and [in which] it is taken for granted that each person will insist, as far as possible, on what he considers his rights."[49]

Rawls set out to model these features of justice in the original position and see what principles of justice they imply. The original position consisted of three key features: the persons in the original position, the problem posed to these persons, and the circumstances in which the problem had to be solved. Rawls depicted the persons in the original position as "mutually self-interested" or interested in their own objective (as opposed to relative) well-being, having "roughly similar needs and interests," and, finally, as rational.[50] Rational, in turn, implied persons who knew their interests, understood the consequences of their actions, and were capable of adhering to plans on which they had decided.[51] Such persons had the task of choosing the principles of justice: principles to adjudicate their complaints. Rawls thought—but did not yet try to show—that once circumstances of justice are imposed on this choice, the rational and mutually self-interested persons would choose the two principles of justice known as "justice as fairness."

In sum, engaging Quine's nonfoundationalism helped Rawls sharpen his philosophical vision. It added new features to his philosophical vocabulary—fixed points and reflective equilibrium—and made it clearer that he was seeking to justify a conception of justice against alternative understandings of justice. By the time Quine's ideas were reflected in Rawls's philosophical framework, Rawls was already outlining different conceptions of justice and introducing greater clarity and effectiveness to the original position—tasks that were central under the new, Quinean, description. However, Quine's ideas helped Rawls explain how these activities fit together in one coherent goal: defending a theory of justice. It is at this point that Rawls's previously separate, if related, philosophical activities firmly became part of one venture. This period may not have contained exciting novelties such as the naturalist considerations discussed in Chapter 6, but it finally brought out Rawls as he is known to the readers of *A Theory of Justice:* an author of a grand, consistent philosophical enterprise.

8

Kantian Autonomy

RAWLS SPENT much of the 1960s elaborating his political vision. As any reader of *A Theory of Justice* knows, it had strong elements of Kantianism. Perhaps for that reason, it is surprising to learn that Rawls considered himself working within utilitarianism until 1960, perhaps even 1962. He did not consider himself a utilitarian, however, and, as we saw, he endorsed a Kantian vision of freedom in 1947. Nonetheless, he thought he "started" his thinking within utilitarianism. Only in 1962 did Rawls start describing himself as a social contract theorist who stood in clear contrast to the utilitarian tradition. Once he accepted this self-description, he drew on Kant to elaborate the key features of "justice as fairness."

The transition took place in two steps, and these steps expressed different visions of Kantianism. Prompted by Rousseau to adopt the social contract theory as his starting point in 1958, Rawls drew on Kantians to explain how we can reach agreement among reasonable persons. To funnel natural feelings in a common direction, one had to take on what Rawls called a "point of view of morality." Following Kurt Baier, Rawls interpreted Kant's main message to be found in his formula of humanity, or the requirement to treat "humanity, whether in your own persons or in the person of any other, never simply as means, but always at the same time as an end."[1] Taking a moral point of view, Rawls now argued, was analyzing what it means to respect persons. It was a slight but consequential shift in emphasis. Until then, Rawls saw ethics as a scientific inquiry aimed at arriving at the principles of justice. This of course remained his aim, but he now added another: to explore what it means to respect persons as persons. The two goals could have been consistent, but they were not the same.

It is important to emphasize that Kant's influence on Rawls expressed itself through the formula of humanity for most of his early career. This fact gets overshadowed by Rawls's own later emphasis on Kant's formulas of universality and autonomy—the requirements to "only act on that maxim through which you can at the same time will that it should become a universal law" and to govern ourselves by a will that "makes universal law"—and by some of his most influential Kantian students, who also placed the emphasis on these two formulas.[2] But Rawls started emphasizing the importance of autonomy and connected it to universality only in the mid-1960s. To be autonomous, he argued, was to be governed by principles of justice that are independent of contingent social and personal facts. This meant that the derivation of the principles of justice should be dependent only on the most general facts about human life. Modeled in this way, the original position became the point of view of eternity—it looked at human beings from all social and temporal points of view.[3]

Working within Utilitarianism

Rawls's relationship with utilitarianism had long been complex. Throughout his career, he borrowed some aspects of utilitarianism while rejecting others. In 1946, when he elaborated his first secular ethical theory, he called it "imperative utilitarianism" to highlight its key Sidgwickian insight that praise and blame are distributed on the basis of usefulness. In his 1955 article "Two Concepts of Rules," Rawls introduced a distinction between justifying a practice and justifying an action that falls under the practice, using the distinction to "defend utilitarianism against those objections which have traditionally been made against it."[4] Later he clarified that in the 1955 article he was not presenting a "complete defense of utilitarianism as a general theory of morals" and only making the claim that "restricting the utilitarian principle to practices . . . strengthened it."[5] In the 1958 "Justice as Fairness" article, Rawls similarly described himself as working out a utilitarian position: "In this paper I take up the question as to how the utilitarian principle itself must be modified."[6] Rawls's emphasis on sympathy in the 1958 naturalistic account of moral feelings also showed the influence of utilitarianism.

Rawls was conscious of these commitments, accepting the links between his argument and utilitarianism willingly. This utilitarian self-understanding is evident in the undated note "What Can Philosophy Do for Politics?," written most likely in 1960. "I happen to feel more at home among the utilitarian tradition," he wrote, "so I am inclined to start out from that."[7] Explaining this preference, Rawls emphasized the valuable tradition of thinking on which he hoped to build. "In my own thinking I like to see where [utilitarianism] goes wrong, if it does," he wrote, "and where it should be corrected. As it has enlisted so many first-rate figures, it is a line of thought worth developing, a good choice of a starting point, although not, of course, the only such choice."[8]

As late as 1960, Rawls described his theory as "combin[ing] both utilitarian and contractarian elements," but one that starts from the utilitarian tradition. "For purely personal reasons," he wrote, "I am inclined to approach moral and political philosophy by asking what are the <u>least</u> changes and amendments which have to be made in the utilitarian tradition, or in some utilitarian writer, eg., Hume or Mill, to render the view stated <u>true</u>."[9] The reading list for the course, however, listed Rawls's own 1958 "Justice as Fairness" under the social contract tradition, together with Kant's "Of the Common Saying: 'This May Be True in Theory but Does Not Apply to Practice'" and Rousseau's *On the Social Contract*. The utilitarian tradition was introduced through John Stuart Mill's *Utilitarianism,* Henry Sidgwick's *Methods of Ethics,* and Hastings Rashdall's *Theory of Good and Evil.*[10]

Only in 1962 did Rawls clearly phrase his theory of justice in contrast to the utilitarian tradition. As he told his students during the first lecture, "The analysis of justice which I shall try to give is derived quite obviously from the theory of the <u>social contract</u>." Rawls still proposed to depart from the core writings of the tradition, but the departures were not conceived as departures from the social contract theory: "I shall attempt to formulate it in a somewhat different manner and I hope, in a more <u>rigorous</u> and <u>comprehensive</u> way."[11]

This self-understanding is somewhat puzzling, especially given the contrast he drew between the social contract tradition and utilitarianism in his 1958 "Justice as Fairness." There, Rawls viewed utilitarianism as presenting a political vision alternative to his own. His own theory, he remarked comparing it to classical utilitarianism, "actually has a different conception of justice standing behind it." Moreover, as he himself argued, that political vision relied on other utilitarian concepts; it was not a stand-alone argument. As Rawls wrote, "The slight alteration of principle reveals another family of notions, another way of looking at the concept of justice."[12] The utilitarian conception "assimilates justice to benevolence and the latter in turn to the most efficient design of institutions to promote the general welfare. Justice is a kind of efficiency."[13] "Justice as fairness," on the other hand, linked justice to fairness and, as we will see, consent.

So, how do we reconcile these conflicting self-descriptions? Rawls must have thought that parts of the utilitarian framework are detachable from others. If so, some parts of utilitarianism could be salvaged and drawn on in fruitful inquiries. That is what Rawls thought himself as doing until 1962. This interpretation is supported by Rawls's understanding of the history of political philosophy. As I have tried to show in this book, Rawls expected to find overlaps among the main values of different conceptions of justice. As his remarks from the 1960 course on Political and Social Philosophy indicate, Rawls thought we could borrow from other traditions and incorporate their concepts into our own framework. Up to a point, this is not, of course, a contestable claim. However, Rawls's thinking presupposed that the main virtues of the rival conceptions of justice did not depend on radically different conceptual frameworks.

This view is evident in Rawls's thoughts on the history of political thought and his own relation to it. He described the differences between theories as mainly the differences in the weights assigned to the same values. As he explained, "The classical social ideals recognize the <u>same</u> virtues but for various reasons, moral and theoretical, assign them <u>dif-</u>

ferent interpretations and priorities." Explaining how one may recognize the same virtues and yet act differently, Rawls gave an example of different economic policies. While "most everyone would agree on the desirability of efficient allocation of resources (per period), full employment, high rate of growth of GNP, price stability, all consistent with distributive justice and liberty," attaching different weights to these goals, different people would recommend different economic policies. Rawls acknowledged the possibility that these different economic policies "presumably express different (underlying) social ideals," but did not hold the conceptual difference as the only possible reason for disagreement.[14]

The belief that rival conceptual frameworks are in large part compatible led Rawls to view political frameworks not as conceptually different but as more or less complete and different in rigor and clarity of expression. "I look at the development of political philosophy," Rawls wrote, "as the development of more precise understanding of moral concepts and principles as they apply to political questions."[15] Rawls's analysis of Aquinas brings out this view best. Instead of arguing that Aquinas's analysis of justice depends at least in part on his theological framework, Rawls described it as "incomplete." Aquinas's account of justice was "not so much incorrect, but . . . not as strong as one would like: that is, it fails to provide a complete account of our judgments about justice."[16] In particular, Aquinas fell short in thinking that all his moral injunctions followed from the concept of natural law, and in being "vague" in his conception of the common good.[17] According to Rawls, contemporary political philosophers had the task of improving the rigor and breadth of previous thinking: "What one should try to do is to make a substantial improvement over what has gone before. . . . It will be a start simply to collect together and try to answer in a consistent way the main questions to be answered in giving an analysis of justice."[18] To do so, one must ask how to build on Aquinas's achievements and search for ways to "strengthen and improve Aquinas's account."[19]

Viewing the history of political philosophy in this cumulative way, Rawls could therefore conceive his own work as part of the utilitarian tradition. On this view of history, not much depended on choosing utilitarianism as the starting point. As Rawls told his students in the 1960 lectures, he began his analysis of justice from within the utilitarian tradition, "but one could equally profitably, I suspect, begin with Rousseau or Kant asking the same question and end up, in either case, in much the same place."[20]

So, why did Rawls reject utilitarianism in the end? It must have been the realization that to build a consistent theory, it was better to choose a different starting point. This rejection had been building up throughout Rawls's career, and many reasons are responsible for it. For example, in a talk to the Socratic Club in 1954, Rawls criticized utilitarianism for insisting that only one major reason—happiness—was used in moral deliberations. As he suggested to the audience, "I'm inclined to say that a broad utilitarian view covers most ordinary 'legislative' decisions, but there are other and more delicate cases which require us to admit other reasons."[21] Undated but clearly later notes show Rawls's dissatisfaction with the fact that utilitarianism in principle allows slavery and caste systems—so long as these can be shown to lead to greatest happiness.[22] But Rawls's criticism was leveled not primarily because such exploitative systems were permitted, but because their possible justice was even contemplated. As he wrote,

> The error is to undertake to balance these claims in the first place. On the conception of justice as reciprocity, since the offices of slave and slaveholder cannot be mutually acknowledged, the claims (and so advantages) of the slave holder cannot be counted: their satisfaction is no <u>reason</u> for having slavery. No reason at all, not even a consideration which happens to be outweighed by other considerations. The mistake of utilitarianism would still obtain even if, whenever the balancing took place, it came down on the right side.[23]

Other criticisms followed as well. As Rawls argued in the 1964 draft of *A Theory of Justice*, "The principle of utility mistakes impersonality for impartiality."[24] Claiming to consider the good of each person equally, utilitarianism actually treated persons' interests equally. Detaching these interests from the persons to whom they belong, they effectively ignored the persons. As he put it in *A Theory of Justice*, the "classical [utilitarian] view results, then, in impersonality, in the conflation of all desires into one system of desire." Doing so, it "fails to take seriously the distinction between persons."[25]

The Turn to Social Contract

If there is a point that marks the beginning of Rawls's transition away from utilitarianism, it is his adoption of the social contract approach. In *A Theory of Justice,* Rawls described his argument as a "traditional theory of the social contract" but "generaliz[ed] and carri[ed] to a higher order of abstraction."[26] This transition to viewing his own work as a social contract theory began in the late 1950s. In the 1958 "Justice as Fairness" article Rawls proposed to bring out an aspect of justice by using "the idea of the social contract."[27] By 1962, as we saw, Rawls already viewed himself as working from the social contract tradition. Summarizing this secular social contract theory that year, Rawls wrote, "Roughly, I want to say that an institution is just if those subject to it <u>could</u> have <u>contracted</u> into it from the <u>original</u> position."[28]

Why did this transition take place? Surely, it took place in the context of dissatisfaction with utilitarianism, as discussed above. However, the realization that the social contract tradition captures reasonable persons' most significant considered judgments must have pushed Rawls to adopt this approach. In a 1972 discussion with Stanley Moore, Rawls highlighted the importance of realizing that Rousseau's *Social Contract* already expressed the ideas Rawls had been developing. He singled out the fourth chapter of Book II, "The Limits of Sovereign Power," and in it the fifth paragraph, which discusses the general will. Key in that paragraph is Rousseau's insistence that the general will be general in nature: it should "spring from all and apply to all." Once it applies to "any particular and circumscribed object," the general will loses its "natural rectitude."[29] The appeal of these insights for Rawls is more intelligible in the context of his naturalist arguments of 1958. There, he argued that while natural feelings lead us to judge ethical questions in the same way, self-interest and sympathy distort our sense of justice by making us prioritize particular persons. To use Rousseau's terms, sympathy turned our focus to a particular object, making our general will lose its natural rectitude. According to Rawls, this passage of Rousseau's fully described the essence of the arguments he had been formulating:

> That passage [of Rousseau's] had a great effect on me. I can first recall reading it (at least with understanding) around 1958. By that time the fundamental intuitive idea of *A Theory of Justice* had long since occurred to me (1950–51), and I had already thought about many of the problems in trying to work it out. With this conception in mind, I was ready to grasp the significance of what Rousseau was saying. The discovery of Rousseau finally dispelled any pretense of originality for the idea I had been thinking about; and led me to recognize that the essential thing was to develop the contract doctrine into a reasonably clear moral theory.[30]

Viewing his own theory as a version of the social contract theory, Rawls brought out several new points of emphasis. First, he started emphasizing the importance of consent. He had already assumed the importance of consent in his earlier analyses of justice, seeking to design a society that resembles a game everyone wants to play—a game to which everyone consents. However, the focus now shifted to those who, he thought, were least likely to agree. So Rawls now emphasized the consent of those who fare most poorly, the "least advantaged persons." As he told his students in the 1962 lectures, he took "from the older theory (e.g. Locke) . . . the notion of <u>unanimity</u> of <u>consent</u> in the <u>original</u> position."[31] "Now it follows," he continued, "that the constitution and the basic social structure, if it is just (as defined by the two principles) can be justified to <u>every</u> member of the society, to <u>every citizen</u>." This in effect meant that the intellectual focus was on the least advantaged persons: if a society can be justified to every person, then "it can be justified to the <u>least fortunate</u> members."[32]

Of course, Rawls did not take on board all aspects of the social contract tradition. Most obviously, he denied that consent was historical: "That the state of nature is a <u>historical</u> state and one of <u>danger</u> etc, is left out of account in the theory."[33] Furthermore, he uprooted this consent from the background of the natural law on which the social contract theory relied. As he put it, his social contract theory was a "secularized" version of its predecessor: "The conception of justice which I shall try to work out is an elaboration of the theory of the <u>social contract</u>: it is a <u>secularization</u> of the <u>natural rights</u> theory [in that] . . . it is a natural rights theory <u>only</u> in the <u>general</u> sense, and I prefer to avoid this sense altogether."[34]

Kant and a Moral Point of View

The return of Kant's influence on Rawls begins to be seen in his formulation of the problem of sympathy in notes most likely made around 1958. As we saw in Chapter 6, Rawls thought that sympathy and self-interest led our ethical judgments to unfairly favor some persons over others. Since Rawls's goal was to show agreement among reasonable persons, this partiality in itself was a problem. However, Rawls thought that it was a problem for other, Kantian, reasons as well. This formulation of the problem shows the influence of Kant's formula of autonomy, but this is the only such mention in the late 1950s. According to Rawls, the directions of our sympathies are influenced by contingencies. As he wrote, "Our sympathies and their intensities are influenced by contingent matters, by accidents of circumstance and place, and likings even (tastes), by things the influence of which we should <u>not</u> offer as <u>reasons</u>."[35] As he clarified, contingent facts, such as the circumstances of one's birth, are problematic because they are not relevant from a moral point of view: "Sympathy reactions <u>may</u> depend on acquaintance, class lines, etc, in the most arbitrary way from a moral point of view; they may be affected by mood, health, etc."[36]

While this formulation of the problem does not quite capture Kant's formula of autonomy, it mentions reasons that were important for Kant. Kant argued that a person is autonomous—self-legislating—when the will "by all its maxims enacts universal law."[37] "Every rational being," he continued, "must be able to regard himself as also the maker of universal law in respect of any law whatever to which he may be subjected."[38] This self-legislation of the will takes place without mention of empirical facts. As he wrote, "All moral concepts have their seat and origin in reason completely *a priori*. . . . They cannot be abstracted from any empirical, and therefore merely contingent, knowledge."[39] Indeed, Kant argued, "we should not dream for a moment of trying to derive the reality of this principle from *the special characteristics of human nature*."[40] And similarly: "Hence everything that is empirical is, as a contribution to the principle of morality, not only wholly unsuitable for the purpose, but is even highly injurious to the purity of morals."[41] In this document, Rawls did not talk about the self-legislation of the will, nor did he mention Kant's distinction between the noumenal or the intellectual world and the phenomenal or the empirical world; but the claim that some reasons made use of contingent facts that are irrelevant from "a moral point of view" was already there.

This discussion of the formula of autonomy should not overshadow Rawls's introduction of a new concept in that same document—"a moral point view." What was a moral point of view, and how did Rawls arrive at this notion? One of the main inspirations seems to have been Kurt Baier and his writings on "the moral point of view" (unlike Rawls, Baier used the definitive article).[42] There were many intellectual affinities between the two thinkers. Baier described the arguments of his *Moral Point of View* as "closest to those of Stephen Toulmin" and thanked Max Black.[43] Moreover, Baier explicitly engaged Kant's ideas, refusing to place emphasis on Kant's formula of universality and instead placing it on Kant's formula of humanity. Baier's "moral point of view" relied on Kant's formula of humanity.

As Kant argued explaining the formula of humanity, "Rational nature exists as an end in itself."[44] Since human beings have that rational nature, they deserve to be treated as ends. As Kant wrote, "Rational beings . . . are called *persons* because their nature already marks them out as ends in themselves." This fact sets limits on how human beings should be treated. Persons, Kant wrote, "are not merely subjective ends whose existence as an object of our actions has a value *for us:* they are *objective ends*—that is, things whose existence is in itself an end."[45] Possessing this absolute value, human beings were not to be treated as means to our interests and aims.

Baier's "moral point of view" rested on this insight. A standpoint from which one could try to answer ethical questions, the moral point of view contained a requirement to conform to "the rules whether or not doing so favors one's own or anyone else's aim."[46] This outlawing of partiality must have been one of the reasons for which Rawls was drawn to Baier's idea. Baier attributed the main idea of the moral point of view to Kant's requirement that one always follow the moral law. As Baier wrote:

> Kant grasped this point even if only obscurely. He saw that adopting the moral point of view involves acting on principle. It involves conforming to rules even when doing so is unpleasant, painful, costly, or ruinous to oneself. Kant, furthermore, argued rightly that, since moral action is action on principle (and not merely in accordance with rules of thumb), a moral agent ought not to make exceptions in his own favor.[47]

But why should one adopt the moral point of view? Baier defended the moral point of view on Kantian grounds. Just as Kant argued that persons should be treated "never simply as means, but always at the same time as an end," so Baier made it clear that adopting the moral point of view was committing oneself to treating persons as ends and not as means.[48] As he wrote:

> We are adopting [this point of view] if we regard the rules belonging to the morality of the group as designed to regulate the behaviour of people all of whom are to be treated as equally important "centres" of cravings, impulses, desires, needs, aims, and aspirations; as people with ends of their own, all of which are entitled, *prima facie,* to be attained.[49]

As Baier put it expressly referencing Kant, "I take this to be the meaning of 'treating [people] as ends in themselves and not merely as means to one's own ends.'"[50]

While drawing on Kant's formula of humanity, Baier made it clear that taking the moral point of view could not be defended by appeal to Kant's formula of universality. Baier interpreted this formula as requiring the test of self-contradiction. As he wrote, "Kant has given a different justification for doing the morally right thing. He claims that wrongdoing is acting in a way contrary to reason. He arrives at this conclusion by way of the categorical imperative."[51] Such a justification, Baier thought, was fruitless, since no practical restrictions followed from the formula of universality. As he put it, "A morality based on the categorical imperative is useless for it rejects as immoral only self-contradictory and self-frustrating maxims."[52] According to him, the formula of universality allowed the practices of "killing, stealing, maiming, lying, and hurting others, without involving ourselves in self-contradiction. Such a code can hardly be described as a morality."[53]

This criticism meant that Baier de-emphasized (but, as we will see later, did not reject) the universalistic strand of Kant. Moreover, he rejected Kant's requirement that moral principles derive from "reason completely *a priori*" and "ought never . . . depend on the special nature of human reason."[54] For Baier, this position had deep flaws. As he wrote, objectively true moral principles "are not true for 'all rational beings'" but "only for human beings, and they would not necessarily remain true for human beings if there were radical changes in human nature."[55] Clearly, Baier was drawing on Kant, but only on part of his arguments.

Later in his career, Rawls shared Baier's downplaying the importance of Kant's formula of universality. As he wrote in the 1967 draft of *A Theory of Justice,*

> It is a mistake, I believe, to emphasize the place of generality and universality in Kant's ethics. That moral principles are general and universal is hardly new with him; and as we have seen these conditions do not in any case take us very far. It is impossible to construct a moral theory on such a slender basis, so to limit the discussion of Kant's doctrine to these notions is to reduce it to triviality. The real force of his view lies elsewhere.[56]

Rather, Rawls believed, the focus should fall on the Kantian understanding of "free and equal rational beings." As he wrote, "Kant supposes that this moral legislation is to be agreed to under conditions that characterize men as free and equal rational beings. The description of the original position is an attempt to interpret this Kantian conception."[57]

In the meantime, when Rawls was thinking about sympathy and its problems in 1958, Baier's emphasis on Kant's formula of humanity was on his mind. At first, likely also in 1958, his primary solution to correct for the partiality of sympathy was the already staple notion of considered judgments. Those were judgments in which the agent was not affected and so had no reason for partiality. They were not hasty or impulsive but rather made after consideration of the relevant facts. These conditions were imposed partly on the grounds we have seen before: "The basis of these conditions is that they void any excuse for mistake."[58] Other grounds, however, were new: the notion of considered judgments was now connected to the recognition of persons as persons. As Rawls wrote, "The absence of personal interests, and involvement, and the hypothesis that there is time to reflect, removes any obstacle there might have been not simply for mistake, but for failure to react to the persons as persons in the situation."[59]

In the years immediately following these writings, Rawls merged the concept of a moral point of view with the already-existing concept of morality and the constraints it imposed on the choice of the principles of justice. Both imposed the same conditions on the choice. For example, in the 1958 "Justice as Fairness" article, Rawls wrote that the principles of justice are chosen in the conditions constrained by the requirements of morality. The chosen principles were to be considered as "binding on future occasions" in order to exclude the possibility of someone tailoring "the canons of a legitimate complaint to fit his own special condition, and then to discard them when they no longer suit his purpose."[60] As Rawls summarized, "The procedure whereby principles are proposed and acknowledged represents constraints, analogous to those of having a morality."[61] In 1963, he would attribute his understanding of the concept of morality to Kant and Baier, among others: "The definition I have used is reasonably standard: it derives from Kant obviously (Hume and Rousseau with Kant the main figures) and appears in recent variants (cf. Baier, *The Moral Point of View*)."[62]

In the later years, however, Rawls related the concept of a moral point of view to the concept of personhood. Thus Kant's formula of humanity and his conception of freedom started playing a more prominent role in Rawls's thought again. Restating his Kantian ideas of 1946 in different terms, Rawls now argued that moral personality is the capacity to "take up a moral point of view and express it in one's conduct."[63] More particularly, he continued, moral personality implies the ability to enact the conclusions of a moral point of view in action: "It means being able to view conflicts of interests, including one's own case, in a certain way, of being able to discuss solutions in accordance with principles satisfying certain general conditions; and being able to live by conclusions settled upon from this viewpoint."[64]

In the 1969 draft of *A Theory of Justice,* Rawls combined two aspects of moral personality that we saw in his writings in the 1940s and 1950s. In those early years of his career, Rawls defended the Kantian conception of freedom as the ability to follow the moral law and the right to determine one's own good as important aspects of autonomy. By 1969 he combined these two aspects of autonomy into one vision. First, Rawls argued, moral persons "are capable of having (and are assumed to have) a conception of their good (as determined by a rational plan of life)." Second, "they are capable of having (and are assumed to acquire) a sense of justice, that is, a normally effective desire to apply and to act upon the principles of justice."[65]

It is clear that this conception of personhood drove Rawls's argument and explained why, according to him, we should take on a moral point of view. Like Baier, Rawls thought that taking on a moral point of view is an expression of respecting persons as moral persons. As he wrote likely in 1963, "The thesis I shall argue is this: that justice is owed to persons equal in capacity for moral personality; that this condition is both necessary and sufficient for the obligation of justice to hold."[66] Thus, although the "original position" was defined in part by constraints of the concept of morality, these very constraints stemmed from the conception of moral personhood.[67]

Autonomy as Independence from Contingencies

By the mid-1960s, Rawls's conception of moral personhood had changed yet further, and this time it was shaped by a Kantian conception of autonomy as independence from contingent circumstances. His papers from that period show a clear shift of emphasis toward Kant's formulas of universality and in particular autonomy. This conception of moral personhood, as Rawls understood it, had two core features. First, to act autonomously was still to express one's nature as a free and rational being: "Kant held, I believe, that a person is acting autonomously when the principles of his action are chosen by him as the most adequate possible expression of his nature as a free and equal rational being." This time, however, he understood expressing one's nature as acting on principles that are independent of contingent facts about ourselves and the societies in which we live. This required that the chosen principles not depend on such contingent circumstances. As Rawls wrote, "The principles he acts upon are not adopted because of his social position or natural endowments, or in view of the particular kind of society in which he lives or the specific things that he happens to want."[68] He compared the principles of justice to Kant's categorical imperatives to capture the link between these principles and the moral conception of the person. "The principles of justice are also categorical imperatives in Kant's sense," he wrote. "For by a categorical imperative Kant understands a principle of conduct that applies to a person in virtue of his nature as a free and equal rational being. The validity of the principles does not presuppose that one has a particular desire or aim."[69]

Rawls also drew comparisons to Kant's other concepts, perhaps exaggerating the kind of independence he wanted to achieve from the historical and social contexts in which ethical judgments are made. The first such concept was "noumenal selves," or selves as they are independent of the phenomenal world in which our experiences arise. Rawls wrote that we should view the original position as "the point of view from which noumenal selves see the world."[70] He disagreed with Kant about the kind of independence this would be, however. Much like Toulmin and his earlier self in 1946, Rawls rejected Kantian metaphysics and insisted that ethics still dealt with actual human life. As he wrote:

> It might appear that Kant meant his doctrine to apply to all rational beings as such. . . . Men's situation in the world may seem to have no role in determining the first principles of justice. I do not believe that Kant held this view, but I cannot discuss this question here. It suffices to say that if I am mistaken in this matter, the Kantian interpretation of justice as fairness is less faithful to Kant's intentions than I am presently inclined to suppose.[71]

This non-Kantian focus on human nature and the world in which ethical questions arise is also intelligible given Rawls's Quinean claim that a defense of a conception of justice rests on a variety of different considerations. The ideal of personhood is only one such consideration. As Rawls wrote already in around 1958, explaining the derivation of the principles of justice, "No attempt is made to derive the principles of justice from the concept of a judgment of a rational being, or offer them as known by intuition."[72] Indeed, Rawls thought that Kant did not place enough emphasis on the situations in which questions of justice typically arose.[73]

Despite this correction of Kant, Rawls clearly intended the principles of justice to be independent of at least some contingent facts about the world—facts that could not be attributed to human nature or the nature of the world as such. This position echoed Baier's argument about "true morality." Rawls was aware of this argument, as shown by his underlining it in his copy of Baier's book.[74] In that argument, Baier discussed some moral statements that are independent of at least some conditions in which they are made. As he wrote,

> True moralities are particular moralities which pass certain tests. We may abstract from all the particular existential conditions of given moralities and think of true morality as a system of true moral convictions not embodied in, but completely independent of, the particular conditions of this or that way of life. There may therefore be true moral convictions which, though possibly no one actually holds them, are true in and for all possible social conditions. But there could be such true moral convictions only if their content had nothing to do with social conditions. It may, of course, be argued that there are no such convictions, but I think there are.[75]

As examples of such convictions, Baier stated the following: "killing is wrong," "harming others is wrong," "lying is wrong," and "misusing the institutions of one's society is wrong." These were, according to Baier, "true quite irrespective of the particular setup of given societies." However, these maxims were not independent of human nature—"they would not necessarily remain true for human beings if there were radical changes in human nature"—but they were independent of the specific circumstances of particular individuals and societies.[76]

From that point onward, Rawls associated a "point of view of morality" with the distance one could achieve from particular social and personal circumstances. In the 1967 draft of *A Theory of Justice*, Rawls captured this intention by an analogy to the Archimedean point, from which one can observe the question in totality or full view. As Rawls wrote, "The upshot of these considerations is that justice as fairness is not at the mercy, so to speak, of existing wants and interests. It does set up an Archimedean point for assessing the social system."[77] In *A Theory of Justice,* Rawls described the point of view of the original position as "sub specie aeternitatis" or "the perspective of eternity." From this point of view, one could "regard the human situation not only from all social but also from all temporal points of view."[78] While in the late 1950s the original position was a viewpoint from which one analyzed what it meant to respect persons, by the mid-1960s it became a point of view that provided distance from contingency.

The two visions of the moral point of view were not inconsistent for Rawls, as they were not inconsistent for Kant either. To respect persons now meant to respect them as rational beings, or beings the treatment of which should not be affected by contingent factors about them and the society in which they live. But it is important to note that respecting persons did not need to be interpreted as respecting their autonomy so understood, and that Rawls himself did not interpret it in this way for most of his early career. For those working with Rawlsian thought, acknowledging this fact might help delineate an account of respect for persons that does not depend on Kant's contestable principle of autonomy.

Rawls's new conception of autonomy started changing the description of the "original position," the viewpoint from which the principles of justice were to be selected. Aspects that were previously described in "physicalist" or Wittgensteinian ways now received a Kantian description. The 1959 discussion of distributive justice is a good illustration of this. In these notes, Rawls already required that persons in the original position not know their natural talents. However, this restriction was not yet defined in a Kantian language. Instead, it was defended on the grounds that inequalities and all that contributes to them should be organized in such a way as to benefit everyone. "Why not regard intelligence, say, as a gift of nature," Rawls suggested.[79] If these natural gifts are distributed by nature "at random," then the designers of a theory of justice should "before one another acknowledge that however they are placed in this distribution, this natural lottery, that the differences are put to work against a background of institutions which insures that they work for the general benefit as the second principle formulates it."[80] According to Rawls, this would only befit a conception of justice that "requires one to reduce as far as possible the effects of chance and fortune . . . and so render[s] such inequalities as do exist acceptable to persons in an original position of liberty and equality."[81] Implicit in this statement is respect for persons: all of them should be able to accept the principles of justice. But the language of autonomy is not yet there. Indeed, that same essay contains Rawls's corrections, made in hand and, judging by ideas expressed in them, written in the later years. The typed statement regarding not knowing one's natural talents reads: "But this is simply the consequence of requiring that they shall not know their place in the system." To this, Rawls added at the end "and of regarding them purely as moral persons."[82] This addition shows how Rawls redescribed his philosophical apparatus to reflect his newly acquired Kantian ideas. Persons were now conceived independently of contingent facts and "purely" as moral persons.

In 1962, Rawls redefined the significance of the constraints of morality that were imposed on the original position. The universality of the principles of justice was now understood to reflect independence from any particular social position. "Moral principles are <u>universal</u>," Rawls wrote. "They apply to persons in virtue of their nature as human persons and not (as the law does) in virtue of their living in a certain territory or holding a certain social position."[83] Rawls redescribed the results of his argument in Kantian terms as well. For example, in the 1968 "Distributive Justice: Some Addenda," he described his second principle of justice in Kantian terms: "The difference principle . . . enables one to give a reasonable interpretation of the concept of fraternity and of the Kantian idea that persons are always to be treated as ends and never as means only."[84] This is because the difference principle "appropriately regulates the influence of the distribution of natural assets and social contingencies on distributive shares."[85]

Other aspects of the original position were modified as well. Restrictions on the knowledge of persons in the original position were meant to express our nature as moral persons. As Rawls put it, the persons in the original position "make a choice together as free and equal rational persons."[86] To make this choice possible, Rawls stipulated that persons in the original position forgot the nature of their complaints against the society, their position in society (rich, poor, slave, master), their natural endowments (intelligence, gender), and the particular circumstances of their society, including its social and political institutions.[87] On the other hand, the parties knew that they had a conception of the good and that they were subject to the circumstances of justice.[88] This was done to make persons in the original position "abandon any attempt to exploit one's place in society and one's good and bad fortune in the natural lottery."[89] This, Rawls thought, made his theory Kantian. As he wrote, "To be sure the analytic construction adds an element to Kant's notion of autonomy; in particular it adds the feature that the principles chosen are to apply to the basic structure of society, but beyond this it is fairly close to Kant's concept." Through Rawls's marks of erasure we can see that the last part of the sentence used to read, "it is fairly close to Kant's conception of autonomy."[90]

Rawls's Kantianism grew and sharpened in 1965, in response to the criticisms of the utilitarian Allan Gibbard. As Gibbard pointed out in his comments on the first draft of *A Theory of Justice*, Rawls's description of the original position did not contain explicit criteria by which the persons therein evaluated rival conceptions of justice. These persons lacked a great deal of particular knowledge. They had some knowledge, including the fact that they have a plan of life, but there was no obvious way of arguing that this general knowledge led the rational persons to choose one conception of justice over another. Without further criteria, the argument from the original position was incomplete.[91] Acknowledging the force of Gibbard's criticism, Rawls introduced the notion of primary goods. The primary goods were "things which rational persons may be presumed to want whatever else they want" and included goods such as liberty, opportunity, income, wealth, health, and self-respect.[92] Rawls reasoned that the primary goods were needed for any worthwhile pursuit and so were not dependent on any particular conception of a good life. This abstraction from particular contextual circumstances— even if it was restricted to the details of the original position—was another way in which Kantianism seeped into Rawls's theory.

Autonomy and Objectivity

Kant's conception of autonomy also led Rawls to add a layer to his conception of objectivity. We have already seen how Rawls's engagement with

Toulmin helped Rawls explain when the principles of justice are objective. With Toulmin, Rawls argued that one can stand one's ground if no concrete doubt is raised about it. Kant's conception of autonomy offered a different picture, which, judging from Rawls's presentation, was not seen as a rival to his earlier conceptions of objectivity. This conception of objectivity arose from its complicated connection to autonomy. On the one hand, Rawls wrote, principles are objective if they are binding for each individual. On the other, autonomy allows me to question the very principles of morality. As Rawls put the worry in his 1966 lectures on ethics, "If moral principles are principles which we give to ourselves as free rational beings, how can they at the same time be objective? But if we abandon objectivity, what happens to the notion of reason in moral deliberation?" His solution was to "weaken" the concept of objectivity: the principles were objective if "every rational being could accept" them, not if they do in fact accept them.[93] As he put it, "We take it to mean that there are reasons sufficient to lead a rational man to want to act on them."[94]

The introduction of Kant's conception of autonomy brought out new features of the original position and gave it a new framing. However, it also created a variety of complications.[95] In particular, the Kantian conception of autonomy was an ideal, and, as it is evident from Rawls's own use of different conceptions of "personhood," a contestable one. The original position, on the other hand, was meant to model intuitions acceptable to all reasonable persons and, in that way, serve as a heuristic device in discovering the principles of justice that explicated everyone's judgments of justice. It is not obvious that the two fit together easily. Rawls's Kantian conception of the person could be part of that explanatory role only if every reasonable person actually sought to live like a Kantian person.

Rawls would have to return to these problems in responses to the critics of *A Theory of Justice*. For now, in 1968, he described Kantian autonomy as an empirical claim. He thought that every creature seeks to express its nature and that human beings seek to express their nature as free and rational beings. As he explained to his students in 1968, we recognize the moral law as "characterizing the conduct that most adequately expresses our nature as free and equal rational beings. It springs from our intelligence and so from our proper self."[96] We want to follow the moral law because "all creatures of whatever kind <u>desire</u> to express their nature, or to <u>realize</u> their nature: to exercise their higher realized capacities."[97] Rawls's return to Kant was therefore not a return to an old and convincing ideal but a turn to a distinct account of personhood that every reasonable person could accept as the best account of their considered judgments.

Indeed, this turn to Kant's formulas of universality and especially autonomy had important implications for the history of political thought. It affected Rawls's own work after *A Theory of Justice,* as he now focused on showing how the principles of justice could be "constructed."[98] These writings are best explained as attempts to show how universal principles can be legislated or—to use Kant's language—"made" by reason. Moreover, Rawls's influential Kantian students emphasized autonomy as well, constructing principles of justice from the standpoint of practical reason and stressing the formula of autonomy in their interpretations of Kant.[99] The turn to Kantian autonomy overshadowed Rawls's earlier focus on respect for persons and their humanity. Doing so, it took Rawlsian liberalism in the direction that we know today, closing off other—perhaps also reasonable—paths.

9

A Theory of Justice

A THEORY OF JUSTICE was an impressive result of the arguments made essentially since the beginning of Rawls's intellectual career. It took him more than six years—the first draft of the book was finished in 1964—to put into a single argument his thoughts on the subject of justice, the nature of social practices, the laws of moral psychology, the implications of having a morality, and the nature of justification in ethics. In its philosophical vision, the book was an analysis of the considered judgments of reasonable persons, aimed at analyzing what it means to respect persons and to treat them as equals. It provided a conception of justice that most accurately explicated these judgments—"justice as fairness"—and justified it by showing that no alternative conception of justice accomplishes this task better. The analysis was to uncover principles that explain our judgments, even if we might be unaware of our commitment to these principles.

The historical narrative I have defended allows us to correct some misinterpretations of Rawls's philosophy. Interpreters from Allan Bloom to Richard Rorty claimed that Rawls did not provide an account of human nature and was merely reshuffling contemporary political convictions. As we saw, however, Rawls did have an account of human nature—one that rested on an account of natural feelings. The agreement that he hoped to discover was not an agreement for the sake of agreement. Nor was it an agreement that was contingent on the particular historical and cultural period in which Rawls worked.

This interpretation of Rawls has important implications for Rawls's understanding of the relationship between philosophy and politics. How much can actual, nonphilosophizing citizens decide about the main laws of our society? While Rawls did not, to use Rorty's terms, detach democracy from philosophy, the space for democratic decisions of actual citizens in Rawls's just society is greater than it may initially appear. It is not right to claim, with Michael Walzer, that Rawls's analysis of justice provides "conversational endings" to any such democratic discussions about justice.[1] This is because the kind of agreement Rawls expected to find among reasonable persons was limited both in scope and in precision. According to Rawls, the principles of justice were "bins of reasons": they highlighted reasons that were relevant in discussions about justice and provided an order to those reasons. Rawls thought that, despite this clarification, philosophy could offer only a "general direction" for politics. Beyond this philosophical boundary of justice, citizens could determine the content of justice by deliberation or, should it fail to reach a consensus, by vote. As we will see, the relation Rawls drew between philosophy and politics would still not satisfy political realists, but it gives much more space to politics than Rawls's critics allow.

Philosophy as Analysis of Considered Judgments

Given the arguments Rawls made in the 1960s, the conception of philosophy guiding *A Theory of Justice* was expectedly nonfoundational. Rawls rejected foundational approaches to political philosophy, claiming that "while some moral principles may seem natural and even obvious, there are great obstacles to maintaining that they are necessarily true, or even to explaining what is meant by this."[2] These considerations led Rawls to reject foundationalism entirely, as he thought that "there is no set of conditions or first principles that can be plausibly claimed to be necessary or definitive of morality and thereby especially suited to carry the burden of justification."[3] His own approach to questions of justice relied on the belief that conceptions of justice were supported by many kinds of considerations and that they were justified as wholes, not absolutely but relative to one another.[4] Justification stopped for the time being when all parties agreed that one conception of justice was superior to alternatives.

Rawls proposed to show that "justice as fairness" is this preferred conception of justice. His central belief was that "justification proceeds from what all parties to the discussion hold in common."[5] As a result, his aim in the book was to gather "widely accepted but weak premises" and show that, once combined, these assumptions imply a single conception of justice or at least "impose significant bounds on acceptable [conceptions] of justice."[6] The idea was to take as premises considerations mentioned in this and earlier chapters: considered judgments most broadly and the "provisional fixed points" or judgments "which we presume any conception of justice must fit."[7]

The structure of A Theory of Justice reflects Rawls's beliefs about the demands of justification. The first part of the book contains the deduction of the principles of justice from considered judgments, formal constraints on the concept of justice, the implications of having a morality, and a conception of the good. The second part of the book demonstrates that the principles of justice do indeed explicate our considered judgments in particular cases and clarify the more difficult cases. The third part of the book shows that the principles of justice are consistent with the laws of moral development.

Rawls's goal was to use an "analytic construction," or a thought experiment, to make "vivid to ourselves the restrictions that it seems reasonable to impose on arguments for principles of justice."[8] As in its previous versions, the thought experiment consisted of a chooser, the circumstances of choice, and a list of alternatives. Each particular description of the thought experiment was meant to reflect considerations relevant to questions of justice: "Each aspect of the contractual situation can be given supporting grounds."[9] Rawls's goal was to argue that, given this defensible description of the situation of choice, two principles of justice, known as "justice as fairness," would be the unique solution to the problem of choice.[10]

The analytic construction was shaped mostly by a conception of the person, which was responsible for the description of the chooser and the considerations in terms of which that person chose the principles of justice. As in the mid-1960s, this conception of the person was embedded in Rawls's interpretation of Kant's principle of autonomy. As Rawls wrote repeating the arguments made in the early drafts of the book, a person acts "autonomously when the principles of his action are chosen by him as the most adequate possible expression of his nature as a free and equal rational being."[11] In practice, that meant that the principles of justice were chosen based on reasons that were not "adopted because of his social position or natural endowments, or in view of the particular kind of society in which he lives or the specific things that he happens to want."[12] The conception of a rational person was unchanged: he was a "moral person," or a person with the capacities to form conceptions of the good and a sense of justice.[13] This double-edged capacity made human beings into "free and equal rational being[s]."[14] Many other features of the rational person were "the outcome of natural chance or the contingency of social circumstances"—these were not essential to being a rational person.[15] These features included the individual's social position, natural endowments, the kind of society in which he lives and the "specific things that he happens to want," and other characteristics such as race and gender.[16] Justifying one's principles of justice with resort to these kinds of facts would be to lose one's autonomy and act heteronomously.

The Kantian conception of autonomy determined the considerations in terms of which the persons in the original position chose principles of justice. It gave reasons—the primary goods—to evaluate alternative conceptions of justice. The content of the primary goods was determined by Rawls's understanding of a moral person; they were goods that any person needed to develop the moral capacities to exercise the sense of justice and to determine one's good. Rawls's assumption was that rational moral persons would prefer more primary goods rather than fewer. This assumption was transferred to the original position, thereby solving the dilemma of providing criteria of choice without falling into the trap of heteronomy.[17] Parties in the original position were to choose as many primary goods as possible.

In the same manner, the Kantian conception of the person excluded considerations, which Rawls thought to be irrelevant to questions of justice. The key tool for this purpose was the "veil of ignorance," blinding persons in the original position from certain kinds of knowledge and thereby preventing them from using certain kinds of reasons in the choice of the principles of justice. Consistent with the Kantian conception of the person, the persons in the original position did not have any knowledge of the particularities of their own person, including their place in society, class position or social status, natural assets and abilities (such as intelligence and strength), or their own beliefs about the good life.[18] Nor did persons in the original position know any particular facts about their own society or the generation to which they belonged. Deliberations about justice were to be carried out without recourse to reasons "arbitrary from a moral point of view."[19]

There is no need to go through Rawls's technical argument leading from these premises to the selection of justice as fairness. From 1965 onward, these "widely accepted but weak premises" were becoming increasingly shaped by the Kantian conception of autonomy, and the "reasonable person" became increasingly coextensive with the "Kantian person." The last chapter of *A Theory of Justice* illustrates the extent of this transformation well. In it, Rawls continued the 1964 comparison of the "original position" with an Archimedean point of view from which we can analyze the subject in its totality, but took it further.[20] The "original position" was a point of view "sub specie aeternitatis": adopting it, we could "regard the human situation not only from all social but also from all temporal points of view."[21] It allowed us to depart from the particularities of the circumstances in which we found ourselves.

Kantian Political Vision, Not Kantian Philosophy

The historical narrative of this book allows us to correct some other misinterpretations of Rawls's argument. While I have argued that Rawls's political vision became Kantian in nature, others have also interpreted his philosophical vision in the Kantian light. However, Rawls did not endorse a Kantian conception of philosophy, however broadly conceived. This can be seen by analyzing Robert S. Taylor's interpretation of Rawls. According to Taylor, Rawls's Kantian conception of the person is a "necessary presupposition or postulate of practical reason."[22] In Kant's theory, as Taylor explained, this conception of the person is established either directly, by showing that it is "something we must presuppose if we are to conceive of ourselves as agents," or indirectly, by showing that it is presupposed in the "fact of reason" that makes us conscious of our freedom.[23] In both cases, Kant's conception of the person is a "self-evident first principle."[24] Thus, according to Taylor, Kantianism as a conception of philosophy is characterized by two key features. First, it is an attempt to derive ethical conclusions from considerations about what it is to make an ethical judgment, or, more broadly, what it is to take the standpoint of practical reason. Second, these conclusions are viewed as necessary given that taking the practical standpoint is unavoidable.

However illuminating this interpretation may be of twentieth-century political thought in general and Rawls's students in particular, it does not explain Rawls's ideas well.[25] Two reasons stand out. First, Rawls throughout his career understood moral philosophy as analysis of considered judgments, and, in the nonfoundational way that he made very explicit in the 1960s, he allowed that, in principle, any considered judgment—as any part of a moral theory—can be rejected as misguided. He reaffirmed this nonfoundationalism in *A Theory of Justice*, emphasizing that "even the judgments we take provisionally as fixed points are liable to revision."[26] As part of these considered judgments, the Kantian conception of the person is also in principle liable to revision, even if in practice Rawls was confident that it described the considered judgments correctly. This way of arriving at the conception of the person is clearly incompatible with Kant's. Rawls did not claim that his conception of the person was self-evident or necessary. In Rawls's own Quinean terms, this would have been a Cartesian move. Instead, he sidelined the concept of "necessity" altogether, claiming that without a broader background in which "necessity" acquires philosophical significance, this concept has no use.

Neither is Rawls's conception of philosophy Kantian in the second respect. Rawls did not defend the principles of justice as implications—whether these implications are necessary or not—of practical reason alone. He disowned this interpretation of his later arguments in *The Law of Peoples,* stating explicitly that "at no point are we deducing the principles of right and justice . . . from a conception of practical reason in the background."[27] While no such explicit statement can be found in *A*

Theory of Justice, Rawls's 1999 disassociation from the Kantian argument applies to this argument in 1971 as well. Rawls did draw implications of making an ethical judgment in *A Theory of Justice:* these were the constraints on the concept of right, including universality and finality. If one makes an ethical judgment, Rawls assumed, it applies to all persons in similar conditions and cannot be changed if it goes against one's interest. These constraints on the concept of right were incorporated into the description of the "original position," but only as part of the many considerations required to deduce the principles of justice. Throughout the 1960s and in *A Theory of Justice,* Rawls maintained that the principles of justice cannot be derived from any one kind of consideration. In particular, he thought, principles of justice could not be derived from formal conditions on the concept of right. Indeed, he even criticized Kurt Baier (among others) for trying to derive principles of morality from the conditions of prescribability and universalizability.[28] Rawls argued that "we cannot . . . derive the content from the formal conditions <u>alone</u>": "this is too <u>slender</u> a basis."[29] Thus, even understood in this Rawlsian way, the practical standpoint played only a partial role in Rawls's argument for principles of justice. *A Theory of Justice* was clearly Kantian in its conception of the person and the content of the principles of justice. But the conception of philosophy driving the book was not Kantian: it did not treat the principles of justice as implications of making an ethical judgment, much less as necessary implications.

Philosopher of Human Nature

While the "original position" detaches us from the contingent facts about ourselves and our societies, it does not aim to detach us from our humanity. To use Stanley Cavell's terms, it does not require us to forget that we are human animals.[30] Unlike Kant, Rawls aimed to remove us from the particularities of our persons and existence, but not from being human as such. Rawls presented human beings as living in the "circumstances of justice." According to him, human beings live in a world in which they coexist with others of roughly similar physical and mental powers. They do so in conditions of "moderate scarcity," which forces them to participate in cooperative schemes. Hence the need for the virtue of justice. Human beings have their own plans of life and different philosophical, political, religious, and other kinds of beliefs.[31] And, as we saw in Chapter 6, they are born with certain natural attitudes and feelings, which under normal social conditions develop into moral attitudes and feelings.

Often, this account of human nature and, indeed, the very fact that Rawls presented it are ignored. For example, Allan Bloom has argued that while Rawls drew on the social contract tradition, unlike that tradition he did not present a theory of human nature. As Bloom wrote, human nature is "*the* permanent standard; what the good man and the good society are, depend on human nature."[32] For this reason, "metaphysics cannot be avoided. If there is to be political philosophy, . . . man must have a nature, and it must be knowable."[33]

Richard Rorty offered a similar interpretation of Rawls, only he, unlike Bloom, delighted in Rawls so understood. According to him, Rawls's goal was to detach political judgments from other, philosophical, claims. As he put it interpreting Rawls, "For purposes of social theory, we can put aside such topics as an ahistorical human nature, the nature of selfhood, the motive of moral behavior, and the meaning of human life."[34] On this view, Rawlsian democratic vision was independent of his philosophical vision. As Rorty wrote directly challenging the historical narrative of this book, this fact distinguished Rawls from intellectual traditions that linked democracy and philosophy, such as logical positivism. All Rawls was doing was collecting the considered judgments of reasonable persons and making them consistent:

> A *Theory of Justice* simply bypasses the metaethical issues which, in Reichenbach's eyes, were the sole connection between philosophy and normative judgments. . . . [It] is a book which descends straight from Kant, Mill, and Sidgwick. The same book could have been written if logical positivism had never existed. It is not a triumph of "analytic" philosophizing. It is simply the best update of liberal social thought which we have.[35]

On this account, Rawls's argument was "thoroughly historicist and anti-universalist" in that, were he to find agreement among reasonable persons, it was due to a historical contingency that in a culture in which

Rawls lived, this agreement was culturally possible.[36] Both Bloom's and Rorty's accounts portray Rawls as a relativist of sorts—someone who merely combines the already-existing attitudes into a more consistent set of assumptions.

As we have seen, however, Rawls did present a theory of human nature. Rorty is right that it was not an account that attributed to all human beings some essential character traits or beliefs. Nonetheless, it was an account of human nature. Rawls interpreted human nature in terms of natural and moral feelings and, using Wittgensteinian analysis, connected them to moral views. This was a novelty that both Bloom and Rorty failed to observe. Rawls argued that natural and moral feelings are compatible with a variety of moral views. Marxists, liberals, conservatives—all can of course develop feelings of regret and shame. Moreover, Rawls thought that natural and moral feelings would lead all reasonable persons to an overlapping set of moral views. One only had to find a proper way to express these feelings so that they did not lead reasonable persons in partial directions. So, to use Bloom's terms, human beings do have a nature, and it is knowable. There is nothing metaphysical about it, and it does not by itself exclude all political views but one. However, if prompted in the right way, this human nature can lead us to endorse one political vision. Such was Rawls's goal in *A Theory of Justice.*

Other interpreters of Rawls's naturalism have erred in the opposite direction and overlooked the flexibility of human nature that Rawls stressed. This was in great part Rawls's own fault, since, inspired by his former colleague Noam Chomsky's work, he offered an analogy between the sense of justice and the sense of grammaticalness.[37] This led interpreters to argue that Rawls's aim in *A Theory of Justice* was to uncover the "universal moral grammar."[38] As John Mikhail put it, "Rawls was one of the first philosophers to grasp the potential implications of Universal Grammar for ethics."[39] Mikhail admitted that Rawls did not actually defend the claim "understood as a hypothesis of natural science," but saw him as committed to the Chomskian vision of morality.[40] However, as we have seen and as I argue below, there is much more tentativeness in Rawls's argument about the implications of natural feelings than in Mikhail's captivating explorations. Rawls's natural feelings permit a variety of concepts that find their place in rival intellectual traditions—such as utilitarianism and Kantianism—and the most we can say is that these concepts overlap over certain moral statements. It is not a grammar that we can find in natural feelings, but much looser "bins of reasons" that sometimes are good enough to solve practical political problems.

Limits of Philosophy, Space for Democracy

Highlighting Rawls's modest philosophical anthropology helps clarify the relationship between democracy and philosophy in his thought. Clarifying our considered judgments, Rawls's philosophical analysis was meant to supplant them with principles of justice. It is clear from *A Theory of Justice* that, taken as an analysis of what reasonable citizens want, the principles would guide the basic structure of our society through constitutional and legal order.[41] Rawls did not suggest that the principles be used as a beginning of a discussion about justice. In that regard, Walzer is correct in saying that Rawls's account of justice is a "conversational ending." Unless a mistake in the argument is found, Rawls's principles of justice should be taken to govern our constitutional and legal order.

While correct, this criticism ignores the fact that Rawls expected the principles of justice to guide the judgments of reasonable persons only in what Rawls called a "general direction." Limited as they are in reach and precision, principles of justice leave large spaces for citizens' decisions. This argument is made most clearly in Rawls's 1970 lectures on ethics, which contrasted two ways of conceiving principles of justice. The first, more ambitious, view resembled Rawls's early "physicalist" account of the mechanical role of principles. Called a "deductive schema," it viewed principles of justice as "the major premises of our moral judgments." When combined with minor premises, of "facts of the case," the principles "generate our considered judgments in full reflective equilibrium."[42] A distinctive feature of such a "deductive schema" is that it did not require intuitive judgment because all reasons relevant to the question at hand weighed univocally in one direction: "No other principle applies and points in another direction (supports some other alternative)."[43] In such a case, "no moral decision (deliberation) is necessary. The answer is obvious."[44]

It is fair to point out that, as late as 1962, Rawls held this view of principles as an ideal, even if he did not think that philosophy could achieve this kind of precision in practice. As he wrote describing the goals of his analysis of justice, "Ideally, we want an account which reduces to <u>zero</u> the need for the other person to rely on his <u>intuitive</u> hunches as to how we will judge."[45] In these ideal situations, the particular judgments would be deduced with machinelike precision:

> One may, with qualification, think of our task in this way: we are trying to formulate the principle that we should have to build into a machine if the machine is to give the same answer as we do when it is given the facts and information which we regard as relevant.[46]

Rawls did not think one could achieve this kind of precision in practice, but the ideal still set his goal. Failing to achieve machinelike deduction from principles to particular judgments, we can try to "greatly <u>reduce</u> the extent to which such reliance [on intuition] is necessary. <u>Every</u> such reduction is a <u>theoretical</u> gain."[47] Rawls held on to this ideal in *A Theory of Justice*. As he wrote, "We should do what we can to reduce the direct appeal to our considered judgments . . . even though the dependence on intuition cannot be eliminated entirely."[48] Even affirming this goal, Rawls noted that situations in which we could deduce judgments from principles were rare and select, and therefore the deductive schema view of ethical theory was fitting "only in <u>special</u> cases."[49]

The alternative—more "realistic and accurate"—way of understanding principles of justice was the "guiding framework" conception.[50] This conception acknowledged the possibility of conflicting reasons and admitted that the priority rules for ordering these reasons would guide our judgment in some but not all cases. As Rawls wrote, even the best of the feasible theories of justice "identifies the relevant considerations and helps us to assign them their correct weights" but does so only in the more important cases. Consequently, the task of such a feasible theory "when addressing the priority problem . . . is that of reducing and not eliminating entirely the reliance on intuitive judgments."[51] Along the same lines, Rawls also compared ethical theory to economic theory, "which largely tells us what to look for."[52] In short, key to the "guiding framework" conception was the acknowledgment that, despite the priority rules, in some cases even the best conception of justice required "the exercise of <u>some</u> judgment [unguided by the priority rules]."[53]

In different parts of his writings, Rawls noted the limits to agreement that his account of ethical principles imposed. In *A Theory of Justice*, he described the agreement not as a strict agreement but as an overlap of different judgments. As he wrote,

> I have assumed that in a nearly just society there is a public acceptance of the same principles of justice. Fortunately this assumption is stronger than necessary. There can, in fact, be considerable differences in citizens' conceptions of justice provided that these conceptions lead to similar political judgments. And this is possible, since different premises can yield the same conclusion. In this case there exists what we may refer to as overlapping rather than strict consensus.[54]

In effect, this meant that while citizens can endorse the same policy, they will do so by appealing to different values or facts. Rawls had made this argument already in 1958, reflecting on Wittgenstein's *Investigations*. Describing the limits of morality, Rawls wrote that "all moralities resemble one another in their <u>principles</u>; they have this sort of family likeness."[55] Albeit resembling one another in some of their principles, these moralities differ "by varying the emphasis and so favoring one principle over another."[56] For example, a publicly financed television station can arguably be endorsed by appealing both to the freedom of speech and to Rawls's difference principle, which requires that the social and economic inequalities be distributed in such a way as to benefit the least advantaged persons. Both arguments would make use of Rawls's principles of justice, but in different ways. Which of these arguments is better is a matter for debate, and Rawls's principles of justice do not settle debates such as this. Thus, even if critics such as Walzer are correct in saying that the judges or lawmakers have the role of only applying these principles of justice, that still leaves a space for debates about how this application should look in practice. That is the space for democratic debate. This space may not satisfy Walzer, but it has to be acknowledged that it exists.

Moreover, Rawls expected that the principles of justice would lead to an agreement—understood in the above, overlapping sense—only over some easier cases. In his 1970 lectures on ethics, Rawls followed Kant in arguing that the principles of justice apply to everyone in virtue of their being a person, regardless of their nationality or beliefs.[57] However, he did not think that all reasonable persons would equally agree on all parts of the proposed theory. Rather, he thought, they would accept a conception of justice in different degrees. "I disagree with Kant," he told his students, "in that I doubt that it can be shown that there is <u>one complete</u> set of ethical principles in regard to which there are sufficient reasons why all rational men, given the circumstances of human life, should accept them." There might be some "objective principles in this sense," he continued, but they would be the broadest of principles, such as "the principle not to inflict unnecessary suffering." However, "this principle does not make up a <u>complete</u> system"—it only belongs to a complete system.[58] On this view, then, systems of morality would contain principles that are more easily justifiable and principles that are more contestable. This was the result of his view that justification is relative. One tries to combine a system of principles and concepts into one coherent system, such as "justice as fairness," and hopes that it stands against objections better than a rival system, also taken as a whole. As Rawls wrote, "I think there are <u>degrees of justification</u> in that certain <u>parts</u> of morality are <u>more justifiable</u>, more objective, than others."[59] Importantly, this opened the possibility that other conceptions of justice might be reasonable as well.

In his 1960 lectures on political philosophy, Rawls was similarly frank about the limits of the principles of justice. Perhaps, he thought, the order we impose on different relevant reasons would be clear enough to determine only the easier cases. In the more difficult cases, which involve many different values and so generate many different reasons, that order would be more difficult to find. Nonetheless, Rawls wrote, we should be satisfied even if philosophy can solve only such easier cases. "It may be true that there are <u>many</u> cases in which grounds of rational preference <u>can</u> be found," he emphasized, "and numerous abstract possibilities, and some actual ones, may possibly be discarded as beyond the bounds of sound opinion altogether—eg., to maximize pain; or various racist doctrines."[60] Despite its limits, philosophy will have done some important work.

While elaborating his own "justice as fairness," Rawls already knew that some of its emphases and even parts of principles would not gain wide adherence. For instance, as Rawls acknowledged in 1967, he expected little agreement about principles of distributive justice. For this reason, he allowed that the argument from the original position may not be decisive in all cases—it may exclude some feasible conceptions of justice but not others. As he wrote, "No doubt we shall be left with several plausible alternatives, at least on such matters as income distribution." In those cases, we "should follow the principle of tolerance: to press for the morality we favor within the limits of equal liberty."[61]

If the number and variety of values make the order imposed by the principles of justice intractable, the space for democratic deliberations opens yet further. Even if justices and lawmakers will be asked to apply the principles of justice to their respective fields, the lack of justification of some principles or some areas of these principles would not only prevent mechanical and even ordered deduction but could in principle preclude the application of these principles altogether. In such cases, votes would replace the philosophical order Rawls created in *Theory*.

And finally, Rawls thought that philosophy offered only a general direction for politics in the sense that it could not consider facts that went beyond its purview. Policy questions require expertise that philosophy cannot be expected to have. Rawls's favorite examples were economic. Indeed, *A Theory of Justice* contains a range of important economic subjects that, according to Rawls, are left undetermined by the principles of justice. Most famously, Rawls acknowledged that justice as fairness did not provide sufficient considerations to decide between the socialist system of ownership and property-owning society. This decision, he wrote, depends "in large part upon the traditions, institutions, and social forces of each country, and its particular historical circumstances"—matters that a theory of justice cannot discuss.[62] Similarly, Rawls did not think that a theory of justice could help determine the extent of legitimate economic power or the rate of savings between different generations.[63]

Rawls did not see these limitations as a failure of philosophy. Rather, he thought they showed the proper limits of the discipline. As he told his students in the 1966 lectures on ethics, "Moral philosophy must stop, qua moral philosophy, at the general framework. For only a careful study of the facts etc can determine what to do in particular situations."[64] Once the limits of moral philosophy are reached, the range of cases approved by the considerations of justice is to be considered equally just: "Justice is to that extent likewise indeterminate. Institutions within the permitted range are equally just, meaning that they could be chosen; they are compatible with all the constraints of the theory."[65]

In *A Theory of Justice,* the determination of what the principles of justice require was left to the "four-stage sequence" of the original position, in which each stage of deliberation was applied to a different subject matter.[66] The first stage deliberated on the principles of justice, the second chose a constitution compatible with the principles of justice, the third examined laws compatible with the constitution, and the last one applied these laws to policies. It is remarkable how open these later stages were insofar as justice was concerned. As Rawls wrote regarding the choice of constitutions—only the second stage of deliberation–"It is not always clear which of several constitutions" would be chosen. By themselves, the principles of justice could not determine the most just constitution for a specific country. According to Rawls, this indeterminacy was not the fault of philosophy. "When this is so," he continued, "justice is to that extent indeterminate."[67] And as justice is indeterminate, the space for democratic deliberation opens up.

I hope to have shown that while the critics are correct to emphasize the hypothetical experiments in which our actual reasons give way to the philosopher's better reasons, this does not make Rawls's theory of justice a "conversational ending." This is because the kind of agreement Rawls expected to find among reasonable persons was much more limited than the grand structure of *A Theory of Justice* and the clarity of Rawls's thought may suggest. While Rawls sought to eliminate the reliance of intuition as much as possible by introducing a list of ordered principles, in reality he recognized that such an order would be imposed only in the simpler cases. Perhaps in that regard he came to a similar realization as Henry Sidgwick, who concluded in the early editions of his *Methods of Ethics* that, unable to decide between rival conceptions of morality, practical reason was divided.[68] Of course, Rawls's argument did not conclude that we are faced with a "dualism of practical reason"—only that the reach of practical reason is limited in the harder cases.[69] The sheer number of conflicting values that bear on such questions and the different weights we assign to these values may make the determination of a proper order of reasons impossible.

I do not want to say that Rawls intended to expand the space for politics and to limit the role of philosophy in politics. Indeed, this book shows the reverse: he sought to impose as much structure to our considered judgments as possible. For Rawls, who set out in 1946 to discover principles that would mechanically lead to judgments about particular situations, this indeterminacy of justice must have seemed disappointing. Given his conception of justification, Rawls had to come to terms with it. Just as he argued when considering a sailor who refused to examine a capsized boat, he now claimed that we can stop defending our view when a clear alternative to it is absent. Or, as he put this point appealing to Quine's ideas, justification is relative to what else we can achieve. "Justice as fairness" was selected not because it imposed a perfectly clear structure on our considered judgments but because it had fewer—and less important—failures to account for our judgments than its rivals. In fact, *A Theory of Justice* is full of reassurances that what we have is the best that we can have. Addressing the indeterminacy of justice, Rawls wrote that it "is not in itself a defect." In fact, it is "what we should expect": "Justice as fairness will prove a worthwhile theory if it defines the range of justice more in accordance with our considered judgments than do existing theories, and if it singles out with greater sharpness the graver wrongs a society should avoid."[70]

Rawls may well be thought of as an author of a grand philosophical vision, but it is his acknowledgment of the limits of philosophy that might be the most admirable and long-lasting part of his work. The political vision he presented was constructed in awareness of these limits, as a vision that might convince a diverse society. Moreover, it was meant to convince reasonable persons of only the most important constitutional questions and only pull them in the general direction of the theory. This may be a less grand Rawls than we know him, but, understood in this way, his political and philosophical visions may bring greater clarity in democratic debates.

Epilogue

A T THE END of this intellectual history, we can step back and look at Rawls's main questions and the problems of liberal political theory with greater clarity. I want to focus on one of its conclusions: that achieving agreement was at least partly a philosophical problem for Rawls. To be able to argue for his theological vision, Rawls had to analyze shared Christian experiences. To conceive ethics as a science, he had to show that it had a subject matter. To demonstrate the absurdity of doubting some ethical propositions, he had to show that they were shared. To portray ethical reasoning as a practice, he had to uncover the shared constitutive rules that governed it. All these were philosophical tasks.

In the later years, especially since concluding that the function of ethics was to solve disagreement, showing the possibility of agreement became a political problem in its own right. To recognize persons as persons was to respect their capacities to determine their own good and to comply with the rules of justice. Respecting persons required showing that they are able to agree to principles of justice that govern their lives. In the mid-1960s, Rawls modified this argument, now requiring that principles of justice not only be accepted but be accepted only on grounds that do not mention contingent facts about ourselves—our aspirations, gender, race, the places in which we were born. The two reasons for finding agreement—the philosophical and the political—were now combined, as shown by the fact that the original position was meant to show both the autonomy of persons and the objectivity of their judgments.[1] The philosophical conclusions imposed limits on the practical agreement to make sure that the agreement is consistent with the main values of persons who entered it.

Reminding ourselves that showing agreement was also a philosophical task helps us understand more clearly that this agreement, were it feasible, is an expression of some deeper truth about what it is to be a reasonable human.[2] Therefore, as we analyze Rawls's reasons for explaining the possibility of agreement among reasonable persons, we should look not at pragmatic strategies but at Rawls's underlying explanation of what it means to be a reasonable human. This, in turn, leads us to the analysis of natural and moral feelings—Wittgenstein's influence on Rawls. It consists of a claim that there exist logical connections between natural feelings and moral feelings, and between moral feelings and moral conceptions. However, this Wittgensteinian argument by itself does not explain why reasonable persons might agree. If reasonable persons have different conceptions of shame, they will experience moral feelings in different circumstances, and perhaps in different ways.

So, to understand Rawls's expectation of finding agreement among reasonable persons, we need to come back to his early writings, especially his later "physicalist" notion of "basic statements." These early writings reveal his belief that some experiences are so basic that all reasonable persons would have them and interpret them in the same way. Why might Rawls have thought so? Explorations of this book lead to a twofold answer. On the one hand, Rawls's first secular ethical writings reveal his belief that at least some ethical judgments can be independent of other concepts in reasonable persons' conceptual frameworks. In 1946, defending "imperative utilitarianism," Rawls analyzed only judgments but not the reasons for which they were made. His interpretation of Wittgenstein, in which he focused on the commonalities—the human form of life—rather than the differences, and his drawing on Quine rather than Kuhn to explain the process of reflective equilibrium are also telling of his belief that some of our judgments are independent of other judgments. Rawls accepted the thesis of meaning holism, but he thought there were limits to it. The second part of the answer is Rawls's understanding of ethical principles. He thought that sharing reasons—or, as he called them, "bins of reasons"—was sufficient to say that we agree. Such an agreement did not require agreement on the particulars of how these reasons should be employed in practice: it was "logically loose." Nor did it require that different persons agree on the system of weighing the values that produced the bins of reasons.

Transition to Political Liberalism

This interpretation of Rawls's theory of justice helps explain the modifications he made to his argument after *A Theory of Justice*. While a proper account of this transition would require another book, the intellectual history given so far allows us to draw a schema that can help illuminate the criticisms Rawls's project received, Rawls's responses to these criticisms, and the subsequent modifications of his views.[3] Both the criticisms and the responses centered on Rawls's claim that at least some of our political judgments are independent of the rest of our beliefs.

The most powerful criticisms of *A Theory of Justice* claimed that Rawls's argument relied on a Kantian conception of the person, which was controversial and crucial for the conclusions rather than, as Rawls believed, widely accepted and weak.[4] Critics also contested Rawls's reliance on the allegedly widely shared scientific knowledge that was made available to the persons in the original position.[5] This knowledge, they claimed, was controversial and could not be incorporated into the "widely shared" premises of the original position.[6]

In essence, critics of *A Theory of Justice* brought to light how controversial and interrelated Rawls's premises were. They saw Rawls's argument as a Kantian vision rather than a vision on which all reasonable persons can agree. The Quinean "fixed points," so the critics argued, in fact relied on a wider and contestable web of beliefs. They stressed that other frameworks of thought would disagree with Rawls's description of the original position because they relied on a different web of beliefs. In short, these critics claimed meaning holism is not as limited as Rawls had assumed.

Rawls's initial response to such criticisms was to reaffirm the independence of the "fixed points" in our ethical judgments from a wider set of beliefs. He argued that the comparison of theories of justice can take place regardless of other areas of inquiry. Thus, in the 1975 article "The Independence of Moral Theory," Rawls argued that the study of considered judgments, although not isolated, is very much an inquiry independent of other types of inquiries. "Much of moral theory is independent from the other parts of philosophy," he wrote. "The theory of meaning and epistemology, metaphysics and the philosophy of mind, can often contribute very little [to questions raised by moral theory]."[7] In particular, Rawls denied links between moral theory and conceptions of the person: "The conclusions of the philosophy of mind regarding the question of personal identity do not provide grounds for accepting one of the leading moral conceptions rather than another."[8] In short, as critics argued that the Kantian conception of the person depended on commitments in other areas of inquiry, such as his reliance on the Kantian laws of moral development, Rawls denied such connections. Initially, then, he believed that the truth of each aspect of his argument could be established within the confines of its own domain, be it in moral theory or in philosophy of mind, without relying on a broader contestable web of beliefs. He reaffirmed the claim that moral theory has its own subject matter, although by 1975 this subject matter expanded to include more than considered judgments of reasonable persons: "The study of substantive moral conceptions and their relation to our moral sensibility has its own distinctive problems and subject matter that requires to be investigated for its own sake."[9]

Within five years of publishing "The Independence of Moral Theory," however, Rawls stopped severing the description of the original position from wider webs of belief. On Rawls's own account, Samuel Scheffler's "Moral Independence and the Original Position," published in 1979 but sent to Rawls in 1977, played a crucial role: it was then that Rawls realized the need to significantly revise the argument of *A Theory of Justice*.[10] Scheffler's article pointed out an inconsistency between the argument in the original position and Rawls's claim that moral theory is independent of other areas of inquiry. In its broadest claim, however, Scheffler's argument was illustrative of the kinds of criticism Rawls's theory had already received: that Rawls's argument relied on deeper commitments that rival theories of justice did not share. It must have been more influential on Rawls than other arguments because it showed precisely how Rawls's argument against rival conceptions of justice in the original position depended on deeper commitments.

Scheffler argued that Rawls's criticism of utilitarianism depended on the Kantian conception of the person and so was not independent of other fields of inquiry, as Rawls had claimed in the 1975 article. Conceiving themselves in terms of long-term life plans and interests, Rawls's Kantian persons rejected the utilitarianism that endangered these long-term interests by permitting inadmissible sacrifices of individual liberties for the common good. But, Scheffler insisted, utilitarianism did not accept the Kantian conception of the person, allowing that a person may in fact be a bundle of immediate desires without the long-term plans and interests. Thus, Rawls's argument against utilitarianism, insofar as it was successful, drew its force from the fact that its implications on the questions of personal identity were more defensible than those of utilitarianism.

By the late 1970s, Rawls increasingly realized the depth and extent of potential disagreement among reasonable persons and acknowledged that disagreement about one subject often leads to disagreement about ethical theories. As a result of this realization, Rawls concluded that rival ethical theories may not have a sufficient number of weak and widely accepted premises from which to derive a conception of justice. This created a dilemma for Rawls: his central assumption that all reasonable persons have overlapping frameworks of beliefs and values that are relatively independent of their other beliefs seemed flawed.

Rawls's subsequent intellectual development can be understood as a response to this dilemma, and his response was to preserve the independence of political judgments as much as possible. He now argued that, despite broader disagreements, reasonable persons shared a political culture. Rawls's solution was twofold. First, he sharply distinguished between different parts of our web of beliefs: the comprehensive and political doctrines. This distinction consisted in demarcating our broader beliefs about the world, intellectual inquiry, and the nature of morality from beliefs about the political sphere alone.[11] The second step was to acknowledge the fact of reasonable disagreement in the comprehensive sphere but then posit the fact of agreement in the public sphere—the existence of a "public political culture." A conception of justice was to be formulated from these shared public beliefs. As he wrote in 1985, "We look, then, to our public political culture itself, including its main institutions and the historical traditions of their interpretation, as the shared fund of implicitly recognized basic ideas and principles. The hope is that these ideas and principles can be formulated clearly enough to be combined into a conception of political justice congenial to our most firmly held convictions."[12]

The key novelty in this argument was the requirement that each different comprehensive doctrine justify the political conception of justice on its own grounds, from within its own broader conceptual framework. Rawls's argument thereby became more contextual and historical: it now acknowledged the different and incompatible starting points of the rival comprehensive frameworks. Despite this new contextualism, Rawls's new argument remained tied to the assumptions that guided him toward *A Theory of Justice*. He continued to hold that reasonable persons' beliefs about the political sphere would overlap sufficiently to inform a political conception of justice. In essence, then, Rawls retained his earlier belief that meaning holism is limited and does not threaten the agreement among reasonable persons. Some judgments would still be sufficiently independent from other judgments for all reasonable persons to make them. He did not think that disagreement about comprehensive frameworks would extend to core parts of political doctrines that deal with "constitutional essentials and basic questions of justice."[13]

Liberal Political Theory: Possible Paths

Rawls's later work, and the work of his followers, is thus a test of how possible it is to attain agreement among reasonable persons. To what extent can our political beliefs be detached from our wider conceptual frameworks? Initially, Rawls himself thought that public reasons that stem from the shared public political culture could decide even controversial questions, such as abortion. Prioritizing "equality of women as equal citizens," Rawls concluded they lead us to "give a woman a duly qualified right to decide whether or not to end her pregnancy."[14] Later, he took back this conclusion as his opinion and not an argument, not denying, however, that a plausible argument for that conclusion can be made.[15] As Rawls stated, one cannot decide the extent of meaning holism without discussing actual cases of moral and political conflict. That is why the plausibility of Rawls's reformulated argument depends on the success of those that try to show the compatibility between a liberal political conception elaborated by Rawls and other, nonliberal points of view.[16] It cannot be decided by a conceptual argument alone.

Here, I want to return to Rawls's intellectual history and suggest some Rawlsian directions just in case such attempts of reconciliation might fail. What would be the damage if we could not show the agreement of reasonable persons? The pillars of Rawls's philosophical vision would survive, even if they would need to be supplemented by new concepts. As Rawls argued following Toulmin, all we can do is give reasons to explain our judgments and views. These reasons stem from conceptual frameworks we have. They may turn out to be unacceptable to others, but they have the force of reasons for us nonetheless. They arise from the beliefs we hold, as a consequence of the beliefs we hold. Because of this logical connection of reasons to wider conceptual frameworks, the claim that arguing about ethics and politics is actually reasoning— an activity governed by rules—would survive unscathed.

Political reasoning, which requires addressing the reasons of others, would be more difficult to reframe. Rawls portrayed arguments about justice as arguments with other persons. As he put it in the early 1950s, justification could stop when it is absurd to raise objections against the view in question. On this view of justification, if objections to the view remain, the political argument cannot stop. Now, in the context of contemporary disagreements about justice, such objections would always be there. However, raising them again and again would be odd in Rawls's conception of justification, since trading objections would not move the argument forward. So, at this point, parties to the argument could agree to stop for the time being and to solve the disagreement by other means, such as voting or postponing the decision. To adopt this revised conception of justification, a Rawlsian would have to place a newfound focus on the virtues of citizens, in particular their ability to judge when the argument cannot be brought further and when others have genuinely laid out their core beliefs.

To see that this revised position is compatible with Rawls's original vision, we may want to return to his observations that principles of justice lead to agreement only in some cases and are, as he put it in 1952, "logically loose." These may help us realize that Rawls's conception of justification already depends on very little agreement among reasonable persons. In *Political Liberalism* Rawls narrowed the scope of expected agreement even further than in the writings analyzed in this book. Reasonable persons were now expected to agree on constitutional essentials, but, for example, the more controversial economic decisions regulated by his second principle of justice were excluded from this expected agreement.[17] Moreover, Rawls's evolving arguments about the ability of public reason to decide even questions of constitutional essentials, such as those of abortion, also raise doubt whether any agreement can be expected even on these more basic questions.

Moreover, the agreement that Rawls expected to find was, to use his earlier terms, "logically loose." According to him, the principles leave a large degree of indeterminacy and therefore space for democratic decisions. As Rawls now argued, "Public reason allows more than one reasonable answer to any particular question." This is not a problem, he thought, because "public reason does not ask us to accept the very same principles of justice, but rather to conduct our fundamental discussions in terms of what we regard as a political conception." In particular, Rawls argued, "We should sincerely think that our view of the matter is based on political values everyone can reasonably endorse."[18] Thus, the scope and character of agreement Rawls expected to obtain were already rather minimal, and the revised position would not be a drastic departure from the views Rawls already expressed.

Rawls's political vision could retain its core shape as well. In *A Theory of Justice*, Rawls tied the notion of respect for persons to agreement about the principles of justice. As he wrote, the notion of respect for persons presupposes shared principles of justice: "To respect persons is to recognize that they possess an inviolability founded on justice that even the welfare of society as a whole cannot override."[19] However, this respect now rested on the requirement that one offer to others reasons that they could accept. The citizens were expected to accept the reasons used, but not the weights of these reasons or the practical conclusions of these reasons. As critics have argued, the concept of reasons that others can accept is permissive, perhaps overly so: the limits of what people can accept are indeterminate.[20] This is especially so if they are not asked to accept the weights of these reasons and their practical implications. As a result, it is not obvious that the concept of reasons that all can accept is adding anything to our respect for others.

The solution to this problem is to either tighten the concept of reasons that all can accept, thereby excluding many actual reasons from this notion, or to allow reasons that others may not accept into political conversations. If we tighten the concept of acceptable reasons, we would have to show why we should accept this new definition. Alternatively, we may allow into the political conversation reasons that genuinely attempt to convince others but cannot realistically be hoped to bring conversion or even change of mind during the discussion. This would have an advantage of accommodating critics such as Michael Walzer, who interpret respect for persons as respect for their actual reasoning.

Can one respect others while offering to them reasons they cannot be expected to accept? To answer this question positively, we may want to return to Rawls's early political views. Interpreting respect for persons, Rawls drew primarily on Kant's formula of humanity that requires us to always treat persons as ends. To elaborate such a vision, we would have to introduce relevant virtues, such as the ability to listen to others, involve them in the decision, and to compromise with them in reaching it.

I believe that such a move would retain the core of Rawls's ideas. As I have tried to show, Rawls thought that in large areas of political life agreement cannot be expected, and that these areas are already left to be decided by the democratic decisions of actual persons. He spent his intellectual career trying to show that the agreement we have left—however narrow, however logically loose—is still worth keeping. And, of course, it is. But should it prove to be more minimal than Rawls expected it, or to not exist, Rawls's intellectual history can remind us that his main motivating idea was to find a way to treat others as moral persons and to acknowledge them as equal. Bringing back this emphasis on respect, rather than agreement, might help us not only better understand Rawls's aims, but also inform our own future inquiries.

APPENDIX A

John Rawls:
Courses Taken and Taught

PRINCETON UNIVERSITY 1939–1942
BA in philosophy, 1942

FALL 1939
Chemistry 105: Chemistry of Metals and Qualitative Analysis, I
English 201: English Literature of the Eighteenth Century
German 103: Intermediate German, I
Mathematics 107: Coordinate Geometry
Music 101: Elementary Harmony, I

SPRING 1940
Chemistry 106: Chemistry of Metals and Qualitative Analysis, II
English 202: The Romantic Movement in English Literature
German 104: Intermediate German, II
Mathematics 108: Differential Calculus
Music 102: Elementary Harmony, II

FALL 1940
Art 101: Freehand Drawing
Art 201: Ancient Architecture
Chemistry 303: Organic Chemistry, I
History 201: Modern European History from the French Revolution to the
    Present, I
Philosophy 201: Elements of Ethics (Walter T. Stace)

SPRING 1941

Art 202: Medieval Architecture

Art 204: Freehand Drawing

Classics 318: Roman History

History 202: Modern European History from the French Revolution to the
Present, II

Philosophy 202: Plato (Theodore M. Greene)

FALL 1941

Art 205: Ancient Art

Art 303: The Revival of Painting in Italy

Oriental Languages 303: Ancient and Medieval Semitic Culture, I

Religious History 303: Christian Thought to the Reformation (George F. Thomas)

Philosophy 401: Kant and the Philosophy of the Nineteenth Century (David F.
Bowers)

SPRING 1942

Philosophy 302: History of Philosophy (Ledger Wood)

Philosophy 303: Philosophy of Science and Scientific Method (Andrew P. Ushenko)

Philosophy 306: Social Philosophy (Norman Malcolm)

FALL 1942

Philosophy 203: Logic (Ushenko)

Philosophy 301: History of Philosophy (Robert Scoon)

Philosophy 305: Theory of Value (Scoon)

PRINCETON UNIVERSITY, 1946–1947
PhD in philosophy, beginning studies

SPRING 1946

Philosophy 501: Philosophy of Plato (Scoon)

Philosophy 520: Logic (Ushenko)

Philosophy 536: Problems of Philosophy (Malcolm)

SUMMER 1946

Philosophy 522: Systematic Ethics (James Ward Smith)

FALL 1946

Philosophy 528: Conception of Consciousness (Wolfgang Köhler)

Philosophy 504: Philosophy of Kant (Edgar Herbert Henderson)

Philosophy 303: Philosophy of Mind (Preceptor for Köhler)

SPRING 1947
Philosophy 503: Philosophy of Aristotle (Scoon)
Philosophy 513: Pre-Kantian Rationalism (Wood)
Philosophy 537: Pragmatism (Lewis E. Hahn)

SUMMER 1947
Prepares for General Examination—history of philosophy, metaphysics,
    epistemology, logic and scientific method, ethics and theory of value,
    philosophy of mind (Ushenko)

CORNELL UNIVERSITY, 1947–1948
PhD in philosophy, studies continued

FALL 1947
Philosophy 595: Informal Course on Ethics, I (Arthur E. Murphy)
Philosophy 39: Seminar on Induction and Probability (Max Black)
History 165: History of Science, I (Henry Guerlac)

SPRING 1948
Philosophy 324: Informal Course on Ethics, II (Murphy)
Philosophy 39: Philosophy of Science (Black)
History 166: History of Science, II (Guerlac)

PRINCETON UNIVERSITY, 1948–1950
PhD in philosophy, 1950

FALL 1948
Philosophy 527: Theory of Knowledge (Stace)
Research: Foundations of Ethical Knowledge (Scoon)

SPRING 1949
Research and work on dissertation (Stace and Scoon)

SUMMER 1949
Preparation for dissertation (Stace)

FALL 1949
Dissertation (Stace)
Economics seminar with Jacob Viner

SPRING 1950

Seminar with Alpheus Mason on the history of U.S. political thought and
constitutional law

May 11: Dissertation accepted

June 13: Degree granted

PRINCETON UNIVERSITY, 1950–1952
Instructor in philosophy

FALL 1950

Philosophy 303: Philosophy of the Nineteenth Century

Philosophy 309: Philosophy of Religion (Preceptor)*

Audits seminar with William Baumol

SPRING 1951

Philosophy 308: Social Philosophy (Preceptor)*

Unofficial study group in economics: Walras's *Elements of Pure Economics,*
Neuman and Morgenstern's *Theory of Games and Economic Behavior*

FALL 1951

Philosophy 307: Ethics

Philosophy 309: Philosophy of Religion (Preceptor)

SPRING 1952

Philosophy 302: History of Philosophy: Modern (Preceptor)*

Philosophy 308: Social Philosophy (Preceptor)

OXFORD UNIVERSITY, 1952–1953
Fulbright Scholar

CORNELL UNIVERSITY, 1953–1959
Assistant professor (1953–1956) and associate professor
(1956–1959) of philosophy

*Walter Kaufman was the instructor of these courses, but the university's Office of the
Dean of Faculty Records also lists Rawls, presumably as preceptor. See Princeton Uni-
versity Archives, Office of the Dean of Faculty Records (AC 118), Box 145, Folders 4 and 5.
The same reasoning applies to Rawls's courses during the academic year 1951-1952.
Ibid., Folders 6 and 7.

FALL 1953
[Philosophy 585: Ethics and Value Theory]*

SPRING 1954
Philosophy 425: Ethical Theory: Christian Ethics

FALL 1954
Philosophy 101: Philosophical Classics I (with others)
Philosophy 325: Ancient and Medieval Political Philosophy
Philosophy 585: Ethics and Value Theory

SPRING 1955
Philosophy 102: Philosophical Classics II (with others)†
Philosophy 103: Elementary Logic (with others)

FALL 1955
Philosophy 101: Philosophical Classics I (with others)
Philosophy 103: Elementary Logic (with others)
Philosophy 585: Ethics and Value Theory

SPRING 1956
Philosophy 326: Political and Social Philosophy
Philosophy 425: Ethical Theory: Contemporary Moral Philosophy

FALL 1956
Philosophy 101: Philosophical Classics I (with others)
Philosophy 103: Elementary Logic (with others)
Philosophy 585: Ethics and Value Theory: Natural Law

SPRING 1957
Philosophy 326: Political and Social Philosophy

FALL 1957
Philosophy 101: Philosophical Classics I (with others)
Philosophy 103: Elementary Logic (with others)
Philosophy 585: Ethics and Value Theory: Natural Law

---

*Rawls is not listed as the instructor of this course (the catalog must have been prepared before his hiring), but it is likely that he taught his "Justice as Fairness" there.
†This course (and introductory courses 101 and 103 listed in Fall 1955) is listed as "Either term," so it is not clear when Rawls taught it.

SPRING 1958
Philosophy 326: Political and Social Philosophy

FALL 1958
Philosophy 103: Elementary Logic (with others)
Philosophy 585: Ethics and Value Theory: Moral Feelings

SPRING 1959
Philosophy 326: Political and Social Philosophy

HARVARD UNIVERSITY, 1959–1960
Visiting professor of philosophy

FALL 1959
Philosophy 169: Ethics

SPRING 1960
Philosophy 171: Political and Social Philosophy
Philosophy 269: Seminar in Moral Feelings

MASSACHUSETTS INSTITUTE OF TECHNOLOGY, 1960–1962
Professor of philosophy

FALL 1960
Humanities 21.75: Moral Philosophy
Humanities 21.77: History of Political and Social Thought

SPRING 1961
Humanities 21.70: Philosophy of the Social Sciences
Humanities 21.78: Political and Social Philosophy

FALL 1961
Humanities 21.61: Philosophical Problems and Systems I
Humanities 21.77: History of Political and Social Thought

SPRING 1962
Humanities 20.70: Moral Philosophy
Humanities 21.78: Political and Social Philosophy

HARVARD UNIVERSITY, 1960–1995
Professor of philosophy

FALL 1962
Philosophy 171: Political and Social Philosophy

SPRING 1963
Philosophy 132: The Philosophy of Idealism
Philosophy 271: Seminar in Political and Social Philosophy: Liberty

FALL 1963
Philosophy 169: Ethics
Philosophy 171: Political and Social Philosophy

SPRING 1964
Philosophy 132: The Philosophy of Idealism
Philosophy 267: Moral Attitudes

1964–1965: GUGGENHEIM FELLOWSHIP (SABBATICAL)

FALL 1965
Philosophy 171: Political and Social Philosophy
Philosophy 269: Theory of Value

SPRING 1966
Philosophy 132: The Philosophy of Idealism
Philosophy 169: Contemporary Ethical Theory

FALL 1966
Philosophy 171: Political and Social Philosophy

SPRING 1967
Philosophy 169: Ethics
Philosophy 267: Duty and Obligation

FALL 1967
Philosophy 171: Political and Social Philosophy

SPRING 1968
Philosophy 169: Ethics
Philosophy 267: Theory of Value

FALL 1968

Philosophy 169: Ethics

Philosophy 171: Political and Social Philosophy

Economics 217: Research Seminar in Advanced Theory (with K. J. Arrows and Amartya Sen)

SPRING 1969

Philosophy 173: Moral Problems

1969–1970: FELLOWSHIP AT THE STANFORD UNIVERSITY CENTER FOR ADVANCED STUDY IN THE BEHAVIORAL SCIENCES (SABBATICAL)

FALL 1970

Philosophy 179: Ethics

SPRING 1971

Philosophy 171: Political and Social Philosophy

FALL 1971

Philosophy 171: Political and Social Philosophy

SPRING 1972

Philosophy 168: Problems in Ethical Theory

APPENDIX B

John Rawls: Publications

1942

"A Brief Inquiry into the Meaning of Sin and Faith." Undergraduate senior
thesis, Princeton University.

1948

"Review of *The Fathers of the Church: The Apostolic Fathers* by Francis X. Glimm,
Joseph M.-F. Marique, Gerald G. Walsh." *Hudson Review* 1: 274–75.
"Review of *Magic, Science, and Religion and Other Essays* by Bronislaw
Malinowski, ed. Robert Redfield." *Philosophical Review* 57: 628.

1950

"A Study in the Grounds of Ethical Knowledge: Considered with Reference to
Judgments on the Moral Worth of Character." PhD diss., Princeton
University.

1951

"Outline of a Decision Procedure for Ethics." *Philosophical Review* 60: 177–97.
"Review of *An Examination of the Place of Reason in Ethics* by Stephen E.
Toulmin." *Philosophical Review* 60: 572–80.

1955

"Two Concepts of Rules." *Philosophical Review* 64: 3–32.
"Review of *Inquiries into the Nature of Law and Morals* by Axel Hägerström." *Mind*
64: 421–22.

1957

"I. Justice as Fairness." *Journal of Philosophy* 54: 653–62.

1958

"Justice as Fairness." *Philosophical Review* 67: 164–94.

1961

"Review of *Philosophy in Mid-Century: A Survey* by Raymond Klibansky."
    Philosophical Review: 131–32.

1963

"Constitutional Liberty and the Concept of Justice." In *Nomos,* vol. 6, *Justice,*
    ed. C. J. Friedrich and John Chapman, 98–125. New York: Atherton Press.
"The Sense of Justice." *Philosophical Review* 72: 281–305.

1964

"Legal Obligation and the Duty of Fair Play." In *Law and Philosophy: A
    Symposium,* ed. Sidney Hook, 3–18. New York: New York University Press.

1965

"Review of *Social Justice* by Richard B. Brandt." *Philosophical Review* 74: 406–9.

1967

"Distributive Justice." In *Philosophy, Politics, and Society,* ed. Peter Laslett and
    W. G. Runciman, 58–82. Oxford: Blackwell.

1968

"Distributive Justice: Some Addenda." *Natural Law Forum* 13: 51–71.

1969

"The Justification of Civil Disobedience." In *Civil Disobedience: Theory and
    Practice,* ed. Hugo Bedau, 240–55. New York: Pegasus.

1971

"Justice as Reciprocity." In *John Stuart Mill: Utilitarianism, with Critical Essays,* ed.
    Samuel Gorovitz, 242–68. Indianapolis: Bobbs-Merrill.
A Theory of Justice. Cambridge, MA: Harvard University Press.

NOTES

Introduction

1. For Rawls's indirect influence on Barack Obama, see James T. Kloppen-berg, *Reading Obama: Dreams, Hope, and the American Political Tradition* (Princeton, NJ: Princeton University Press, 2011), 85–149; and Paul Schu-maker, "John Rawls, Barack Obama, and the Pluralist Political Consensus," *American Political Thought: A Journal of Ideas, Institutions, and Culture* 5 (2016): 628–57. Andreas Follesdal, "Rawls in the Nordic Countries," *European Journal of Political Theory* 1 (2012): 192 notes Finland's prime minister dis-cussing Rawls's key concept, the "difference principle." Infrequently, Rawls took part in politics himself. For his involvement in the debates about the military draft, see Katrina Forrester, "Citizenship, War, and the Origins of International Ethics in American Political Philosophy," *Historical Journal* 57 (2014): 780.
2. Charles Larmore, *Patterns of Moral Complexity* (Cambridge: Cambridge University Press, 1987), 50–55.
3. Jonathan Quong, *Liberalism without Perfection* (Oxford: Oxford University Press, 2011), 5.
4. John Rawls, *Political Liberalism* (New York: Columbia University Press, 1995), 223–27. For a valuable critical discussion of this approach, see James Bohman and Henry S. Richardson, "Liberalism, Deliberative Democracy, and 'Reasons That All Can Accept,'" *Journal of Political Philosophy* 17 (2009): 253–74.

5. For the term "high liberalism," see William Galston, "Realism in Political Theory," *European Journal of Political Theory* 9 (2010): 385.

6. For agonistic democracy, see Bonnie Honnig, *Political Theory and the Displacement of Politics* (Ithaca, NY: Cornell University Press, 1993); and Chantal Mouffe, *On the Political* (London: Routledge, 2005). For political realism, see especially the first two chapters of Raymond Geuss, *Outside Ethics* (Princeton, NJ: Princeton University Press, 2005); Bernard Williams, *In the Beginning Was the Deed* (Princeton, NJ: Princeton University Press, 2005); William A. Galston, "Two Concepts of Liberalism," *Ethics* 105 (1995): 516–34.

7. For the discussion of the distinction between respect for persons' beliefs and respect for persons, see Larmore, *Patterns of Moral Complexity*, 63. I thank Athmeya Jayaram for discussions on this topic. My framing of the problem of liberalism owes much to these discussions and his work. See, for example, Athmeya Jayaram, "Public Reason and Private Bias," PhD diss., University of California, Berkeley, 2018.

8. Michael Walzer, "A Critique of Philosophical Conversation," *Philosophical Forum* 21 (1989): 182.

9. Michael Walzer, "Philosophy and Democracy," *Political Theory* 9 (1981): 386.

10. For example, Samuel Freeman claims that "Rawls's research agenda was only mildly influenced by the contemporary discussions in moral and political philosophy" and that "though raised within the Anglo-American analytic tradition in philosophy, Rawls is mainly responding to problems set forth by the major moral and political philosophers since Hobbes." Samuel Freeman, *Rawls* (New York: Routledge, 2007), 12, 28.

11. Plato, *The Republic*, ed. G. R. F. Ferrari, trans. Tom Griffith (Cambridge: Cambridge University Press, 2008); Immanuel Kant, *Groundwork of the Metaphysic of Morals*, trans. H. J. Paton (New York: Harper Torchbooks, 1956); William D. Ross, *The Right and the Good* (Oxford: Clarendon Press, 1930).

12. John Rawls, *A Theory of Justice* (Cambridge, MA: Harvard University Press, 1971), 19–21.

13. Ibid., 302.

14. Ibid.

15. Ludwig Wittgenstein, *Philosophical Investigations*, trans. Gertrude E. M. Anscombe (Upper Saddle River, NJ: Prentice Hall, 1958), 226.

16. Allan Bloom, for instance, argued that, unlike the tradition of political philosophy, Rawls sets aside considerations about human nature. See Allan Bloom, "Justice: John Rawls vs. The Tradition of Political Philosophy," *American Political Science Review* 69 (1975): 648–62.

17. S. Aybar, J. Harlan, and W. Lee, "John Rawls: For the Record," *Harvard Review of Philosophy* 1 (Spring 1991): 44.

18. Rawls, *Theory of Justice*, 51.

19. For the argument that the transformation of the Christian concepts "agape" and *"Imago Dei"* into secular terms is also a typical story of modern democratic thought, see James T. Kloppenberg, *Toward Democracy: The Struggle for Self-Rule in European and American Thought* (Oxford: Oxford University Press, 2016), 16.

20. John Rawls, *A Brief Inquiry into the Meaning of Sin and Faith,* ed. Thomas Nagel (Cambridge, MA: Harvard University Press, 2009). To my knowledge, the thesis was discovered by Eric Gregory. See his "Before the Original Position: The Neo-Orthodox Theology of the Young John Rawls," *Journal of Religious Ethics* 35 (2007): 179–206.

21. John von Neumann and Oskar Morgenstern, *Theory of Games and Economic Behavior* (Princeton, NJ: Princeton University Press, 1944).

22. Stephen Toulmin, *An Examination of the Place of Reason in Ethics* (Cambridge: Cambridge University Press, 1950).

23. John Rawls, "Essay V" (Harvard University Archives, 1958–1962), "How Moralities May Differ," 1i, HUM 48, Box 8, Folder 1, John Rawls Faculty Papers. Rawls numbered only the recto in his handwritten notes. I marked the recto as (i) and, when applicable, the verso as (ii), here and throughout the book. So, sheet 1 might consist of both 1i and 1ii. The underlining is Rawls's—here and in the rest of the book.

24. See Rawls's remarks in "Kantian Constructivism in Moral Theory." John Rawls, *Collected Papers,* ed. Samuel Freeman (Cambridge, MA: Harvard University Press, 1999), 305–6.

25. Hilary Putnam, *Realism with a Human Face,* ed. James Conant (Cambridge, MA: Harvard University Press, 1990).

26. Kant, *Groundwork of the Metaphysic of Morals,* 96 (AK 4:429). For scholarly continuity, I will also include references to the German edition of Kant's works (known as the *Akademie* edition), both here and in the rest of the book. See *Kant's Gesammelte Schriften* (Berlin: Königlich Preußische Akademie der Wissenschaften, 1900–).

27. Ibid., 98 (AK 4:431).

28. Richard Rorty, "The Priority of Democracy to Philosophy," in *Objectivity, Relativism, and Truth* (Cambridge: Cambridge University Press, 1991), 175–96.

29. Ibid., 185, 181.

30. I make this argument in Andrius Gališanka, "Just Society as a Fair Game: John Rawls and Game Theory in the 1950s," *Journal of the History of Ideas* 78 (2017): 299–308. For a similar interpretation of Rawls's democratic vision, see P. Mackenzie Bok, "'The Latest Invasion from Britain': Young Rawls and His Community of American Ethical Theorists," *Journal of the History of Ideas* 78 (2017): 275–85. For rival interpretations of Rawls's conception of democracy, see David A. Reidy, "Results on Philosophy and Democracy: Lessons from the Archived Papers," *Journal of the History of*

Ideas 78 (2017): 265–74; and Daniele Botti, "Rawls on Dewey before the Dewey Lectures," *Journal of the History of Ideas* 78, no. 2 (2017): 287–98.

31. Rawls, *Political Liberalism,* 212–54.

1. Protestant Beginnings

1. John Rawls, "On My Religion," in *A Brief Inquiry into the Meaning of Sin and Faith,* ed. Thomas Nagel (Cambridge, MA: Harvard University Press, 2009), 261.

2. Thomas Pogge, *John Rawls: His Life and Theory of Justice* (Oxford: Oxford University Press, 2007), 5.

3. Ibid.

4. Rawls, "On My Religion," 261.

5. "John Rawls Undergraduate File" (Princeton University Mudd Manuscript Library, 1943), "John Rawls Undergraduate Transcript," Undergraduate Academic Files, Series 3, AC198.03, Box 63. Rawls's initial art and archeology major is crossed out and replaced by the philosophy major.

6. See, for example, Rawls's first article: John Rawls, "Contest on Baker Field Will Provide Acid Test for Freshmen Playing without Star Halfback," *Daily Princetonian,* October 25, 1940, 1, 3. His first article on music was the cowritten John Rawls and William P. Carton, "Budapest Quartet Presents Concert," *Daily Princetonian,* November 23, 1940, 1, 4. Rawls's articles in the *Daily Princetonian* are too numerous to list. He was announced as editor of the News section for the issue of October 30, 1940.

7. John Rawls, "Spengler's Prophecy Realized," *Nassau Literary Magazine* 95 (June 1941): 53.

8. Ibid., 46, 48.

9. Ibid., 53.

10. "John Rawls Undergraduate File," "John Rawls Undergraduate Transcript."

11. Princeton University, *Princeton University Course Catalog, 1950–51* (Princeton, NJ: Princeton University Press, 1950), 166–67.

12. John Rawls, "Christianity and the Modern World," *Nassau Literary Magazine* 100 (May 1942): 140–50.

13. Ibid., 141–43.

14. Ibid., 145.

15. Ibid., 150.

16. "Norman Malcolm Faculty File" (Princeton University Mudd Manuscript Library, n.d.), Faculty Card, 1, AC107.13, Faculty and Professional Staff files 1764–2014.

17. Ibid., Department Chair evaluation by Robert Scoon, December 15, 1941.

18. Pogge, *John Rawls,* 11.

19. John Rawls, *A Theory of Justice* (Cambridge, MA: Harvard University Press, 1971), 3.

20. Eric Gregory, "Before the Original Position: The Neo-Orthodox Theology of the Young John Rawls," *Journal of Religious Ethics* 35 (2007): 185–88; Robert M. Adams, "The Theological Ethics of the Young John Rawls and Its Background," in *A Brief Inquiry into the Meaning of Sin and Faith*, 25–32.

21. David Reidy, "Rawls's Religion and Justice as Fairness," *History of Political Thought* 31 (2010): 315–16; John Rawls, *A Brief Inquiry into the Meaning of Sin and Faith*, ed. Thomas Nagel (Cambridge, MA: Harvard University Press, 2009), 254.

22. "Various Changes Made at Trustees' Meeting," *Daily Princetonian*, June 19, 1923, 2.

23. The lectures were individually announced in the various 1929 issues of the *Daily Princetonian*. See, for example, "The Third Elective," *Daily Princetonian*, March 5, 1929, 3, where Scoon's "The Bases of Morality" is announced.

24. "Forum on Religion Starts Tomorrow," *Daily Princetonian*, December 6, 1941, 1. George F. Thomas presided over that meeting.

25. Paul J. Tillich, Theodore M. Greene, George F. Thomas, Edwin A. Aubrey, and Henry van Dusen, *The Christian Answer* (London: Nisbet, 1945).

26. Immanuel Kant, *Religion within the Limits of Reason Alone*, trans. Theodore M. Greene (Chicago: Open Court Publishing, 1934).

27. "George F. Thomas Faculty File" (Princeton University Mudd Manuscript Library, n.d.), "Religion in an Age of Secularism: The Inaugural Lecture" (October 24, 1940), AC107, Faculty and Professional Staff files 1764–2014.

28. "John Rawls, Graduate School Records" (Cornell University Library. Division of Rare and Manuscript Collections, n.d.), George F. Thomas Recommendation, 1i, 12-5-636, Box 153 c.1, Cornell University Graduate School student records.

29. Ibid., Robert Scoon's Recommendation, 1i.

30. "Total of 126 Awarded Departmental Honors 'Highest Honors' Go to 14 While 43 Receive 'High Honors' for Departmental Work—69 'Honors' Also Given to Members of the Class of '43," *Daily Princetonian*, January 30, 1943, 5.

31. Princeton University, *Princeton University Course Catalog, 1941–42* (Princeton, NJ: Princeton University Press, 1941), 148.

32. "John Rawls, Graduate School Records," "Answer 9," 1i.

33. Ibid.

34. "Norman Malcolm Faculty File," Biographical File, 1.

35. For the claim that liberal Protestantism is best characterized as relying on the experiences of the Christian community, see Gary Dorrien, *The Making of American Liberal Theology: Imagining Progressive Religion 1805–1900* (Louisville, KY: Westminster John Knox Press, 2001), xiii, 1. My argument in this chapter is indebted to his account of liberal Protestantism.

36. Thomas Albert Howard, *Religion and the Rise of Historicism* (Cambridge: Cambridge University Press, 2000), 39–40.

37. W. M. L. de Wette quoted in ibid., 38.

38. Adolf von Harnack, *Outlines of the History of Dogma,* trans. Edwin Knox Mitchell (Boston: Starr King Press, 1957), 7–8.

39. Albrecht Ritschl, *The Christian Doctrine of Justification and Reconciliation,* trans. H. R. MacIntosh and A. B. Macaulay (Edinburgh: T. & T. Clark, 1902), 197.

40. Dorrien, *American Liberal Theology,* 358.

41. Charles Briggs quoted in Dorrien, *American Liberal Theology,* 340–42.

42. Ibid., 351, 340–42, 66, 196. See also Brown's statement that theology is a "normative science, whose function it is to discriminate that which is essential and permanent in Christian faith from that which is accidental and temporary." William Adams Brown, *Christian Theology in Outline* (New York: Charles Scribner's Sons, 1919), 6.

43. Brown, *Christian Theology in Outline,* 21.

44. Ibid., 31–32, 408.

45. Theodore M. Greene, "Christianity and Its Secular Alternatives," in *The Christian Answer,* ed. Paul J. Tillich et al., 101.

46. Ibid., 104.

47. Ibid.

48. Ibid., 113.

49. Ibid., 104–5.

50. Ibid., 107.

51. Ibid., 111.

52. George F. Thomas, "Central Christian Affirmations," in *The Christian Answer,* ed. Paul J. Tillich (London: Nisbet, 1946), 180.

53. Ibid., 132 (emphasis in original).

54. Ibid., 136.

55. Ibid., 130 (emphasis in original).

56. Ibid., 180 (emphasis in original).

57. Karl Barth, "An Answer to Professor Adolf von Harnack's Open Letter," in *Revelation and Theology: An Analysis of Barth-Harnack Correspondence of 1923,* ed. H. Martin Rumscheidt (Cambridge: Cambridge University Press, 1972), 45–46 (emphasis in original).

58. Ibid., 44.

59. Ibid., 42.

60. For the most detailed account of the origins of personalism, see Jan Olof Bengtsson, *The Worldview of Personalism: Origins and Early Development* (Oxford: Oxford University Press, 2006). A shorter, more encyclopedic, summary can be found in Thomas D. Williams and Jan Olof Bengtsson, "Personalism," in *The Stanford Encyclopedia of Philosophy,* ed. Edward N. Zalta, n.d., https://plato.stanford.edu/archives/sum2016/entries/personalism/.

61. Jacques Maritain, *The Person and the Common Good,* trans. John J. Fitzgerald (New York: Charles Scribner's Sons, 1947), 2. The first chapter, from which the citation comes, is a revised version of "The Human Person and Society," a lecture given at Oxford University on May 9, 1939.

62. For this broader story, see Samuel Moyn, *Christian Human Rights* (Philadelphia: University of Philadelphia Press, 2015).

63. For this history, see Terence Renaud, "Human Rights as Radical Anthropology: Protestant Theology and Ecumenism in the Transwar Era," *Historical Journal* 60 (2017): 493–518.

64. For the Boston School personalism, see Dorrien, *American Liberal Theology,* 286–355.

65. Emil Brunner, *The Mediator: A Study of the Central Doctrine of the Christian Faith,* trans. Olive Wyon (London: Lutterworth Press, 1934), 30; Emil Brunner, *The Theology of Crisis* (New York: Charles Scribner's Sons, 1929), 31–33.

66. Tillich et al., *The Christian Answer*; George F. Thomas, *Spirit and Its Freedom* (Chapel Hill: University of North Carolina Press, 1939), 19.

67. Thomas, "Religion in an Age of Secularism," 20 (emphasis in original).

68. For earlier helpful arguments linking Rawls's political vision to personalism, see P. Mackenzie Bok, "To the Mountaintop Again: The Early Rawls and Post-Protestant Ethics in Postwar America," *Modern Intellectual History* 14 (2017): 153–85; Moyn, *Christian Human Rights,* 17.

69. Rawls, *Meaning of Sin and Faith,* 219.

70. Ibid., 114.

71. Jurgen Habermas, "The 'Good Life'—a 'Detestable Phrase': The Significance of the Young Rawls's Religious Ethics and His Political Theory," *European Journal of Philosophy* 18 (2010): 443–54.

72. Rawls, *Meaning of Sin and Faith,* 121.

73. Ibid., 207.

74. Ibid., 138.

75. Ibid., 153.

76. Ibid.

77. Ibid., 112.

78. Ibid., 205.

79. Ibid.

80. Ibid., 122.

81. Ibid., 124, 122.

82. Jeremy Waldron, "Persons, Community, and the Image of God in Rawls's Brief Inquiry," New York University Public Law and Legal Theory Working Papers, 2011, 1–23.

83. Rawls, *Meaning of Sin and Faith,* 206.

84. Thomas, *Spirit and Its Freedom,* 140.

85. Ibid., 18.

86. Rawls, *Meaning of Sin and Faith,* 198.

87. Ibid., 197.

88. Ibid., 254. Rawls lists *Babylonian Captivity of the Church* and *On Christian Liberty* as relevant works.

89. Martin Luther, *Babylonian Captivity of the Church* (N.p.: n.p., 1520), 211, https://babel.hathitrust.org/cgi/pt?id=njp.32101066133651;view =1up;seq=5; Rawls, *Meaning of Sin and Faith,* 241.

90. Rawls, *Meaning of Sin and Faith,* 241.

91. Ibid., 240.

92. Ibid., 224.

93. Ibid., 115, 117–18.

94. Ibid., 117.

95. Rawls, "Spengler's Prophecy Realized," 54.

96. Ibid., 49, 48.

97. Rawls, *Meaning of Sin and Faith,* 187.

98. Rawls, *Theory of Justice,* 130–36.

99. Thomas, *Spirit and Its Freedom,* 74.

100. Ibid., 145.

101. Ibid., 147.

102. Rawls, *Meaning of Sin and Faith,* 193; Philip Leon, *The Ethics of Power: Or the Problem of Evil* (London: George Allen & Unwin, 1935), 23–24, 38. For Leon's turn to personalism, see Philip Leon, *The Philosophy of Courage: Or the Oxford Group Way* (London: George Allen & Unwin, 1939).

103. Rawls, *Meaning of Sin and Faith,* 194.

104. Ibid., 194–95.

105. Ibid., 215.

106. Rawls, "Christianity and the Modern World," 150.

107. Ibid.

108. Ibid.

109. Rawls, *Meaning of Sin and Faith,* 233.

110. Ibid., 110.

111. Ibid.

112. Ibid., 224.

113. Ibid. Rawls also allowed that by reason we can learn that God is intelligent, powerful, and eternal, but he denied that reason can get us any further than that. Ibid.

114. Rawls, *Meaning of Sin and Faith,* 223.

115. Adams, "The Theological Ethics of the Young John Rawls," 96; Rawls, *Meaning of Sin and Faith,* 124–25, 233–34.

116. Rawls, *Meaning of Sin and Faith,* 233.

117. Ibid., 113.

118. Ibid., 254.

119. Ibid., 236.

120. Ibid., 111.

121. Ibid., 153. This reliance on experience has a different form in Rawls's "Christianity and the Modern World," which precedes Rawls's thesis by several months. In it, Rawls writes that "reason," which presumably consists of the various Christian experiences, might not "fully grasp" the "final truths." Faith might be required to grasp such truths. Even if there is a disagreement between the earlier and later positions, Rawls's earlier position gives an important role to experience. Rawls, "Christianity and the Modern World," 150.

122. Rawls, *Meaning of Sin and Faith*, 234–35.

123. Ibid.

124. Ibid.

125. This view can be seen in his choice of words: Rawls wrote that the rival view of sin "does not accord with the facts," that "examination of our actions bears him out," and that the concept of "will" is "a false representation of personal experience." See ibid., 181, 161, 220.

126. Ibid., 120.

127. See, for example, ibid., 161–62.

128. Anders Nygren, *Agape and Eros* (Philadelphia: Westminster Press, 1952).

129. Thor Hall, *Anders Nygren* (Waco, TX: Word Books Publishers, 1978), 36; Anders Nygren, *The Essence of Christianity: Two Essays,* trans. Philip S. Watson (London: Epworth Press, 1960), 12, 57. Nygren's original argument was that agape had undergone a series of changes since its inception, especially when contaminated by the Greek concept of love, eros. Because of these contaminations, it was no longer evident what the "essential meaning" of agape was, and the task of theology was to clarify it.

130. Nygren, *Agape and Eros,* 29–30.

131. Rawls, *Meaning of Sin and Faith,* 120–21.

132. Ibid., 162.

133. Ibid., 161, 114.

134. Ibid., 122–23, 206.

135. Ibid., 212, 213 (emphasis in original).

136. Ibid., 121.

137. Ibid., 244.

138. Ibid., 208.

139. Rawls, "On My Religion," 261.

140. Pogge, *John Rawls,* 12.

141. Rawls, "On My Religion," 261.

142. Ibid., 262.

143. Ibid.

144. Ibid.

145. Ibid.

146. John Rawls, "Rational Theology" (Harvard University Archives, n.d.), "Review of Paul Ramsey's Basic Christian Ethics," 1–5, Published in *Perspectives:*

A Princeton Journal of Religion, May 1951, HUM 48, Box 7, Folder 17, John
Rawls Faculty Papers.

147. "John Rawls, Graduate School Records," Robert Scoon's Recommendation, 1ii.

148. Rawls, *Meaning of Sin and Faith,* 262.

149. Bok, "To the Mountaintop Again."

150. Peter Berkowitz, "God and John Rawls," *Policy Review,* June and July 2009,
http://www.hoover.org/research/god-and-john-rawls; Keeho Kim, "From
Neo-Orthodox Theology to Rationalistic Deism: A Study of the Religious
Influences on the Development of John Rawls's Political Philosophy," PhD
diss., Baylor University, 2012, esp. 79.

151. John Rawls, "Remarks on Ethics" (Harvard University Archives, 1947), Section 6, 20, HUM 48, Box 9, Folder 15, John Rawls Faculty Papers.

152. Ibid., Section 6, 21.

153. John Rawls, "Christian Ethics: Class at Cornell" (Harvard University Archives, 1953), "Some General Remarks on Christian Ethics," 4i–5i, HUM
48, Box 8, Folder 5, John Rawls Faculty Papers.

2. Drawing on Logical Positivism

1. Rudolf Carnap, *Philosophy and Logical Syntax* (London: Kegan Paul, Trench,
Trubner, 1935); Rudolf Carnap, *Introduction to Semantics and Formalization
of Logic* (Cambridge, MA: Harvard University Press, 1942); Hans Reichenbach, *Experience and Prediction* (Chicago: University of Chicago Press, 1938);
Karl R. Popper, *The Logic of Scientific Discovery* (New York: Basic Books, 1959).

2. This popular narrative originates mainly from Peter Laslett and W. G.
Runciman's provocative assessments of the state of political philosophy
in the 1950s. See Peter Laslett and W. G. Runciman, eds., *Philosophy, Poli-
tics and Society,* 1st ed. (Oxford: Basil Blackwell, 1963 [1956]), vii–ix; Peter
Laslett and James Fishkin, eds., *Philosophy, Politics and Society,* 5th ed. (New
Haven, CT: Yale University Press, 1979), 2.

3. For an example of such criticisms, see Alfred Jules Ayer, *Language, Truth,
and Logic* (New York: Dover, 1946), 114–20.

4. James Ward Smith, A. Leland Jamison, and Nelson R. Burr, *Religion in
American Life.* Princeton Studies in American Civilization (Princeton, NJ:
Princeton University Press, 1961).

5. James Ward Smith, "Should General Theory of Value Be Abandoned?,"
Ethics 57 (1947): 274–88.

6. James Ward Smith, "Senses of Subjectivism in Value Theory," *Journal of Philosophy* 45 (1948): 393–405.

7. Norman Malcolm, "Are Necessary Propositions Really Verbal?," *Mind* 49
(1940): 189–203; Norman Malcolm, "The Nature of Entailment," *Mind* 49

(1940): 333–47; Norman Malcolm, "Defending Common Sense," *Philosophical Review* 58 (1949): 201–20.

8. "John Rawls, Graduate School Records" (Cornell University Library. Division of Rare and Manuscript Collections, n.d.), "John Rawls's Application to Cornell University," "Answer 9," 1, 12-5-636, Box 153 c.1, Cornell University Graduate School student records.

9. Wolfgang Köhler, "Value and Fact," *Journal of Philosophy* 41 (1944): 197–212.

10. "John Rawls, Graduate School Records," "John Rawls's Application to Cornell University," "Answer 9," 1.

11. For logical positivism's relationship with American pragmatism, see Alan W. Richardson, "Logical Empiricism, American Pragmatism, and the Fate of Scientific Philosophy in North America," in *Logical Empiricism in North America*, ed. Gary L. Hardcastle and Alan W. Richardson (Minneapolis: University of Minnesota Press, 2003), 1–24; and Cornelius Delaney, "Realism, Naturalism, and Pragmatism," in *The Cambridge History of Philosophy 1870–1945*, ed. Thomas Baldwin (Cambridge: Cambridge University Press, 2003), 449–60. Both Richardson and Delaney emphasize scientific aspirations of the two traditions, but it also needs to be added that in the mid to late 1930s, when logical positivism had become nonfoundational, reliance on experience became very similar in the pragmatist and logical positivist traditions, and was perceived so by the representatives of these traditions. See, for example, Herbert Feigl's "Method without Metaphysical Presuppositions," *Philosophical Studies* 5 (1954): 17–29, in which he notes that pragmatism's most valuable contribution to epistemology was its claim that one can vindicate (as opposed to validate by proof) theories only by showing their usefulness to human purposes. Ibid., 26.

12. "John Rawls, Graduate School Records," "John Rawls's Application to Cornell University," "Answer 9," 2.

13. Ibid.

14. Rudolf Carnap, *The Logical Structure of the World: Pseudoproblems in Philosophy*, trans. Rolf A. George (Berkeley: University of California Press, 1969); Moritz Schlick, "The Turning Point in Philosophy," in *Logical Positivism*, ed. Alfred Jules Ayer, trans. David Rynin (Westport, CT: Greenwood Press, 1959), 53–59.

15. Carnap, *Logical Structure of the World*, 7, 19, 102; Schlick, "Turning Point in Philosophy," 57.

16. Ayer, *Language, Truth, and Logic*, 91. For a brief yet excellent account of the development of logical positivism from foundationalism to nonfoundationalism, see Carl G. Hempel, "On the Logical Positivists' Theory of Truth," *Analysis* 2 (1935): 49–59. Also valuable are Ernest Nagel, "Impressions and Appraisals of Analytic Philosophy in Europe. I," *Journal of Philosophy* 33 (1936): 5–24; Ernest Nagel, "Impressions and Appraisals of

Analytic Philosophy in Europe. II," *Journal of Philosophy* 33 (1936): 29–53; and Thomas E. Uebel, "Anti-foundationalism and the Vienna Circle's Revolution in Philosophy," *British Journal for the Philosophy of Science* 47 (1996): 415–40. For Carnap's first turn away from foundationalism, see Rudolf Carnap, "On Protocol Sentences," *Noûs* 21 (1987 [1932]): 457–70; as well as Richard Creath, "Some Remarks on 'Protocol Sentences,'" *Noûs* 21 (1987): 471–75.

17. Karl Popper, *The Logic of Scientific Discovery* (New York: Basic Books, 1959), 111 (emphasis removed).

18. The term "basic statements" is Karl Popper's, while "protocol sentences" is Rudolf Carnap's and "protocol statements" Otto Neurath's. See Creath, "Some Remarks on 'Protocol Sentences.'"

19. Popper, *Logic of Scientific Discovery,* 84, 100–103.

20. Ibid., 102–3.

21. Ibid., 104.

22. Curt J. Ducasse, "The Nature and Function of Theory in Ethics," *Ethics* 51 (1940): 22–37; Curt J. Ducasse, *Philosophy as a Science: Its Matter and Method* (New York: O. Piest, 1941).

23. For the relationship between logical positivism and modernism, see Peter Galison, "Aufbau/Bauhaus: Logical Positivism and Architectural Modernism," *Critical Inquiry* 16 (1990): 709–52; and Peter Galison, "Constructing Modernism: The Cultural Location of the Aufbau," in *Origins of Logical Empiricism,* ed. Ronald N. Geire and Alan W. Richardson (Minneapolis: University of Minnesota Press, 1997), 17–44.

24. Jacques Rueff, *From the Physical to the Social Sciences: Introduction to a Study of Economic and Ethical Theory,* trans. Herman Green (Baltimore: Johns Hopkins University Press, 1929), 65.

25. Ducasse, "Nature and Function of Theory in Ethics," 28–29.

26. Ibid.; Ducasse, *Philosophy as a Science,* 74.

27. Ducasse, "Nature and Function of Theory in Ethics," 29.

28. John Rawls, *A Theory of Justice* (Cambridge, MA: Harvard University Press, 1971), 17–21, 46–53.

29. Ducasse, "Nature and Function of Theory in Ethics," 30.

30. Ibid., 29, 32.

31. Ibid., 35.

32. Ibid., 35–36.

33. John Rawls, "A Brief Inquiry into the Nature and Function of Ethical Theory" (Harvard University Archives, 1946), HUM 48, Box 7, Folder 3, John Rawls Faculty Papers.

34. "John Rawls, Graduate School Records," "John Rawls's Application to Cornell University," "Answer 9," 2.

35. Rawls, "Nature and Function of Ethical Theory," 5.

36. Ibid., 11.

37. Ibid., 12.
38. Ibid., 9. Rawls's reference is to *Erkenntnis* 3:2 (1932 / 1933), which contains Neurath's "Protocol Statements," 204–214, and Carnap's "On Protocol Sentences," 215–228.
39. Rawls, "Nature and Function of Ethical Theory," 61.
40. Ibid., 9.
41. Rawls added "A Brief Inquiry into" to Ducasse's title and changed "Theory in Ethics" to "Ethical Theory."
42. Rawls, "Nature and Function of Ethical Theory," 7–8.
43. Ibid., 7.
44. Ibid., 53–54, 9.
45. Ibid., 29.
46. Ibid., 20.
47. Ibid., 7.
48. Ibid., 19.
49. Ibid., 9.
50. Ibid.
51. Ibid., 20–21. In his argument, Rawls referred to Charles Morris, *Signs, Language and Behavior* (New York: Prentice Hall, 1946), 28–29.
52. Rawls, "Nature and Function of Ethical Theory," 31.
53. Ibid.
54. Rawls, *Theory of Justice,* 252.
55. Rawls, "Nature and Function of Ethical Theory," 31.
56. Ibid., 53–54.
57. Ibid., 20.
58. Ibid.
59. Ibid., 48.
60. Ibid., 38–39; Henry Sidgwick, *The Methods of Ethics,* 7th ed. (Indianapolis: Hackett, 1981), 428.
61. Rawls, "Nature and Function of Ethical Theory," 30.
62. Ibid., 25.
63. Sidgwick, *Methods of Ethics,* 77. Unlike Rawls, however, Sidgwick did not believe that one could systematize our cognitions so as to arrive at only one theory. See his discussion of rational egoism and utilitarianism as two plausible theories in ibid., 496–509.
64. Ibid., 419.
65. Ibid., 422.
66. Ibid.
67. Rawls, "Nature and Function of Ethical Theory," 29.
68. See, for example, Ludwig Wittgenstein, *The Blue and Brown Books / Preliminary Studies for the "Philosophical Investigations"* (New York: Harper Torchbooks, 1965), 17–18.
69. Rawls, "Nature and Function of Ethical Theory," 56.

70. Ibid., 56. Rawls also describes semantic meaning as the "linguistic function" of a word. Ibid., 25.

71. Rawls, "Nature and Function of Ethical Theory," 56.

72. Ibid., 29–30.

73. John Stuart Mill, *On Liberty, Utilitarianism, and Other Essays,* ed. Mark Philip and Frederick Rosen (Oxford: Oxford University Press, 2015), 121.

74. Sidgwick, *Methods of Ethics,* 411.

75. Rawls, "Nature and Function of Ethical Theory," 35–36.

76. Sidgwick, *Methods of Ethics,* 382.

77. Rawls, "Nature and Function of Ethical Theory," 43.

78. Ibid.

79. Ibid., 53–54; Ducasse, "Nature and Function of Theory in Ethics," 36.

80. Rawls, "Nature and Function of Ethical Theory," 6–7.

3. Engagement with Wittgensteinian Philosophy

1. "John Rawls Graduate Student File" (Princeton University Mudd Manuscript Library, 1950), Letter from the Dean of Graduate School, August 30, 1947, 1i, AC105.03, Graduate Alumni Records 1930–1959, Box 120. The letter states that Rawls "will return to Princeton to take his doctorate after a year at Cornell."

2. Robert Scoon's letter of recommendation, in "John Rawls, Graduate School Records" (Cornell University Library. Division of Rare and Manuscript Collections, n.d.), 12-5-636, Box 153 c.1, Cornell University Graduate School student records.

3. Arthur E. Murphy, "Can Speculative Philosophy Be Defended?," *Philosophical Review* 52 (1943): 135–43.

4. Ernest Nagel, "Review of Arthur E. Murphy's *The Uses of Reason*," *Journal of Philosophy* 41 (1944): 666.

5. It is unclear whether this essay still exists.

6. Arthur E. Murphy, *The Uses of Reason* (New York: Macmillan, 1943), 32.

7. Ibid.

8. Max Black, "Induction—Seminar (1947–48)" (Cornell University Library. Division of Rare and Manuscript Collections, 1947), November 11, 1947 Seminar Notes by John Rawls, 2, 14-21-2466, Box 1, Max Black Papers.

9. Ibid., November 11, 1947 Seminar Notes by John Rawls, 3.

10. Karl Popper, "Replies to My Critics," in *The Philosophy of Karl Popper,* ed. Paul Arthur Schilpp (La Salle, IL: Open Court, 1974), 1016.

11. John Rawls, "Remarks on Ethics" (Harvard University Archives, 1947), HUM 48, Box 9, Folder 15, John Rawls Faculty Papers.

12. Ibid., Section 8, 14.

13. Ibid., Section 4, 19–20.

14. Ibid., Section 4, 20.
15. Ibid.
16. Ibid., Section 4, 20–21. Cf. John Rawls, "A Study in the Grounds of Ethical Knowledge: Considered with Reference to Judgments on the Moral Worth of Character," PhD diss., Princeton University, 1950, 276.
17. Rawls, "Grounds of Ethical Knowledge," 45.
18. Rawls, "Remarks on Ethics," Section 5, 18. For Rawls's quick dismissal of the American legal realists Karl Llewellyn's and Jerome Frank's view that divergence of moral opinions is insurmountable, see ibid., Section 5, 11.
19. For Rawls's remarks that ethical theory is an empirical theory, see Rawls, "Remarks on Ethics," Section 4, 2, and Section 5, 1.
20. Ibid., Section 5, 20.
21. Ibid., Section 5, 21.
22. Ibid., Section 8, 12.
23. Ibid., Section 5, 18.
24. Ibid., Section 5, 20.
25. Rawls, "Grounds of Ethical Knowledge," 60, 66.
26. Ibid., 45–49.
27. Ibid., 49–52, 52–57, 57–60.
28. Rawls, "Remarks on Ethics," Section 2, 1.
29. Ibid., Section 1, 1, Section 7, 11, and Section 8, 21.
30. Ibid., Section 8, 21.
31. For the concept of "meaning holism," see Mark Bevir, *The Logic of the History of Ideas* (Cambridge: Cambridge University Press, 1999), 89–96, 106–16.
32. See in particular the first two chapters of Raymond Geuss's *Outside Ethics* (Princeton, NJ: Princeton University Press, 2005).
33. John Rawls, *Political Liberalism,* expanded ed. (New York: Columbia University Press, 2005), 56–57.
34. Rawls, "Remarks on Ethics," Section 8, 12.
35. Charles L. Stevenson, *Ethics and Language* (New Haven, CT: Yale University Press, 1944), 31.
36. Rawls, "Remarks on Ethics," Section 8, 24.
37. Ibid.
38. Ibid., Section 8, 22.
39. Ibid., Section 8, 23.
40. Ibid., Section 8, 24.
41. Ibid., Section 3, 7.
42. Rawls, *Political Liberalism,* 35–40, 133–72.
43. Ibid., 133–72, esp. 138.
44. Rawls, "Grounds of Ethical Knowledge," 110.
45. Ibid., 120.

46. Rawls, "Remarks on Ethics," Section 5, 16.

47. Ibid., Section 5, 17.

48. Ibid., Section 4, 3, 4, 12, 15.

49. Ibid., Section 4, 6–11.

50. Ibid., Section 5, 2.

51. Ibid., Section 5, 1.

52. In his description of the principles, Rawls refers to Kant, but his actual defense of these principles relies on linguistic philosophy's notion of absurdity. Ibid., Section 5, 14–15.

53. Ibid., Section 5, 1.

54. Ibid., Section 8, 18; Samuel Butler, *Erewhon, or, Over the Range* (London: Ballantyne Press, 1880).

55. Butler, *Erewhon*, 71–83.

56. Rawls, "Remarks on Ethics," Section 8, 18.

57. Ibid., Section 8, 19.

58. Ibid., Section 5, 7.

59. John Rawls, "A Brief Inquiry into the Nature and Function of Ethical Theory" (Harvard University Archives, 1946), 20, HUM 48, Box 7, Folder 3, John Rawls Faculty Papers.

60. Rawls, "Remarks on Ethics," Section 8, 10–11.

61. Ibid., Section 4, 18–19.

62. John Rawls, "Theory of Goods" (Harvard University Archives, 1952), "Considerations of Some Objections," 1i, HUM 48, Box 8, Folder 2, John Rawls Faculty Papers.

63. Rawls, "Grounds of Ethical Knowledge," 47–48, 277–78.

64. Ibid., 278.

65. John Rawls, "Outline of a Decision Procedure for Ethics," in *John Rawls: Collected Papers,* ed. Samuel Freeman (Cambridge, MA: Harvard University Press, 1999), 4; Rawls, "Grounds of Ethical Knowledge," 43, 36.

66. Rawls, "Grounds of Ethical Knowledge," 49.

67. Ibid., 48–49.

68. Ibid., 278.

69. Rawls, "Theory of Goods," Lecture 7, 7i.

70. Rawls, "Grounds of Ethical Knowledge," 72.

71. Ibid., 73. This view sharply differs from contemporary conceptions of ethical principles that trace their origins to Rawls's work. See, for example, Rawls's student Onora O'Neill's *Toward Justice and Virtue: A Constructive Account of Practical Reasoning* (Cambridge: Cambridge University Press, 1996), 77–90, which defends a more open-ended and nonmechanistic account of ethical principles.

72. Rawls, "Grounds of Ethical Knowledge," 75.

73. Ibid., 77.

74. Ibid., 76f.

75. Ibid., 77.

76. Rawls, "Grounds of Ethical Knowledge," 78. Carl Hempel, "A Purely Syntactical Definition of Confirmation," *Journal of Symbolic Logic* 8 (1943): 122–43; Carl Hempel, "Studies in the Logic of Confirmation," *Mind* 54 (1945): 1–26; Rudolf Carnap, "On Inductive Logic," *Philosophy of Science* 12 (1945): 72–97; Rudolf Carnap, "The Two Concepts of Probability," *Philosophy and Phenomenological Research* 5 (1945): 513–32. The reference to these works is found in Rawls, "Grounds of Ethical Knowledge," 73f.

4. The Fair Games of Autonomous Persons

1. Princeton University, *Princeton University Course Catalog, 1941–42* (Princeton, NJ: Princeton University Press, 1941), 148.
2. Henry Sidgwick, *The Methods of Ethics,* 7th ed. (Indianapolis: Hackett, 1981).
3. Walter T. Stace in his letter of recommendation. "John Rawls, Graduate School Records" (Cornell University Library. Division of Rare and Manuscript Collections, n.d.), 12-5-636, Box 153 c.1, Cornell University Graduate School student records.
4. J. B. Schneewind, "Sixty Years of Philosophy in a Life," in *Portraits of American Philosophy,* ed. Steven M. Cahn (New York: Rowman and Littlefield, 2013), 30.
5. John von Neumann and Oskar Morgenstern, *Theory of Games and Economic Behavior* (Princeton, NJ: Princeton University Press, 1944).
6. John Rawls, "Remarks on Ethics" (Harvard University Archives, 1947), Section 6, 1, HUM 48, Box 9, Folder 15, John Rawls Faculty Papers.
7. Ibid., Section 6, 11.
8. Ibid., Section 6, 2.
9. Ibid., Section 6, 13.
10. Ibid., Section 6, 4, 8.
11. Ibid., Section 6, 3.
12. Ibid., Section 6, 14.
13. Ibid., Section 6, 18.
14. Ibid., Section 7, 12.
15. Ibid., Section 8, 6.
16. Ibid., Section 8, 7.
17. Ibid.
18. Ibid.
19. Ibid., Section 6, 14.
20. Ibid.
21. Ibid.
22. Ibid., Section 6, 9.
23. Ibid., Section 6, 10.

24. In the 1951–1952 academic year, Rawls studied Stephen Toulmin, *An Examination of the Place of Reason in Ethics* (Cambridge: Cambridge University Press, 1950). Accordingly, his writings began to be marked by an analogy between reasoning and games—an analogy that is not present in John Rawls, "Delimitation of the Problem of Justice" (Harvard University Archives, [1950]), HUM 48, Box 9, Folder 13, John Rawls Faculty Papers.

25. Rawls, "Delimitation of the Problem of Justice," 1.

26. Ibid., 5.

27. Ibid., 2–4.

28. Ibid., 11.

29. Ibid., 49–53.

30. Von Neumann and Morgenstern, *Theory of Games and Economic Behavior,* 9.

31. Ibid., 43.

32. Ibid., 17–30.

33. Ibid., 31.

34. John Rawls, "[1949–52] King Street, Princeton" (Harvard University Archives, 1949–1952), "Society as a Game," 4i, HUM 48, Box 8, Folder 3, John Rawls Faculty Papers.

35. Ibid., "On the Function of Government," 1i.

36. Frank H. Knight, *The Ethics of Competition and Other Essays* (New York: Harper & Brothers, 1935). Pogge writes that Rawls used Knight's ideas for a different purpose in 1952–1953, but it is conceivable that other parts of the book influenced Rawls earlier. Thomas Pogge, *John Rawls: His Life and Theory of Justice* (Oxford: Oxford University Press, 2007), 16–17. I thank David M. Levy for access to Rawls's annotated copy of Knight's *Ethics*.

37. Knight, *Ethics of Competition,* 297.

38. Rawls, "[1949–52] King Street, Princeton," "What Would Happen If Everybody Did It?," 2.

39. John Rawls, *A Theory of Justice* (Cambridge, MA: Harvard University Press, 1971), 12, 51.

40. Rawls, "[1949–52] King Street, Princeton," "Society as a Game," 12i.

41. Rawls, "Delimitation of the Problem of Justice," 38.

42. Ibid., 39.

43. Rawls, "[1949–52] King Street, Princeton," "Society as a Game," 16i.

44. Rawls did not consider whether an economic system can shape the individual's conception of the good. Compare with his *Theory of Justice,* 258–265; and Knight, *Ethics of Competition,* 52–53.

45. John Rawls, "Theory of Justice [1951–52]" (Harvard University Archives, c. 1951–1952), "On Justice," 2, HUM 48, Box 7, Folder 14, John Rawls Faculty Papers.

46. Ibid., 10i.

47. Ibid., 11i.

48. Ibid., 13i.

49. Rawls, "[1949–52] King Street, Princeton," "On the Function of Government," 2i.

50. Ibid., "Society as a Game," 14i.

51. Rawls, "Oxford Notes, Spring 1953," "Justice (Just) and Fairness (Fair): Contrasting Uses," 1i.

52. John Rawls, "Justice as Fairness, Cornell Seminar 1953 Fall" (Harvard University Archives, 1953), "Reasoning and Games," 2, HUM 48, Box 7, Folder 11, John Rawls Faculty Papers.

53. Ibid.

54. Knight likely influenced this formulation of the problem, as he too compared discussion to games that are conducted by rules. Knight, *Ethics of Competition,* 352. Rawls departed from Knight in formulating the content of the thought experiment, however.

55. John Rawls, "On Explication Oxford" (Harvard University Archives, 1952–1953), 11, HUM 48, Box 7, Folder 18, John Rawls Faculty Papers.

56. Ibid., 68.

57. Rawls's 1951–1952 lectures also draw analogies between reasoning and games when these apply to choices of one's good. John Rawls, "Theory of Goods" (Harvard University Archives, [1952]), "On Prudential Reasoning," 1i–2i, HUM 48, Box 8, Folder 2, John Rawls Faculty Papers.

58. John Rawls, "Oxford Notes, Spring 1953" (Harvard University Archives, 1953), "Are the Principles Strong Enough?," 10, HUM 48, Box 7, Folder 10, John Rawls Faculty Papers.

59. Rawls, *Theory of Justice,* 12, 19.

60. The term "pure case" appears in Rawls, "Oxford Notes, Spring 1953," "Justice," 4.

61. Ibid., 4, 2.

62. Ibid.

63. Rawls, "Oxford Notes, Spring 1953," "Justice," 2; Rawls, "Theory of Justice [1951–52]," "On the Application of Our Criterion to Concrete Cases," 2.

64. Rawls, "Theory of Justice [1951–52]," "On the Application of Our Criterion to Concrete Cases," 1.

65. Ibid.

66. Ibid., 3.

67. According to Pogge, the idea was inspired by Knight. Pogge, *Rawls,* 15–16. Knight imposed conditions on the process by which one can legitimately arrive at an agreement. Knight, *Ethics of Competition,* 345.

68. Rawls, "On Explication Oxford," 49.

69. Ibid., 50.

70. Rawls, "Oxford Notes, Spring 1953," "Are the Principles Strong Enough?," 17.

71. S. Aybar, J. Harlan, and W. Lee, "John Rawls: For the Record," *Harvard Review of Philosophy* 1 (Spring 1991): 40, 39.

72. John Rawls, "Justice as Fairness," in *John Rawls: Collected Papers,* ed. Samuel Freeman (Cambridge, MA: Harvard University Press, 1999), 48.

5. Practices of Reasoning

1. William Frankena, "Main Trends in Recent Philosophy: Moral Philosophy at Mid-Century," *Philosophical Review* 60 (1951): 44–55.

2. For key arguments in the "good reasons" approach, see Stephen Toulmin, *An Examination of the Place of Reason in Ethics* (Cambridge: Cambridge University Press, 1950); Kurt Baier, "Good Reasons," *Philosophical Studies* 4 (1953): 1–15; Kurt Baier, "Proving a Moral Judgment," *Philosophical Studies* 4 (1953): 33–44; Kai Nielsen, "The 'Good Reasons Approach' and 'Ontological Justifications' of Morality," *Philosophical Quarterly* 9 (1959): 116–30.

3. Thomas Pogge, *John Rawls: His Life and Theory of Justice* (Oxford: Oxford University Press, 2007), 16.

4. Stanley Cavell, *The Claim of Reason: Wittgenstein, Skepticism, Morality, and Tragedy* (Oxford: Oxford University Press, 1999). See in particular Stuart Hampshire, *Justice Is Conflict* (Princeton, NJ: Princeton University Press, 2001).

5. I discuss this emphasis on commonality among Wittgensteinians in the 1950s in "Wittgenstein and Mid-20th Century Political Philosophy: Naturalist Paths from Facts to Values," in *Wittgenstein and Normative Inquiry,* ed. Mark Bevir and Andrius Gališanka (Leiden: Brill Press, 2016), 152–73.

6. John Rawls, "Review of Stephen Toulmin's *An Examination of the Place of Reason in Ethics,*" *Philosophical Review* 60 (1951): 572.

7. Ludwig Wittgenstein, *Philosophical Investigations,* trans. Gertrude E. M. Anscombe (Upper Saddle River, NJ: Prentice Hall, 1958), §§355, 7.

8. Ibid., §§355, 345.

9. Hence Wittgenstein's argument against the possibility of a private language, where criteria for correct application of a word are known to the user of that language alone. See ibid., §§269–75.

10. Ibid., §241 (emphasis in original).

11. Ibid., §23 (emphasis in original).

12. Ibid., §§7, 17 (emphasis in original).

13. Ibid., §§18, 23.

14. Toulmin, *Reason in Ethics*, 38.

15. Ibid., 81.

16. Ibid., 137.

17. Ibid., 148.

18. Ibid., 148–52.

19. Ibid., 202–3.
20. Ibid., 163.
21. Ibid., 203.
22. Ibid., 204–12.
23. Ibid., 208.
24. Ibid., 161 (emphasis in original).
25. Nielsen, "Good Reasons Approach," 117, 121.
26. Baier, "Good Reasons."
27. James Opie Urmson, "On Grading," *Mind* 59 (1950): 169.
28. Stuart Hampshire, "Fallacies in Moral Philosophy," *Mind* 58 (1949): 478 (emphasis in original).
29. Ibid., 481.
30. Herbert L. A. Hart, "The Ascription of Responsibilities and Rights," *Proceedings of the Aristotelian Society* 49 (1948): 174, 181.
31. Princeton University, *Princeton University Course Catalog, 1950–51* (Princeton, NJ: Princeton University Press, 1950), 259.
32. John Rawls, "On Values" (Harvard University Archives, [1952]), HUM 48, Box 7, Folder 9, John Rawls Faculty Papers; John Rawls, "Ethics and Its Reasoning" (Harvard University Archives, [1952]), HUM 48, Box 8, Folder 4, John Rawls Faculty Papers; John Rawls, "Diseases of Ethical Reasoning" (Harvard University Archives, [1952]), HUM 48, Box 7, Folder 14, John Rawls Faculty Papers.
33. John Rawls, "On Explication Oxford" (Harvard University Archives, 1952–1953), HUM 48, Box 7, Folder 18, John Rawls Faculty Papers; John Rawls, "Oxford Notes, Spring 1953" (Harvard University Archives, 1953), HUM 48, Box 7, Folder 10, John Rawls Faculty Papers.
34. Rawls, "Ethics and Its Reasoning," Lecture 2, 1.
35. Rawls, "On Explication Oxford," 45.
36. John Rawls, "Christian Ethics: Class at Cornell" (Harvard University Archives, 1953), "Some General Remarks on Christian Ethics: (Lectures 1 and 2)," 1, HUM 48, Box 8, Folder 5, John Rawls Faculty Papers.
37. Ibid.
38. Rawls, "Ethics and Its Reasoning," Lecture 3, 1.
39. Rawls, "On Explication Oxford," 77.
40. Rawls, "Ethics and Its Reasoning," Lecture 1, 3.
41. Rawls, "On Explication Oxford," 64.
42. Rawls, "Review of Toulmin," 574.
43. For a description of the "reasonable person," see John Rawls, "Remarks on Ethics" (Harvard University Archives, 1947), Section 5, 18–22, HUM 48, Box 9, Folder 15, John Rawls Faculty Papers. For considered judgments, see John Rawls, "A Study in the Grounds of Ethical Knowledge: Considered with Reference to Judgments on the Moral Worth of Character," PhD diss., Princeton University, 1950, 47–60.

44. Rawls, "Review of Toulmin," 574.

45. Ibid.

46. Rawls, "On Explication Oxford," 64.

47. Rawls, "Review of Toulmin," 574–75.

48. Rawls, "Ethics and Its Reasoning," Lecture 3, 15.

49. Rawls, "Christian Ethics: Class at Cornell," 15.

50. Ibid.

51. Ibid., 21.

52. Toulmin, *Reason in Ethics,* 137.

53. Rawls, "Christian Ethics: Class at Cornell," Some Questions, 4i.

54. Rawls, "Oxford Notes, Spring 1953," 13.

55. Ibid.

56. Rawls, "Christian Ethics: Class at Cornell," 20.

57. Rawls, "Oxford Notes, Spring 1953," "The Fundamental Problem of Ethical Theory: Are Principles Strong Enough?," 1.

58. John Rawls, "Justice as Fairness, Cornell Seminar 1953 Fall" (Harvard University Archives, 1953), 15, HUM 48, Box 7, Folder 11, John Rawls Faculty Papers.

59. John Rawls, *Political Liberalism,* expanded ed. (New York: Columbia University Press, 2005), 144–50.

60. John Rawls, "Delimitation of the Problem of Justice" (Harvard University Archives, [1950]), 1–4, HUM 48, Box 9, Folder 13, John Rawls Faculty Papers; Rawls, "Justice as Fairness, Cornell Seminar 1953 Fall," 3.

61. Rawls, "Diseases of Ethical Reasoning," 34.

62. Ibid., 38.

63. Toulmin, *Reason in Ethics,* 146.

64. John Rawls, "Two Concepts of Rules," *Philosophical Review* 64 (1955): 3–32.

65. Rawls, "Diseases of Ethical Reasoning," 6.

66. Ibid.

67. Ibid., 27.

68. John Rawls, *A Theory of Justice* (Cambridge, MA: Harvard University Press, 1971), 10–11.

69. Rawls, "Review of Toulmin," 577–78.

70. Ibid., 578 (emphasis in original).

71. Rawls, "Ethics and Its Reasoning," "Meaning of Good," 1. Rawls's criticism of Toulmin is not entirely fair. See Toulmin, *Reason in Ethics,* 48, where Toulmin acknowledges that principles are not expected to be helpful in every situation that requires judgment.

72. Rawls, "Diseases of Ethical Reasoning," "On the Application of Our Criterion in Concrete Cases," 5.

73. Rawls, "On Explication Oxford," "The Fundamental Problem of Ethical Theory: Are Principles Strong Enough?," 2.

74. Rawls, "On Values," 15.
75. Rawls, "Diseases of Ethical Reasoning," 2.
76. Rawls, "On Explication Oxford," "The Fundamental Problem of Ethical Theory: Are Principles Strong Enough?," 2.
77. Rawls, "Diseases of Ethical Reasoning," 2.
78. Ibid., "On the Application of Our Criterion in Concrete Cases," 1.
79. Rawls, "Justice as Fairness, Cornell Seminar 1953 Fall," 22.
80. Ibid., 22, 1.
81. Rawls, "Diseases of Ethical Reasoning," 5.

6. Natural Bases of Justice

1. Stanley Cavell, *The Claim of Reason: Wittgenstein, Skepticism, Morality, and Tragedy* (Oxford: Oxford University Press, 1999), 207.
2. John Rawls, "Wittgenstein Investigation, Lexicon" (Harvard University Archives, 1953), HUM 48, Box 60, John Rawls Faculty Papers; John Rawls, "Wittgenstein Criteria" (Harvard University Archives, 1953), HUM 48, Box 9, Folder 8, John Rawls Faculty Papers; John Rawls, "Wittgenstein Investigations" (Harvard University Archives, 1953), HUM 48, Box 9, Folder 2, John Rawls Faculty Papers.
3. John Rawls, "Moral Feeling I (1958)" (Harvard University Archives, 1958), Topic VII, 1i, HUM 48, Box 34, Folder 19, John Rawls Faculty Papers.
4. John Rawls, "Twofold Basis of Justice" (Harvard University Archives, [1958]), 1i, HUM 48, Box 9, Folder 1, John Rawls Faculty Papers.
5. Ibid.
6. John Rawls, "Moral Psychology, 1964–65" (Harvard University Archives, 1964), Seminar V, 3i, HUM 48, Box 35, Folder 6, John Rawls Faculty Papers.
7. John Rawls, *A Theory of Justice* (Cambridge, MA: Harvard University Press, 1971), 51, 479–90.
8. Cavell, *Claim of Reason,* 173–74.
9. Ludwig Wittgenstein, *Philosophical Investigations,* trans. Gertrude E. M. Anscombe (Upper Saddle River, NJ: Prentice Hall, 1958), §30.
10. Cavell, *Claim of Reason,* 93.
11. Ibid., 88 (emphasis in original).
12. Ibid., 90 (emphasis mine).
13. Wittgenstein, *Philosophical Investigations,* 230. See also Ludwig Wittgenstein, *On Certainty,* ed. G. E. M. Anscombe and G. H. von Wright, trans. Denis Paul and G. E. M. Anscombe (New York: Harper Torchbooks, 1969), §63: "If we imagine the facts otherwise than as they are, certain language-games lose some of their importance, while others become important."

14. See also P. M. S. Hacker, *Wittgenstein's Place in Twentieth Century Analytic Philosophy* (Oxford: Blackwell Publishers, 1996), 219; and Lynn Rudder Baker, "On the Very Idea of a Form of Life," *Inquiry* 27 (1984): 277–89.

15. I discuss these appropriations of Wittgenstein in Andrius Gališanka, "Wittgenstein and Mid-20th Century Political Philosophy: Naturalist Paths from Facts to Values," in *Wittgenstein and Normative Inquiry*, ed. Mark Bevir and Andrius Gališanka (Leiden: Brill Press, 2016), 152–73.

16. Rawls, "Moral Feeling I (1958)," Topic VII, 1i.

17. Ibid., "Procedure," 1i.

18. Gališanka, "Paths from Facts to Values."

19. John Niemeyer Findlay, "The Justification of Attitudes," *Mind* 63 (1954): 145–61; Philippa Foot, "When Is a Principle a Moral Principle?," *Proceedings of the Aristotelian Society*, Supp. Vol. 28 (1954): 95–134.

20. Philippa Foot, "Moral Beliefs," *Proceedings of the Aristotelian Society* 59 (1958–1959: 83–104.

21. G. E. M. Anscombe, *Intention* (Cambridge, MA: Harvard University Press, 2000 [1957]), 68.

22. Ibid., 71.

23. Ibid., 91.

24. Rawls, "Moral Feeling I (1958)," "Topic IX: Compassion," 5i.

25. For an analysis of Wittgenstein's discussion of pain and recognition of a person as a person, see Joel Isaac, "Pain, Analytical Philosophy, and American Intellectual History," in *The Worlds of American Intellectual History*, ed. Joel Isaac, James T. Kloppenberg, Michael O'Brien, and Jennifer Ratner-Rosenhagen. (New York: Oxford University Press, 2016), 202–17.

26. John Rawls, "Justice as Fairness," in *John Rawls: Collected Papers*, ed. Samuel Freeman (Cambridge, MA: Harvard University Press, 1999), 62f.

27. Wittgenstein, *Philosophical Investigations*, §287 and §§281–286.

28. Rawls, "Moral Feeling I (1958)," Topic III, 4ii.

29. John Rawls, "Fellow Feeling and Sympathy" (Harvard University Archives, [1960]), "Remarks re Sympathy, Pity, and Compassion," 1i, HUM 48, Box 34, Folder 15, John Rawls Faculty Papers.

30. Ibid.

31. Rawls, *Theory of Justice*, 494–95.

32. Rawls, "Twofold Basis of Justice," 10i.

33. Ibid., 12i.

34. John Rawls, "Essay V" (Harvard University Archives, 1958–1962), 1i, HUM 48, Box 8, Folder 1, John Rawls Faculty Papers. See also Rawls's remarks on Jean Piaget in Rawls, "Moral Feeling I (1958)," "Topic IX: Compassion," 5i.

35. Rawls, "Essay V," "Notes on the Growth of Morality," 1i.

36. Rawls, "Moral Feeling I (1958)," "Procedure," 3i; "Topic II," 1ii–2ii; "Topic III," 4ii.

37. John Rawls, "Moral Feelings, 1960" (Harvard University Archives, 1960), "Seminar III: Concept of Moral Attitude + Classification of Moral Feelings," 4ii, HUM 48, Box 35, Folder 1, John Rawls Faculty Papers.

38. Rawls, "Moral Feeling I (1958)," "Topic IX," 1i.

39. Rawls, "Moral Feelings, 1960," "Topic VI," 1i.

40. Rawls, "Moral Psychology, 1964–65," "Seminar IV—Excellence and Shame (I)," 2ii; Rawls, "Moral Feelings, 1960," "Seminar V—Remorse," 3ii.

41. Jean Piaget, *The Moral Judgment of the Child,* trans. Marjorie Gabain (London: Kegan Paul, Trench, Trubner, 1932), 57.

42. Piaget, *Moral Judgment,* 194.

43. Rawls, "Moral Feelings, 1960," "Topic IX: Compassion," 5i.

44. Ibid., "Seminar VI—Authority Guilt," 4ii.

45. John Rawls, "The Sense of Justice" (Harvard University Press, 1961), "Moral Feelings and Natural Attitudes," 23, HUM 48, Box 36, Folder 7, John Rawls Faculty Papers.

46. Rawls, "Moral Feelings, 1960," "Topic VI," 9i. The manuscript says "within," but the context requires "without."

47. Rawls, "Essay V," "The Natural Response + Morality," 2i–2ii.

48. Rawls, *Theory of Justice,* 494–95.

49. Rawls, "Moral Feelings, 1960," "Topic VI," 9i; Rawls, "Moral Feeling I (1958)," "Procedure," 2i.

50. Rawls, "Moral Feelings, 1960," "Seminar I: The Point + Procedure in the Study of Moral Feelings," 3ii.

51. Ibid., "Topic VI," 9i; Rawls, "Moral Feeling I (1958)," "Procedure," 2i.

52. Rawls, *Theory of Justice,* 489.

53. Rawls, "Moral Feeling I (1958)," "Summary," 3ii.

54. Rawls, "Moral Feelings, 1960," "Topic VII: Concept of Morality," 2ii.

55. Rawls, "Moral Feeling I (1958)," "Topic IX," 3i.

56. Ibid., "Topic IX," 3i.

57. Ibid.

58. Ibid., "Topic IX," 2i; Richard M. Hare, *The Language of Morals* (Oxford: Clarendon Press, 1952).

59. Rawls, "Moral Feeling I (1958)," "Summary," 3i.

60. Ibid., "Topic IX," 2i.

61. Ibid., "Summary," 4ii.

62. Rawls, "Twofold Basis of Justice," 2i.

63. Rawls, "Essay V," "How Moralities May Differ," 1i.

64. Wittgenstein, *Philosophical Investigations,* §66.

65. Rawls, "Essay V," "How Moralities May Differ," 1i.

66. Ibid.

67. Ibid., "Arguments for Morality Part of Seeing Persons as Persons," 1i.

68. John Rawls, "Problems of Akrasia and Moral Feelings" (Harvard University Archives, 1958), "Concept of Morality and Conditions of Considered Judgments," 3i, HUM 48, Box 34, Folder 18, John Rawls Faculty Papers.

69. Rawls, "Fellow Feeling and Sympathy," "Necessary Distinction in Regard to Sympathy," 2ii.

70. Ibid., "Questions re Altruism, Reason and Sympathy," 1i.

71. Ibid., "Necessary Distinction in Regard to Sympathy," 2ii.

72. Rawls, "Twofold Basis of Justice," 1i.

73. John Rawls, "Equality XIX–XXI" (Harvard University Archives, n.d.), 28i, HUM 48, Box 35, Folder 16, John Rawls Faculty Papers.

74. Rawls, "Problems of Akrasia and Moral Feelings," "Concept of Morality and Conditions of Considered Judgments," 3i.

75. John Rawls, "Philosophy 171, Class Lectures" (Harvard University Archives, 1963), Lecture V, 1, HUM 48, Box 27, Folder 5.

76. John Rawls, *Political Liberalism,* expanded ed. (New York: Columbia University Press, 2005), xxxvii.

77. Rawls, *Theory of Justice,* 44, 489.

78. Rawls, "Moral Psychology, 1964–65," "Introductory Remarks," 2ii.

79. Ibid., "Seminar II," 4i.

80. Rawls, *Theory of Justice,* 501. See also ibid., 438.

81. John Rawls, "Philosophy 169. Part I. Lectures I–IV" (Harvard University Archives, 1970), "Chapter III: The Original Agreement," 77, HUM 48, Box 5, Folder 2, John Rawls Faculty Papers.

82. Ibid., 78.

83. Ibid., 79.

84. John Rawls, "A Theory of Justice, Second Version, Chapters V–IX" (Harvard University Archives, 1969), "Chapter VIII: The Sense of Justice," 229, HUM 48, Box 10, Folder 11, John Rawls Faculty Papers.

85. Ibid., 228.

86. Ibid., 229.

87. Ibid.

88. Rawls, *Theory of Justice,* 496, 499–501.

7. No Shortcuts in Philosophy

1. Hilary Putnam, *Realism with a Human Face,* ed. James Conant (Cambridge, MA: Harvard University Press, 1990), 268.

2. John Rawls, "Autobiographical Notes" (Harvard University Archives, 1993), 21, HUM 48, Box 42, Folder 12, John Rawls Faculty Papers; John Rawls, *A Theory of Justice* (Cambridge, MA: Harvard University Press, 1971), xi. For

Rawls's annotations of Quine's *From a Logical Point of View* (1953), *Word and Object* (1960), *The Ways of Paradox and Other Essays* (1966), and *Ontological Relativity and Other Essays* (1969), see Books from the Personal Library of John Rawls, Harvard University Archives, HUM 48.1, Box 6. On Rawls's reflections of Burt Dreben and Dreben's influence on him, see John Rawls, "Afterword: A Reminiscence," in *Future Pasts: The Analytic Tradition in Twentieth Century Philosophy,* ed. Juliet Floyd and Sanford Shieh (Oxford: Oxford University Press, 2001), 417–30, especially 423, where Rawls states, "I can't think of any of my basic ideas that I got from Burt, yet I am convinced that replying to his criticisms always enormously improved the clarity and the organization of my thought." For Rawls's collaboration with Dreben, see ibid., 424.

3. Willard V. O. Quine, "Homage to Carnap," in *Dear Carnap, Dear Van,* ed. Richard Creath (Berkeley: University of California Press, 1990), 463–64.

4. Ibid.

5. Willard V. O. Quine, *Word and Object* (Cambridge, MA: MIT Press, 1960), 1.

6. See, for instance, ibid., 22.

7. Willard V. O. Quine, "Two Dogmas of Empiricism," *Philosophical Review* 60 (1951): 39.

8. W. V. Quine, "Two Dogmas in Retrospect," *Canadian Journal of Philosophy* 21 (1991): 272.

9. Willard V. O. Quine, "Epistemology Naturalized," in *Ontological Relativity and Other Essays* (New York: Columbia Press, 1969), 79.

10. Ibid., 85–86.

11. Ibid., 86–87.

12. Thomas S. Kuhn, *The Structure of Scientific Revolutions* (Chicago: University of Chicago Press, 1962), 125–29.

13. Ibid., 129.

14. Ibid., 202f.

15. Ibid., 199. See 198–210 for the full argument.

16. Michael Polanyi, *Science, Faith, and Society* (London: Geoffrey Cumberlege, 1946); Norwood Russell Hanson, *Patterns of Discovery: An Inquiry into the Conceptual Foundations of Science* (Cambridge: Cambridge University Press, 1958).

17. Quine, "Epistemology Naturalized," 87.

18. Ibid., 88.

19. W. V. O. Quine, "Reply to Morton White," in *The Philosophy of W. V. Quine,* ed. Lewis Hahn and Paul A. Shilpp (La Salle, IL: Open Court, 1986), 664.

20. W. V. O. Quine, "On the Nature of Moral Values," in *Theories and Things* (Cambridge, MA: Harvard University Press), 62. It did, however, mean that "a coherence theory of truth is evidently the lot of ethics." Ibid., 63.

21. John Rawls, "Philosophy 171, Lectures I–IV 1966–1967" (Harvard University Archives, 1966), "Question of Justification," 3i, HUM 48, Box 36, Folder 10, John Rawls Faculty Papers.

22. John Rawls, "Analytic Ethics and Justification, 1966–1967" (Harvard University Archives, 1966–1967), 1967 Ethics, 2ii, HUM 48, Box 5, Folder 6, John Rawls Faculty Papers.

23. John Rawls, "Goodness as Rationality" (Harvard University Archives, 1965), 1i–1ii, HUM 48, Box 35, Folder 17, John Rawls Faculty Papers.

24. Rawls, "Analytic Ethics and Justification. 1966–1967," 1967 Ethics 169, 2ii–3i.

25. John Rawls, "Philosophy 171, Class Lectures" (Harvard University Archives, 1963), Lecture X, 2i, HUM 48, Box 27, Folder 5.

26. Quine, "Two Dogmas in Retrospect," 272; Rawls, "Philosophy 171, Lectures I–IV 1966–1967," "Question of Justification," 3i–3ii.

27. John Rawls, "Philosophy 169. Part I. Lectures I–IV" (Harvard University Archives, 1970), Lecture IV, 6i, HUM 48, Box 5, Folder 2, John Rawls Faculty Papers.

28. Rawls, "Analytic Ethics and Justification. 1966–1967," 1966 Philosophy 169, 9i–9ii.

29. Ibid., 8ii–9i.

30. John Rawls, "Philosophy 171. Chapters on Justice. Draft of A Theory of Justice Reproduced to Students" (Harvard University Archives, 1965), 2–3, HUM 48, Box 18, Folder 4, John Rawls Faculty Papers.

31. Rawls, "Analytic Ethics and Justification. 1966–1967," 1966 Philosophy 169, 8ii–9i.

32. Ibid., 11ii.

33. John Rawls, "Philosophy 169. Part II. Lectures V–IX" (Harvard University Archives, 1970), Lecture VIII, 3b., HUM 48, Box 5, Folder 3, John Rawls Faculty Papers. For Rawls's reasons to call these conditions "formal," see ibid., Lecture VII, 2ii–3i: "The term 'formal' is merely a label. That is, I shall not attempt to define it, and I do not know how to do so. Presumably, since it seems a natural term to use, it expresses some intuitive notion; but what this notion is I am not able to say. Thus by formal conditions I mean those conditions on first principles that are given by a certain list (by enumeration)."

34. Rawls, *Theory of Justice,* 52.

35. John Rawls, "Moral Psychology, 1964–1965" (Harvard University Archives, 1964), Seminar I, 2i, HUM 48, Box 35, Folder 6, John Rawls Faculty Papers. The essay referred to is William Frankena, "Obligation and Motivation in Recent Moral Philosophy," in *Essays in Moral Philosophy,* ed. A. I. Melden (Seattle: University of Washington Press, 1958), 40–81.

36. John Rawls, "Natural Law, 1962–1965" (Harvard University Archives, 1962–1965), 1965 Lecture VIII, 1i–1ii, HUM 48, Box 35, Folder 13, John Rawls Faculty Papers.

37. Rawls, "Analytic Ethics and Justification. 1966–1967," 1967 Ethics 169, "Lecture on Justification," 1i.

38. Rawls, "Moral Psychology, 1964–65," Seminar V, 3ii.

39. John Rawls, "Nature of Political and Social Thought and Methodology" (Harvard University Archives, n.d.), 1960 Lecture I, 4i, HUM 48, Box 35, Folder 10, John Rawls Faculty Papers.

40. See Rawls's critical discussion of intuitionism in Rawls, *Theory of Justice,* 34–46.

41. Rawls, "Nature of Political and Social Thought and Methodology," 1960 Lecture II, 3i.

42. For "equilibrium of reflection," see John Rawls, "Liberty, of Person and Thought" (Harvard University Archives, 1962), Political Philosophy 171, Lecture XVI, 2i, HUM 48, Box 35, Folder 11, John Rawls Faculty Papers. For "reflective equilibrium," see Rawls, "Philosophy 171. Chapters on Justice," 18.

43. Rawls, "Nature of Political and Social Thought and Methodology," 1962 Political Philosophy 171, Lecture IX, 2i.

44. John Rawls, "Justice as Fairness," in *John Rawls: Collected Papers,* ed. Samuel Freeman (Cambridge, MA: Harvard University Press, 1999), 47, 71.

45. Ibid., 47.

46. Rawls, *Theory of Justice,* 21, 18.

47. Four drafts of *A Theory of Justice* are noticeably different from the published book: one in 1964 (the very first draft), two in 1965 (although, given that there is little difference between them, they can be considered as the same draft), one in 1967, and one in 1969. Rawls considered the 1964 and 1965 drafts as one draft. The 1964 draft can be found in John Rawls, "Essay on Justice. First Draft of *A Theory of Justice,* 1 of 2" (1964), John Rawls Faculty Papers, Harvard University Archives, HUM 48, Box 17, Folder 2. The first 1965 draft can be found in John Rawls, "Justice, second draft of *A Theory of Justice,* March 1965," John Rawls Faculty Papers, Harvard University Archives, HUM 48, Box 17, Folder 4. The second 1965 draft, distributed to students, can be found at John Rawls, "Philosophy 171. Chapters on Justice. Draft of *A Theory of Justice* reproduced to students" (1965 Fall), John Rawls Faculty Papers, Harvard University Archives, HUM 48, Box 18, Folder 4. The 1967 draft can be found at John Rawls, "Justice as Fairness II" (1967), John Rawls Faculty Papers, Harvard University Archives, HUM 48, Box 10, Folders 1–5. There are later, 1969, revisions as well, and these approach *A Theory of Justice* closer and closer. See John Rawls Faculty Papers, Harvard University Archives, HUM 48, Boxes 11–12.

48. Rawls, "Justice as Fairness," 54.

49. Ibid.

50. Ibid., 52–53.

51. Ibid., 52.

8. Kantian Autonomy

1. Immanuel Kant, *Groundwork of the Metaphysic of Morals,* trans. H. J. Paton (New York: Harper Torchbooks, 1956), 96 (AK 4:429).
2. Ibid., 88 (AK 4:421), 98 (AK 4:431). For Kant's students relying on these formulas, see Christine Korsgaard, *The Sources of Normativity* (Cambridge: Cambridge University Press, 1996); and Onora O'Neill, *Toward Justice and Virtue: A Constructive Account of Practical Reasoning* (Cambridge: Cambridge University Press, 1996). For Rawls's students' interpretations of Kant, see Onora O'Neill, "Autonomy, Plurality and Public Reason," in *New Essays on the History of Autonomy: A Collection Honoring J. B. Schneewind,* ed. Natalie Brender and Larry Krasnoff (Cambridge: Cambridge University Press, 2004), 181–94.
3. John Rawls, *A Theory of Justice* (Cambridge, MA: Harvard University Press, 1971), 587.
4. John Rawls, "Two Concepts of Rules," in *John Rawls: Collected Papers,* ed. Samuel Freeman (Cambridge, MA: Harvard University Press, 1999), 21.
5. John Rawls, "Justice as Fairness," in *John Rawls: Collected Papers,* ed. Samuel Freeman (Cambridge, MA: Harvard University Press, 1999), 51f.
6. Ibid.
7. John Rawls, "Nature of Political and Social Thought and Methodology" (Harvard University Archives, [1960]), "Philosophy and Social Thought," 3i, HUM 48, Box 35, Folder 10, John Rawls Faculty Papers.
8. Ibid.
9. Ibid., 1960 Lecture II, 5i.
10. John Rawls, "Bibliographies and Topics for Philosophy 171" (Harvard University Archives, n.d.), 1, HUM 48, Box 24, Folder 7, John Rawls Faculty Papers.
11. Rawls, "Nature of Political and Social Thought and Methodology," 1962 Lecture I, 6.
12. Rawls, "Justice as Fairness," 71.
13. Ibid., 64.
14. Rawls, "Nature of Political and Social Thought and Methodology," 1962 Lecture I, 3.
15. Ibid., 1962 Lecture I, 1i.
16. John Rawls, "Natural Law" (Harvard University Archives, 1962–1965), 1962 Lecture VIII, 1i, HUM 48, Box 35, Folder 13, John Rawls Faculty Papers.
17. Ibid., 1962 Lecture VIII, 7i.
18. Rawls, "Nature of Political and Social Thought and Methodology," 1962 Lecture I, 1i.
19. Rawls, "Natural Law," 1962 Lecture VIII, 1ii.
20. Rawls, "Nature of Political and Social Thought and Methodology," 1960 Lecture II, 5i.

21. John Rawls, "Philosophy 171, Lectures, I–IV" (Harvard University Archives, 1966–1967), "Talk to Socratic Club, Apr 1954," 2i, HUM 48, Box 36, Folder 10, John Rawls Faculty Papers.

22. John Rawls, "Liberty, Essay IV" (Harvard University Archives, n.d.), "Chapter IV: Liberty and Equality," 2, 2a., HUM 48, Box 36, Folder 2, John Rawls Faculty Papers.

23. Ibid., "Chapter IV: Liberty and Equality," 2i.

24. John Rawls, "Essay on Justice. First Draft of A Theory of Justice, 1 of 2" (Harvard University Archives, 1964), 98, HUM 48, Box 17, Folder 2, John Rawls Faculty Papers.

25. Rawls, *Theory of Justice*, 188, 187.

26. Rawls, "Essay on Justice. First Draft of A Theory of Justice, 1 of 2," viii.

27. John Rawls, *Collected Papers*, ed. Samuel Freeman (Cambridge, MA: Harvard University Press, 1999), 47.

28. John Rawls, "Justice as Reciprocity, IX–X" (Harvard University Archives, n.d.), Lecture IX, 3i, HUM 48, Box 35, Folder 12, John Rawls Faculty Papers.

29. Jean-Jacques Rousseau, *The Social Contract*, trans. Maurice Cranston (London: Penguin, 1979), 75.

30. John Rawls, "Reply to Stanley Moore" (Harvard University Archives, 1972), 1i, HUM 48, Box 19, Folder 4, John Rawls Faculty Papers.

31. Rawls, "Justice as Reciprocity, IX–X," Lecture XI, 7ii.

32. Ibid., Lecture XI, 1ii.

33. Ibid., Lecture XI, 7ii. See also Rawls, *Collected Papers*, 59.

34. Rawls, "Justice as Reciprocity, IX–X," Lecture IX, 1i–1ii.

35. John Rawls, "Fellow Feeling and Sympathy" (Harvard University Archives, n.d.), "Necessary Distinction in Regard to Sympathy," 2ii, HUM 48, Box 34, Folder 15, John Rawls Faculty Papers.

36. Ibid., "Remarks re Sympathy, Pity, and Compassion," 2ii.

37. Kant, *Groundwork of the Metaphysic of Morals*, 99 (AK 4:432).

38. Ibid., 105 (AK 4:438).

39. Ibid., 79 (AK 4:411).

40. Ibid., 92 (AK 4:425) (emphasis in original).

41. Ibid., 93 (AK 4:426).

42. Kurt Baier, "The Point of View of Morality," *Australasian Journal of Philosophy* 32 (1954): 104–35; Kurt Baier, *The Moral Point of View* (Ithaca, NY: Cornell University Press, 1958).

43. Baier, *Moral Point of View*, viii.

44. Kant, *Groundwork of the Metaphysic of Morals*, 96 (AK 4:429).

45. Ibid., 96 (AK 4:428) (emphasis in original).

46. Baier, *Moral Point of View*, 191.

47. Ibid.

48. Kant, *Groundwork of the Metaphysic of Morals*, 96 (AK 4:429).

49. Baier, "Point of View of Morality," 123.

50. Ibid.
51. Baier, *Moral Point of View,* 9.
52. Ibid., 9–10.
53. Ibid., 10.
54. Kant, *Groundwork of the Metaphysic of Morals,* 79 (AK 4:411–12).
55. Baier, *Moral Point of View,* 182.
56. John Rawls, "A Theory of Justice, First Draft of the Manuscript, Equal Liberty, Chapter IV" (Harvard University Archives, 1967), 54, HUM 48, Box 10, Folder 7, John Rawls Faculty Papers.
57. Ibid., 54a.
58. John Rawls, "Problems of Akrasia and Moral Feelings" (Harvard University Archives, 1958), "Concept of Morality and Considered Judgments," 3i, HUM 48, Box 34, Folder 18, John Rawls Faculty Papers.
59. Ibid.
60. Rawls, "Justice as Fairness," 53.
61. Ibid., 54.
62. John Rawls, "Philosophy 171, Class Lectures" (Harvard University Archives, 1963), "Lecture X," 2, Box 27, Folder 5.
63. John Rawls, "Equality XIX–XXI" (Harvard University Archives, n.d.), 27i, HUM 48, Box 35, Folder 16, John Rawls Faculty Papers.
64. Ibid.
65. John Rawls, "A Theory of Justice, Second Version, Chapters V–IX" (Harvard University Archives, 1969), Chapter VIII, 230, HUM 48, Box 10, Folder 11, John Rawls Faculty Papers.
66. Rawls, "Equality XIX–XXI," 26i.
67. In *A Theory of Justice,* respect for persons is treated as a specific duty dependent on the principles of justice. Likely to distinguish himself from other Kantian positions, Rawls specified that he is not using respect for persons to derive the principles of justice. As he wrote, "The notion of respect or of the inherent worth of persons is not a suitable basis for arriving at these principles." Rawls, *Theory of Justice,* 586. However, Rawls also permitted a broader meaning of respect for persons. To take part in the original position thought experiment is to explore what it means to respect persons. This initial disposition to treat and respect others as persons is the notion I use in this book. See also ibid., 337–38.
68. Rawls, "A Theory of Justice, First Draft of the Manuscript, Equal Liberty, Chapter IV," 54a–55.
69. Ibid., 56i.
70. Ibid., 59i.
71. Ibid., 61i.
72. John Rawls, "Justice as Fairness and Notes, Essay 2, APA" (Harvard University Archives, [1958]), "Additional Notes: Symposium Paper," 1ii, HUM 48, Box 8, Folder 9, John Rawls Faculty Papers.

73. Ibid., [1958] "Additional Notes: Symposium Paper," 2i.
74. John Rawls, "Personal Copy of Kurt Baier's *The Moral Point of View* (1958)" (Harvard University Archives, n.d.), HUM 48.1, Box 15, Books from the Personal Library of John Rawls, 1915–2002.
75. Baier, *Moral Point of View,* 182.
76. Ibid.
77. Rawls, "A Theory of Justice, First Draft of the Manuscript, Equal Liberty, Chapter IV," Chapter V, 5i.
78. Rawls, *Theory of Justice,* 587.
79. John Rawls, "Distributive Justice, Part II" (Harvard University Archives, 1959), 20, HUM 48, Box 36, Folder 4, John Rawls Faculty Papers.
80. Ibid.
81. Ibid.
82. Ibid.
83. Rawls, "Justice as Reciprocity, IX–X," 1962 Political Philosophy, Lecture IX, 6i–6ii.
84. John Rawls, "Distributive Justice: Some Addenda," in *John Rawls: Collected Papers,* ed. Samuel Freeman (Cambridge, MA: Harvard University Press, 1999), 155.
85. Ibid.
86. Rawls, "Essay on Justice. First Draft of A Theory of Justice, 1 of 2," 74.
87. Ibid., 50.
88. Ibid., 50–53, 60.
89. Ibid., 57.
90. Ibid., 74.
91. Rawls thanks Allan Gibbard for mentioning this shortcoming in the preface to *A Theory of Justice* and explains that the outcome of Gibbard's comments was the introduction of the notion of primary goods. Rawls, *Theory of Justice,* x.
92. Rawls, "Distributive Justice: Some Addenda," 158.
93. John Rawls, "Analytic Ethics and Justification. 1966–67" (Harvard University Archives, 1966–1967), 1966 Philosophy 169, "Justification and Remarks concerning Objectivity and Autonomy," 4ii, HUM 48, Box 5, Folder 6, John Rawls Faculty Papers.
94. Ibid., 1966 Philosophy 169, "Justification and Remarks concerning Objectivity and Autonomy," 5i.
95. For an analysis of the problems that arguably stem from Rawls's reliance on the Kantian conception of the person, see Michael J. Sandel, *Liberalism and the Limits of Justice* (Cambridge: Cambridge University Press, 1982).
96. John Rawls, "Kant Lectures, Philosophy 169" (Harvard University Archives, 1968), 1968 Fall, Philosophy 169: Ethics, Lecture XVIII, 6ii, HUM 48, Box 5, Folder 14, John Rawls Faculty Papers.
97. Ibid., 1968 Fall, Philosophy 169: Ethics, Lecture XVIII, 7i.

98. John Rawls, "Kantian Constructivism in Moral Theory," in *John Rawls: Collected Papers,* ed. Samuel Freeman (Cambridge, MA: Harvard University Press, 1999), 303–58.

99. Korsgaard, *Sources of Normativity;* O'Neill, "Autonomy, Plurality and Public Reason."

9. A Theory of Justice

1. Michael Walzer, "A Critique of Philosophical Conversation," *Philosophical Forum* 21 (1989): 182.

2. John Rawls, *A Theory of Justice* (Cambridge, MA: Harvard University Press, 1971), 578.

3. Ibid.

4. Ibid., 21, 579.

5. Ibid., 580.

6. Ibid., 18.

7. Ibid., 20. For Rawls's references to such fixed points, see ibid., 104, 206, 311.

8. Ibid., 18.

9. Ibid., 21.

10. Ibid., 119.

11. Ibid., 252.

12. Ibid.

13. Ibid., 12.

14. Ibid., 252.

15. Ibid., 12.

16. Ibid., 252.

17. Ibid., 142.

18. Ibid., 137.

19. Ibid., 15.

20. Ibid., 160–261.

21. Ibid., 587.

22. Robert S. Taylor, *Reconstructing Rawls: The Kantian Foundations of Justice as Fairness* (University Park: Pennsylvania State University Press, 2011), 234.

23. Ibid.

24. Ibid., 234–35.

25. This conception of Kantianism captures the main goals of Rawls's students Barbara Herman, Christine Korsgaard, and Onora O'Neill. See Barbara Herman, *The Practice of Moral Judgment* (Cambridge, MA: Harvard University Press, 1993); Onora O'Neill, *Toward Justice and Virtue: A Constructive Account of Practical Reasoning* (Cambridge: Cambridge University Press,

1996); Christine Korsgaard, *The Sources of Normativity* (Cambridge: Cambridge University Press, 1996).

26. Rawls, *Theory of Justice,* 20.

27. John Rawls, *The Law of Peoples* (Cambridge, MA: Harvard University Press, 2001), 86.

28. For Rawls's description of Richard Hare as a formalist, see John Rawls, "Philosophy 169. Part II. Lectures V–IX" (Harvard University Archives, 1970), Lecture IX, 4i, HUM 48, Box 5, Folder 3, John Rawls Faculty Papers. Rawls also includes Jonathan Harrison and Henry D. Aiken among formalists. See Rawls, Lecture IX, 5ii. For Rawls's classification of Baier as a formalist, see Rawls, Lecture VII.

29. Rawls, "Philosophy 169. Part II. Lectures V–IX," Lecture VIII, 3b. See also Rawls, *Theory of Justice,* 251, 51.

30. Stanley Cavell, *The Claim of Reason: Wittgenstein, Skepticism, Morality, and Tragedy* (Oxford: Oxford University Press, 1999), 207.

31. Rawls, *Theory of Justice,* 126–27.

32. Allan Bloom, "Justice: John Rawls vs. the Tradition of Political Philosophy," *American Political Science Review* 69 (1975): 651 (emphasis in original).

33. Ibid.

34. Richard Rorty, "The Priority of Democracy to Philosophy," in *Objectivity, Relativism, and Truth* (Cambridge: Cambridge University Press, 1991), 180.

35. Richard Rorty, "Philosophy in America Today," *American Scholar* 51 (1982): 188.

36. Rorty, "Priority of Democracy," 180.

37. Rawls, *Theory of Justice,* 47. Rawls refers to Noam Chomsky, *Aspects of the Theory of Syntax* (Cambridge, MA: MIT Press, 1965), 3–9.

38. John Mikhail, *Elements of Moral Cognition* (Cambridge: Cambridge University Press, 2011), 11.

39. Ibid., 34.

40. Ibid., 73.

41. Rawls, *Theory of Justice,* 195–201.

42. Rawls, "Philosophy 169. Part II. Lectures V–IX," Lecture VI, 1i.

43. Ibid., Lecture VI, 6i.

44. Ibid.

45. John Rawls, "Nature of Political and Social Thought and Methodology" (Harvard University Archives, n.d.), Lecture IX, 2i, HUM 48, Box 35, Folder 10, John Rawls Faculty Papers.

46. Ibid.

47. Ibid.

48. Rawls, *Theory of Justice,* 41.

49. Rawls, "Philosophy 169. Part II. Lectures V–IX," Lecture VI, 6i–6ii.

50. Ibid., Lecture VI, 2i.

51. Rawls, *Theory of Justice*, 44–45, 364, 41.

52. John Rawls, "Philosophy 171, Lectures I–IV 1966–1967" (Harvard University Archives, 1966), Lecture I, 2ii, HUM 48, Box 36, Folder 10, John Rawls Faculty Papers.

53. Ibid.

54. Rawls, *Theory of Justice*, 387–88.

55. Ibid.

56. John Rawls, "Essay V" (Harvard University Archives, 1958–1962), "How Moralities May Differ," 1, HUM 48, Box 8, Folder 1, John Rawls Faculty Papers.

57. Rawls, "Philosophy 169. Part II. Lectures V–IX," Lecture VII, 6i. See also the appendix to this same lecture, 2i. See also John Rawls, "Essay on Justice. First Draft of A Theory of Justice, 1 of 2" (Harvard University Archives, 1964), 9i, HUM 48, Box 17, Folder 2, John Rawls Faculty Papers, where Rawls claims that the conception of justice applies to "all possible societies."

58. John Rawls, "Analytic Ethics and Justification, 1966–1967" (Harvard University Archives, 1966–1967), 1967 Ethics 169, "Lecture on Justification," 1ii–2i, HUM 48, Box 5, Folder 6, John Rawls Faculty Papers. See also John Rawls, "Philosophy 169. Part I. Lectures I–IV" (Harvard University Archives, 1970), Lecture IV, 1i–1ii, HUM 48, Box 5, Folder 2, John Rawls Faculty Papers.

59. Rawls, "Analytic Ethics and Justification, 1966–1967," 1967 Ethics 169, "Lecture on Justification," 1ii–2i.

60. John Rawls, "Political Philosophy 171" (Harvard University Archives, 1960), Lecture II, 2i–2ii, HUM 48, Box 35, Folder 12, John Rawls Faculty Papers.

61. Rawls, "Analytic Ethics and Justification, 1966–1967," 1967 Ethics 169, "On Justification," 6ii.

62. Rawls, *Theory of Justice*, 274.

63. Ibid., 278, 287. For Rawls's explanation as to why one cannot require precision when determining the rate of savings, see ibid., 362.

64. Rawls, "Analytic Ethics and Justification, 1966–1967," 1966 Philosophy 169, "Analytic Ethics: Metaethics," 7i.

65. Rawls, *Theory of Justice*, 201. See also ibid., 199.

66. Ibid., 195–201.

67. Ibid., 201.

68. The first edition of the book concludes with the admission that "the prolonged effort of the human intellect to frame a perfect ideal of rational conduct is seen to have been foredoomed to inevitable failure." Henry Sidgwick, *The Methods of Ethics*, 1st ed. Bristol: Thoemmes Press, 1996 [1874]), 473.

69. Henry Sidgwick, *The Methods of Ethics,* 7th ed. (Indianapolis: Hackett, 1981), xxi.

70. Rawls, *Theory of Justice,* 201.

Epilogue

1. John Rawls, *A Theory of Justice* (Cambridge, MA: Harvard University Press, 1971), 513–20.

2. Indeed, in a revised edition of *A Theory of Justice,* rewritten for the German translation in 1975, Rawls clarified that his goal was to explore "a moral conception of the person that embodies a certain ideal." John Rawls, *A Theory of Justice,* rev. ed. (Cambridge, MA: Harvard University Press, 1999), xi, xiii.

3. See, for example, Paul Weithman, *Why Political Liberalism? On John Rawls's Political Turn* (Oxford: Oxford University Press, 2011).

4. Michael J. Sandel, *Liberalism and the Limits of Justice* (Cambridge: Cambridge University Press, 1982).

5. Leon H. Craig, "Contra Contract: A Brief against John Rawls' Theory of Justice," *Canadian Journal of Political Science* 8 (1975): 68–71.

6. For a well-known criticism of Kohlberg's laws of moral development, see Carol Gilligan, *In a Different Voice* (Cambridge, MA: Harvard University Press, 1982).

7. John Rawls, "The Independence of Moral Theory," in *John Rawls: Collected Papers,* ed. Samuel Freeman (Cambridge, MA: Harvard University Press, 1999), 286.

8. Ibid., 296.

9. Ibid., 287.

10. Samuel Scheffler, "Moral Independence and the Original Position," *Philosophical Studies* 35 (1979): 397–403. For Rawls's remarks about the paper, see John Rawls, *Political Liberalism,* expanded ed. (New York: Columbia University Press, 2005), xxxii–xxxiii.

11. John Rawls, "Justice as Fairness: Political, Not Metaphysical," in *John Rawls: Collected Papers,* ed. Samuel Freeman (Cambridge, MA: Harvard University Press, 1999), 47–72; and Rawls, *Political Liberalism,* 1–15.

12. Rawls, "Political, Not Metaphysical," 393.

13. Rawls, *Political Liberalism,* 10, 225.

14. Ibid., 243f.

15. Rawls, "Political, Not Metaphysical," 479f. The text is "The Idea of Public Reason Revisited," published in 1997.

16. See, for example, Andrew F. March, *Islam and Liberal Citizenship* (Oxford: Oxford University Press, 2009).

17. Rawls, *Political Liberalism*, 228–30.
18. Ibid., 241.
19. Rawls, *Theory of Justice*, 586.
20. James Bohman and Henry S. Richardson, "Liberalism, Deliberative Democracy, and 'Reasons That All Can Accept,'" *Journal of Political Philosophy* 17 (2009): 258.

ACKNOWLEDGMENTS

One of the greatest pleasures of writing this book was the many stimulating conversations and the generous help I received from colleagues and friends. They made the book better and my life more enjoyable.

Thank you to Mark Bevir, Kinch Hoekstra, David Hollinger, and Hans Sluga. Their work showed me what political theory and intellectual history can be. Mark's and Kinch's influence can be felt throughout the book. The History of Analytic Philosophy reading group, which Mark prompted, helped develop my early arguments. My thanks go to its members Richard Ashcroft, Jason Blakely, Naomi Choi, and Toby Reiner. Conversations about political liberalism with Athmeya Jayaram have been invaluable and enjoyable. I was fortunate to be at Berkeley with these people at that time.

The argument of this book developed further in the later years. I have benefited from discussions with Kenzie Bok, Daniele Botti, and David Reidy, as well as from their work. The helpful advice of my colleagues at Wake Forest University also improved the book. My thanks go to Michaelle Browers, Wayne Hall, and Lucas Johnston. I want to express a special thank you to Michael Lamb and David Weinstein, with whom I spent numerous enjoyable hours discussing the manuscript. I am also grateful to Athmeya, Kinch, and Toby for their continued discussions and advice.

Thank you also to my editor Jeff Dean and for two anonymous reviewers for Harvard University Press for their constructive and detailed suggestions. Responding to their comments made the book better and engaging their thought was enlightening and enjoyable. I am also grateful to Liz Schueler and Cheryl Hirsch for their valuable editorial help.

Most of all, a sincere thank you to Ellen Heck, who commented on the manuscript countless times over these years. Supporting and encouraging me, she was crucial in bringing this book to completion. Thank you, Ellen.

The book relies on many archival materials. Thank you to the Harvard University Archives for permission to publish, and to the staff of the Harvard University Archives, Princeton University Archives, and Cornell University Archives for their generous help.

Thank you to Wake Forest University's Dean of the College for the Summer Research Award, which helped me finish the manuscript.

Chapter 5 builds on ideas first discussed in "Just Society as a Fair Game: John Rawls and Game Theory in the 1950s," published by the University of Pennsylvania Press in the *Journal of the History of Ideas* 78, no. 2 (April 2017): 299–308.

INDEX

Anscombe, Elizabeth: drawing the boundaries of the concept "want," 119; Rawls attending her lectures at Oxford, 119; Rawls not following her focus on intentions, 120

Aquinas, St. Thomas: mistakes of a naturalist, 38–39; Rawls's analysis of revealing the nature of his meaning holism, 155

Archimedean point: for assessing the social system, 166–167; and the perspective of eternity, 167; relation to the original position, 177

Aristotle: Aquinas and Augustine drawing on, 39; Rawls studying at Princeton, 48, 201

Augustine of Hippo, St.: Rawls's courses on, 19, 22, 23; analyzing the Christian experience incorrectly, 38–39; as a naturalist, 39; the historical origins of his mistakes, 117

Austin, J. L., 102

Autonomy, formula of: and respecting persons, 9–10; and following the moral law, 12, 86–88, 95; Rawls's emphasis on, 14, 152, 159, 164–165; and the ability to choose one's good, 90–92, 94, 116, 120; Piaget's interpretation of, 122–123; and independence from contingencies, 152, 159, 164–169; and the original position, 167–169, 176–177; as an empirical claim, 170–171

Ayer, Alfred Jules: Smith's argument against, 47; as a positivist but not physicalist, 53; ethical terms as imperatives, 58; Rawls's criticism of, 58

Baier, Kurt: good reasons approach, 102; emphasis on the formula of humanity, 151, 160–161; and the moral point of view, 160–161; Rawls's deb to, 163–164; and true morality, 166; Rawls's criticism of, 179

Barth, Karl, 27, 29

Basic experiences: and Rawls's, interpretation of Wittgenstein's concept "family likeness," 13; as records of observable events, 49–50; and the belief that scientific observers will agree in their observations, 50; and Rawls's account of ethical judgments, 57; and meaning holism, 72

Basic judgments, made by all reasonable persons, 8, 11, 76

Basic statements: Popper on, 11; relation to observational statements and protocol statements, 49–50; Rawls's ethical judgments modeled on, 54–55, 57; and meaning holism, 72; in Rawls's Wittgensteinian framework, 76–77, 106

Basic structure of society: as the subject matter of justice, 109–111, 169; institutions part of, 110; and relation to reciprocity, sympathy, and altruism, 134; if just, can be justified to every member of society, 158; principles of justice guiding it through constitutional and legal order, 182

Bible, 18; as the last word in matters of religion, 20, 37; role in justifying the Christian framework, 23; biblical criticism questions the status of as a revelation, 24; revelation of God as recorded in, 25–26; liberal Protestant conception of, 28; neo-orthodox conception of, 28; as Rawls's chief source, 32

Biblical essentialism, 8, 24, 25

Biblical historicism, 24, 39

Black, Max: as a Wittgensteinian, 11; at Cornell, 64; on the justification of induction, 66–67, 76; Baier's relation to, 160; Rawls's courses with, 201

Bloom, Allan, 173, 180–181

Bowers, David, 21, 83, 200

Brunner, Emil, 29

Burdens of judgment, 71, 114
Butler, Bishop, 19
Butler, Samuel, 76

Calvin, John, 23
Carnap, Rudolf: Rawls following the physicalist example of, 45, 53; Rawls studying in the context of pragmatism, 47; as a positivist, 53; Rawls drawing on to defend logical physicalism as applied to ethics, 80; Quine's studies with, 138
Cavell, Stanley: emphasizing the diversity of experiences, 8, 13; as Rawls's Harvard colleague, 13; interpreting Wittgenstein, 98; and Wittgenstein bringing the human animal back to philosophy, 115; analysis of pain, 117; concept of normalcy, 117–118; Harvard as a center of Wittgensteinian thought, 137; original position and the human animal, 179
Chomsky, Noam: sense of justice and sense of grammaticalness, 181; Rawls as drawing the implications of the Universal Grammar for ethics, 181–182
Church, Alonzo, 47
Circumstances of justice, 179–180
Common good: political philosophy organizes the main values, including, 146, 147; as social utility, 147; Aquinas's conception of is vague, 155; utilitarianism's impermissible sacrifices of liberties in the name of, 193
Community: as the end in itself, 30; and personhood, 30; and proper relation to God, 31; and *Imago Dei*, 31–32; participatory, 32; of equals, 35; ways to bring it about, 35; natural appetitions cannot lead to, 38; humans always have the capacity to create, 40
Compassion, 120–121, 129

Considered judgments: philosophy as analysis of, 5, 6, 9, 38, 68, 80, 173, 174–177; political vision implicit in, 7; as stemming from natural feelings, 13, 131; and nonfoundationalism, 51–52; a reasoning game to explain, 93–94; as stopping justification, 106–107; not sufficient by themselves to derive a conception of justice, 145, 146–147; explained by the social contract tradition, 157; correcting the faults of sympathy, 162–163; explained by Kantianism, 171; aim to reduce direct appeal to, 183; aim to impose structure to, 188; analysis of as an independent inquiry, 192
Cornell University: Rawls's application to, 22, 53, 63–64; Department of Philosophy, 63–66

Daily Princetonian, The, Rawls's role in, 17–18
Democracy: agonistic, 2; Walzer's conception of a democratic conversation, 3; philosophy as a conversational ending to, 3, 174, 182, 187; Spengler's prophecy for, 18; participatory, 32, 33–34; Rawls's condemnation of the centralized America, 33–34; Rawls detaching philosophy from, 174, 180–181; principles of justice guiding only in a general direction, 182–187; philosophy cannot decide a system of property ownership, 186; philosophy cannot decide constitutions for, 187
Dewey, John, 47
Difference principle: addresses the differences in natural assets and social contingencies, 168; as an interpretation of Kant's formula of humanity, 168; some moralities put greater emphasis on, 184; Finland's prime minister discussing, 209n1

Impartiality: rational judgment as, 70; impartial sympathetic person, 130; justice as an impartial treatment of persons, 130; considered judgments seek, 131; utilitarianism mistaking impersonality for, 156

Intuitionism: as a foundational framework, 4–5; not providing an order to rank values, 146; and Rawls's mechanical conception of judgment, 183; and Rawls's "guiding framework" conception of principles, 183, 187

James, William, 47

Judgment: theory guiding, 4; rational, 68–70, 75, 77, 78; mechanical conception of, 79–80, 182–183; intuitive, 79, 89, 106, 182–183; "boxes of reason" conception of, 111–114. See also Considered judgments

Justice: and democracy, 1–3, 6, 182–188; and the task of political philosophy, 5–6; principles of, stated, 6, 93–95; as respect for persons, 9, 19; Rawls's account of applies universally, 13; theory of as a theory of moral sentiments, 13; as expression of person's nature as free and equal rational beings, 56; Rawls's turn to the study of, 88; the subject matter of, 88–90, 98, 103, 109–111; connected to and contrasted with fairness, 92; as recognizing persons as persons, 106; and the basic structure of society, 109–111; and its natural basis, 118–126, 128–132; and stability, 132–135; the original position bringing out its features, 147; utilitarian conception of, 154, 156

Justificatory holism, 139, 141, 175, 185–186, 188. See also Meaning holism

Kant, Immanuel: and Rawls's political vision, 9; and following the moral law, 12; Rawls's coursework on, 23, 48, 83, 200, 201; and Kelsen, 56; and autonomy, 85–87; Rawls's rejection of his metaphysics, 87–88, 165–166; and Baier's moral point of view, 159–162; and the completeness of justification, 185. See also Autonomy, formula of; Humanity, formula of; Universality, formula of

Kelsen, Hans, pure theory of law, 56

Knight, Frank: competitiveness at the heart of the political and economic games, 90; liberal economics and liberal politics the same kind of game, 90; sees himself as part of liberalism, 90; contrasted with Rawls, 226n44, 227n54; other influences on Rawls, 227n67

Köhler, Wolfgang: Rawls studying with, 47, 200; Rawls teaching for, 200

Korsgaard, Christine, 238n2, 242n99, 242n25–243n25

Kuhn, Thomas: as emphasizing the diversity of experiences, 8; as a historicist, 8; conception of meaning holism, 140; justification of scientific theories, 140; observational statements presuppose a background of concepts, 140; Quine's criticism of, 140; reflective equilibrium not reflecting the ideas of, 190

Larmore, Charles, 209n2, 210n7

Least advantaged persons, 6, 94, 133, 158, 184

Leon, Philip, 19, 35

Liberalism: Rawls's understanding of political philosophy as guiding light to, 1; its conception of freedom, 1–2; its two strategies for overcoming disagreement, 1–2; the crisis of, 1–3; freedom deemed to require agreement of citizens, 2; high, 2; leaves the political out of political philosophy, 2; Rawls reinvigorating high liberalism, 2; focus on reasonable and not actual persons, 2–3; liberal philosophy providing conversational endings to liberal democracy, 3; respects beliefs rather than persons, 3; Rawls's conception of does not rest on pragmatism, 14; Rawls's conception of committed to a philosophical anthropology, 15; respect for persons in, 16; personalism's criticism of, 29–30; and Rawls's early religious beliefs, 31; Rawls's conception of not relying on unstated religious grounds, 43; and the goal of ethical reasoning, 107; Rawls's conception of and Kantian autonomy, 171

Liberal Protestantism, 10, 20, 21, 23–28, 39, 41

Locke, John, 23, 158

Logic: inductive, 65–66, 76; deductive, 66; of ethical arguments, 100, 104, 112

Logical positivism: and basic statements, 8; Rawls drawing on, 11, 45–46; Quine as logical positivist, 14, 137–140; dismissive of religious thought, 46; and pragmatism, 47; foundationalism of, 48–49; conception of scientific inquiry, 48–53; nonfoundationalism of, 49–51; Rawls's conception of scientific theory drawing on, 54; Rawls's criticism of, 62; and Rawls's conception of metaphysics, 72–73; and agreement of reasonable persons, 78–79; Rawls's relation to, 180

Luther, Martin: Rawls studying at Princeton, 23; and rejection of merit, 32–33; Lutheran pastor's falsehoods, 41

Malcolm, Norman: Rawls studying with, 11–12, 22, 46, 64, 200; course on religious ethics, 19; Scoon's opinion of, 19; joining Princeton, 21, 47; Rawls's description of Malcolm's course on religious ethics, 22; and Rawls's transfer to Cornell, 22; and Rawls's undergraduate thesis, 23; and his engagement with logical positivism, 47; and Wittgenstein, 47; Rawls's conversations with, 76; Rawls's engagement with Wittgensteinian philosophy, 98

Maritain, Jacques, 29

Massachusetts Institute of Technology, Department of Philosophy, 137

Meaning: semantic contrasted with intentional, 59–60; intentional, 70, 79–80

Meaning holism: defined, 71; and historicist criticisms of Rawls, 71; Rawls accepts the thesis of but limits its reach, 71; compromises the notion of basic statements, 72; Rawls aiming to detach ethical judgments from background beliefs, 73; and the analytic-synthetic distinction, 138–139; Quine's conception of, 138–140; Kuhn's conception of, 140; and Rawls's understanding of the contrast between utilitarianism and justice as fairness, 154–156; limited, 194; implications of not discussed in actual cases, 195. See also Justificatory holism

Merit, rejection of: Rawls drawing on Luther's argument for, 32–33; merit denies equality, 33; merit is rooted in sin, 33; one's achievements depend on the help of others, 33

Mikhail, John, Rawls drawing the implication of the Universal Grammar for ethics, 181–182

Mill, John Stuart, 60

Modus vivendi, 109

Moore, G. E.: as Malcolm's teacher, 47; recapitulating Sidgwick, 58

Moore, Stanley, and the conversation about the influence of Rousseau, 157

Moral feelings: a theory of justice as a theory of moral sentiments, 8; Rawls's philosophical anthropology rests on account of, 15; as part of Rawls's conception of morality as a natural phenomenon, 118; Foot's and Findlay's role in beginning the analysis of, 119; defined, 120, 122; develop from natural feelings, 122; logically connected to natural feelings, 122; laws of psychological development exhibiting the development of, 123–124; logical connections between moral views and, 124; connection to natural feelings helps answer the moral skeptic, 124–126

Moral point of view: and respect for persons, 152, 164; as abstracted from contingencies, 159–161, 166–167; Baier's conception of, 160–161; Rawls's conception of, 162–163; as the Archimedean point, 166–167; veil of ignorance and reasons arbitrary from a, 177

Morgenstern, Oskar, 12, 84, 89–90, 95, 202

Murphy, Arthur Edward: Rawls's engagement with, 63–66; and ethical skepticism, 77; Rawls's courses with, 201

Natural feelings: explain the overlap of all moralities, 3, 116, 128–131; analysis of prompted by Wittgenstein's concept of the "form of life," 8; moral reasons as extensions of, 13; compatible with a variety of moral views, 15; defined, 120; enumerated, 120; and recognition of persons as persons, 120; natural since acquired without specific training, 121; logically connected to moral feelings, 122; natural since need not be justified, 122; and Rawls's account of psychological development, 123–124; connection to moral feelings helps answer the moral skeptic, 124–126; deducing moral and political views from, 126–128; biases of sympathy, 129–131; and stability, 132–135

Naturalism: and the emphasis on natural and moral feelings, 13; the influence on Rawls of Wittgenstein's, 13; explaining the agreement of reasonable persons, 13, 116, 128–132; Quine as a naturalist, 14; Aquinas and Augustine as naturalists, 38; the origins of Augustine's and Aquinas's naturalist mistake, 39; Köhler's conception of value, 47; naturalist turn in analytic philosophy, 115; Rawls's conception of, 115–126; and human form of life, 116; and recognizing persons as persons, 116, 128; and Wittgenstein's analysis of pain, 120; answering the moral skeptic, 124–126; and implications for moral and political views, 128–132; and stability, 132–135; Rawls's account of ignored by interpreters, 180–182; Mikhail's interpretation of Rawls's, 181–182

Necessity, 141–143

Needs: defined, 85–86; and Kantian conception of the person, 85–87; and moral freedom, 86; and rights, 87

Neo-orthodoxy, 20, 23–24, 27–30, 88

Neumann, John von, 12, 84, 89–90, 95, 202

Neurath, Otto: as a physicalist, 45, 53; Rawls's engagement with in the context of pragmatism, 47; Rawls drawing on to defend logical physicalism as applied to ethics, 80

Niebuhr, Reinhold, 19, 22

Nietzsche, Friedrich: suffering the consequences of egotism, 39; showing that experience does not depend solely on conceptual framework, 40

Nonfoundationalism: Rawls's early religious, 37; logical positivism's turn to, 48–50; Sidgwick's conception of, 58–59; linguistic philosophers' conception of, 100–102; Rawls's good reasons approach to, 106–109; and Rawls's naturalism, 124–126; Quine's conception of, 137–140; Rawls following Quine on, 141–146, 149; of *A Theory of Justice*, 174–177

Nygren, Anders, 39

Obama, Barack, Rawls's influence on, 209n1

Objectivity: of scientific statements, 67–68; of ethical statements, 67–75, 77–79, 108–109, 170, 190; and autonomy, 169–171

Observational statements: as part of nonfoundational justification, 48–49; as singular statements of fact, 49–50; relation to basic statements and protocol statements, 49–50; Quine on, 139–140; Kuhn on, 140

O'Neill, Onora, 224n71, 238n2, 242n99, 242n25–243n25

Original position: as exhibiting our considered judgments, 3, 9, 93, 146, 147–148; four versions of, 148; as point of view of eternity, 152, 167; as an interpretation of persons as free and equal rational beings, 162; as allowing independence from the empirical world, 165; as the point of view of noumenal selves, 165; and primary goods, 169, 176; and veil of

ignorance, 177; four-stage sequence of, 187

Overlapping consensus: and the independence of political doctrines from comprehensive doctrines, 9; contrasted with Rawls's conception of ethical judgments as independent of other beliefs, 73; Wittgenstein's influence on the concept of, 128–129; natural and moral feelings leading to, 181; contrasted with strict consensus, 184; only over easier cases, 185; origins of, 193

Parker, Dewitt, 77

Peirce, Charles Sanders, 47

Person: and *Imago Dei*, 10, 28, 30–31, 33, 40, 77; God as a, 27, 30; recognizing others as, 31–36, 91–92, 93–94, 116–117, 120, 125, 128–131, 163, 189; requiring an open society, 32; contrasted with means, 34; personal contrasted with natural, 38–39, 116–117; Kantian conception of, 85–86, 90–92, 160; and natural feelings, 124–126, 127–128; as ends in themselves, 160; as moral, 168; and shared principles of justice, 196–197. *See also* Respect for persons

Personalism, 28–30

Physicalism: modeling ethics after science, 45, 48; ethical theory as empirical theory, 51–58, 62, 68–70, 103, 105, 131; contrasted with positivism, 53; ethical judgments as perceptions, 68–69; and scientific temper, 72; Rawls's transition from it to Wittgensteinian philosophy, 76–77, 99, 131, 144; Rawls's self-description as part of, 80–81; its conception of analysis, 89; Rawls's conception of re-described in Kantian terms, 167; its account of principles, 182; and basic statements, 190

Piaget, Jean, 121, 122–123
Plato: foundational arguments of, 4;
    Rawls studying at Princeton, 19, 22,
    46, 200; Scoon and Greene teaching
    the ideas of, 21; Augustine and
    Aquinas drawing on, 39; his
    naturalist conception of ethics, 39
Pogge, Thomas, 212n2
Polanyi, Michael, 140
Political philosophy: as correcting
    democratic disagreement, 1; Rawls
    taking the political out of, 2; as
    providing a conversational ending
    to democracy, 3, 174, 187; task of, 5,
    100; as analysis, 7; guides practice
    only in a general direction, 15, 174,
    186–187; as analysis of experience,
    19; should take the right to choose
    one's good on life as a central value,
    91–92; relation to democracy, 174,
    180, 182–188
Political realism, 2, 10, 91, 107, 174
Popper, Karl: conception of basic
    statements, 11; nonfoundationalism
    of, 49; expected agreement among
    scientific observers, 50; Rawls drawing
    on, 54–55, 57; and the justification of
    induction, 57, 66; as a logical
    physicalist, 80
Practical reason: political views not
    implications of, 178–179; the unity
    of, 187–188
Princeton University: Rawls's decision
    to join, 17; Committee on Religious
    Instruction, 18, 21–22; Department
    of Religion, 18, 21–22, 29; Department
    of Philosophy, 19, 20–21, 45, 46–48,
    63; assessment of Rawls at, 22, 63,
    84; and the birth of game theory, 84;
    the Institute of Advanced Studies,
    84; Urmson's visiting year at, 103
Principles, ethical and political:
    ordered list of, 5–6; as indeterminate,
    9; their role in practice, 9, 52, 109,

113–114, 129–131; mechanical
    conception of, 79–80; need not be
    explicitly used by reasonable persons,
    80; as boxes of reasons, 111–114, 174,
    191; apply to people who reason from
    different conceptual frameworks,
    113; independent of contingent facts,
    164–165; and the limits of philos-
    ophy, 182–187
Principles of justice. See Justice:
    principles of, stated
Protocol statements: relation to
    observational statements and basic
    statements, 49; of a universal
    scientific community, 49; as reports
    of physical reality, 78
Public reason, 15, 194, 196

Quine, W. V. O.: seeing philosophy as
    analysis, 7; and fixed points, 8, 191;
    as a naturalist, 14; relation to logical
    positivism, 14, 137–140; his meaning
    holism, 138–141; conception of
    observational sentences, 138–141;
    expected agreement in ethics,
    140–141; on necessity, 142; and
    reflective equilibrium, 190

Rashdall, Hastings, 153
Reasonable persons: contrasted with
    actual persons, 1, 3; defined, 2, 69;
    and normal observers, 68–70; three
    characteristics of, 69; and their
    scientific temper, 72–73; as part of
    nonfoundational justification, 75,
    80–81; defined in relation to the
    objective factor, 78; understood
    universally, 106; their agreement
    loose, 112; naturalism used to
    explain the agreement of, 116, 131;
    and partiality, 159; seeking to live
    as Kantian persons, 170, 177
Reciprocity: as a central natural
    reaction, 120; and its importance for

Kant and Kantianism, 121; Piaget's account of, 122–123; its role in Rawls's account of moral development, 123–124; as a deep psychological fact, 125; and stability, 125–126, 133–135

Reflective equilibrium: defined, 5; state of contrasted with process of, 5; Quine's influence on Rawls's conception of, 8, 14, 138, 141–147, 190; liberal Protestantism's influence on Rawls's conception of, 20; and scientific observers, 51; and rational judgments, 68

Reichenbach, Hans, 45, 180

Respect for persons: is actually respect for beliefs in liberalism, 3, 15; and the original position, 9; initially interpreted in terms of humanity and not autonomy, 9, 14; is detachable from Kantian autonomy, 10, 15; is possible with only narrow and fragile agreement, 15; leading to inviolability founded on justice, 19; and personalism, 28; requires treating them equally unless relevant differences shown, 94; and for their values, 109; and taking a moral point of view, 152, 164; as respect for rational beings, 167; and shared principles of justice, 189, 196–197; basing it on the formula of humanity, 197

Revelation: as part of liberal Protestantism's lived Christian experience, 10; neo-orthodox emphasis on, 20; self-revelation of God, 20; and Christ, 20, 27; knowledge of God depends on, 23, 24; Bible as a record of, 24, 26, 37; biblical essentialist understanding of, 25; Greene's understanding of, 26; Thomas's understanding of, 26–27; liberal Protestantism and everyday, 28; as active on the part of all participating

in, 33; Rawls's account of challenged by the Second World War, 42

Rights: Rawls studying at Princeton, 22; Maritain's defense of, 29; Protestant personalism linking the concept of persons to, 29; cannot sacrifice persons' for the welfare of society, 31; Rawls not defending the notion of, 31; Rawls uses the concept of, 83; and equality, 85; personhood and the concept of, 85; moral principles and grounds for, 85, 87; contrasted with maxims, 87; persons as bearers of, 87; and treating persons as ends, 87; the state protecting, 88; theory of natural, 158–159

Ritschl, Albrecht, 24

Rorty, Richard, 14, 173–174, 180–181

Rousseau, Jean-Jacques: Rawls prompted by to adopt the social contract approach, 151; Rawls teaching on the social contract tradition, 153; can begin one's inquiries either within utilitarianism or the social contract tradition, 155–156; Rawls's conversation with Moore about the importance of, 157–158; Rawls's definition of morality drawing on, 163

Rueff, Jacques, 51, 54

Ryle, Gilbert, 102

Sachs, David, 137

Scheffler, Samuel, 192–193

Schneewind, J. B., Rawls urging to read Sidgwick, 84

Scientific theory: logical positivism's conception of, 48–50; Rawls modeling ethical theory on, 48, 53–57; observational statements as the subject matter of, 50–51; Ducasse modeling ethical theory on, 51–52; objectivity of its statements, 67–68; and the scientific temper, 71–73

Scoon, Robert: opinion of Malcolm, 19; relation to liberal Protestantism, 21–22; opinion of Rawls, 22; describing Rawls as religious, 42; Rawls's courses with, 46, 48, 200–201; recommendation letter for Rawls, 63

Self-respect, 132, 133

Sidgwick, Henry: Rawls's imperative utilitarianism, 58–60; Rawls encountering Kant through, 84; on the usefulness of praise and blame, 152; and Rawls's depiction of utilitarianism, 153; and the dualism of practical reason, 187–188

Sin: neo-orthodox emphasis on, 10; and the commonality of experiences, 12, 39–40; humans inevitably falling into, 19; liberal Protestantism and, 20; and relation to God, 31; individualizing achievement as, 33; merit rooted in, 33; egoism as, 34–35; egotism as, 35; aloneness as experience of, 39; and *Imago Dei*, 40; Nietzsche's experiences of, 40; remnants of Rawls's focus on, 88

Smith, Adam, 92, 130

Smith, James Ward, 46–47, 53, 200

Social contract, doctrine of: Rawls seeing his work as part of, 151, 153, 157–158; Rawls's rejection of its original background, 158–159

Socialism, justice and the means of production, 9, 186

Stability of a conception of justice, 132–135

Stace, Walter, 21, 23, 63, 199, 201

Sympathy: as a natural feeling, 120–121; and inclination to partiality, 130–131; and stability, 133–134; Kantian reasons for distrusting it, 159

Taylor, Robert: interpretation of Rawls as a Kantian, 177–178; Rawls as a foundationalist, 177–178

Thomas, George F.: theology as analysis of experience, 10; and Princeton's Committee on Religious Instruction, 18; as Rawls's teacher, 21–23, 200; his conception of theology, 26–28; political implications of theology, 29–30, 32, 34–35

Toulmin, Stephen: influence on Rawls, 12; on practices and their logic, 97, 99–100; goal of ethical reasoning, 98, 107; conception of nonfoundationalism, 100–101; influence in analytic philosophy, 102; Rawls's review of *Place of Reason in Ethics*, 105–107; influence on Rawls's conception of the basic structure of society, 110–112; Rawls's drawing on his nonfoundationalism, 125, 141, 165, 170, 195; Baier claiming affinity with his arguments, 160

Universal Declaration of Human Rights, 29

Universality, formula of: Rawls's emphasis on, 152, 164, 171; Baier shifting emphasis from, 161–162; Rawls shifting emphasis from, 162–163

Urmson, James Opie, 98, 102, 103

Ushenko, Andrew, 21, 46, 48, 200, 201

Utilitarianism: analyzing shared experiences, 38; imperative, Rawls's conception of, 57–60, 190; Rawls seeing himself as working within, 60, 151, 152–156; Rawls's defense of, 110; and sympathy, 121, 130–131; and recognition of persons as persons, 128; its relative instability, 133–135; Rawls's rejection of, 133–135, 156–157, 193; mistaking impersonality with impartiality, 156

Veil of ignorance, 93, 177

Walzer, Michael: criticism of Rawls, 3, 174, 182, 184, 187; addressing Walzer's criticism of Rawls, 197

Wittgenstein, Ludwig: concept of the "form of life," 8, 13, 115–120, 122, 135, 190; post-analytic themes in his thought, 11; and Rawls's conception of moral feelings, 13, 190; as Malcolm's interlocutor, 19, 47; family resemblance, 59, 128–129; influence on Cornell's philosophy department, 64, 66; influence on Stephen Toulmin, 97; and the good reasons approach, 98; conception of language as a practice, 99–100; influence on Rawls's naturalism, 114–119; concept of normalcy, 125; and agreement of reasonable persons, 184, 190

Wood, Ledger, 48, 83, 200, 201